EASTERN WINDOWS

EASTERN
WINDOWS

F. D. OMMANNEY

READERS UNION

LONGMANS

LONDON 1962

This RU edition was produced in 1962 for sale
to its members only by Readers Union Ltd at
Aldine House, 10–13 Bedford Street, London
W.C.2 and at Letchworth Garden City, Herts.
Full details of membership may be obtained from
our London address. The book is set in 11
point Bell type leaded and has been reprinted by
Ebenezer Baylis & Son Ltd, Worcester. It was
first published by Longmans, Green & Co. Ltd.

Contents

Illustrations

Part One

LANDSCAPE: SINGAPORE

1

Evening Ride

My view of the East is a restricted one, for I have been here a mere seven years. I look upon it with love and loathing in roughly equal proportions and cannot speak any of its languages. A little kitchen Malay is all I ever acquired in spite of the hours I have spent following the adventures of 'Sang Kanchil' and 'Hang Tuah'. I know little about the history of these bright lands and, in fact, like most Englishmen, I greeted the idea that any of them existed at all before the days of Clive and Warren Hastings with faint incredulity. Singapore, of course, had no existence before the arrival of Stamford Raffles, though this is in fact nearer the truth than many of the things we are brought up to believe. I brought to the East only my eyes and my senses and, perhaps most important of all, my nose.

I did not come to the East until I was nearly fifty, which they, whoever 'they' may be, say is much too late. I am inclined to think that they are right in this case, for at that age it is difficult to get used to the heat, to the constant stickiness and to the disconcerting mistimed drip of sweat. At critical moments it drips on to the paper as you write, on to the cheque you are signing, on to the goods you are examining in a shop, into the drink you are lifting to your lips. It trickles warmly, like the tip of a feather running down your side, under the evening shirt into which you have just laboriously changed. You do not easily get used to the incessant noise which drills into your brain and blankets your senses. Noise is all part of the Eastern scene. Radios are always turned on at full blast. It is unusual, certainly in Singapore, to find anywhere out of the sound of canned music. Voices are strident and most laughter is a shrill cackle. The Chinese love noise and fire off crackers to frighten away evil spirits. Motor-horns are used as an expression of the emotions, to ventilate impatience, anger, scorn and even pride. And then the smells! The smell of rotten eggs near the water-front, which results from decaying garbage. The smell of dried fish and spices and the smell of pig manure which, for some reason, results from the processing of rubber. The smell of durian, sickly sweet and rotten; the smell of ghee, over-powering and rancid; the smell of garlic breathed down the back of your neck, for, owing to the spiced food they eat, nearly all Asians have breath which seems to be almost in-candescent. About three o'clock in the afternoon in Singapore something used to happen to me that I had never experienced anywhere else in the world. My brain stopped working. I could sit at my desk with my mouth open and, I have no doubt, a glazed look in my eye like that of a landed fish. Nothing was going on in my head at all and very little would, in fact, take place in that high echoing vault until after breakfast the follow-ing morning. And sometimes I would be conscious of a short-ness of temper and a mounting rage, that terrible and futile rage of the European in hot, damp countries that makes him shout and blaspheme and curse. There used to be a time when the East trembled at this rage, but now it only laughs.

But though you hate all these things there is much that enters into your heart and never leaves it. These are the things that make up that mysterious disease, which is still very real and catching and compelling, called 'the Call of the East'. I believe it remains as a kind of ache, in serious cases, long after you have left the area of infection and forgotten the heat, the noise and the smells. For you never can forget the beauty and grace of the people, their blue-black hair and the exquisite drawing of the oriental eye. Everybody laughs and everyone is running about with nothing much on. Thighs and breasts and hips move with a gayer, lighter rhythm. Landscapes and vistas have a colour and intensity always to be recalled, and yet already known because artists of matchless skill and intense observation have recorded them all centuries ago on silk or on fabric or on stone. It was always astonishing to discover how closely the oriental scene resembles the pictures of it that artists drew very long ago. Those craggy mountains, bearing tufts of trees, wreathed in the dawn mist, might be a Chinese scroll-painting come to life. So might those fishermen in their conical hats, rowing their high-prowed canoe upon the glassy water which mirrors the last light. In my garden in Singapore tiny yellow sunbirds with curved beaks used to perch on the bending stems of a slender, reed-like plant called *Juncaea* and tickle the vitals of the scarlet bells that hung along it. They, too, seemed to me known and familiar, painted for me centuries before it was given to me to see them. Sometimes, when my Indian gardener thought I was not looking, I would see him standing idle in an attitude of supple grace, leaning on the long handle of a broom or a spade, an expression of calm, wrapt contemplation on his clean-cut, angular black face. I doubt if much contemplation were going on really behind that mystic look, and since I did not think I ought really to pay him to contemplate in these graceful attitudes, I usually, after a moment to admire his pose and the picture that he made, gave a discreet cough to reveal my presence. But something ancient and familiar was implicit in the way he stood and moved. And certainly something familiar about the way he leapt into life and began to sweep with unaccustomed energy when he heard me cough.

I came to Singapore as an officer in the Research branch of the Colonial Service with an assignment to direct an as yet unborn Fisheries Research project in the Colony. It was June 1952 when I made my bow to the Orient from the deck of the big Dutch ship which had brought me from East Africa. It was raining in torrents and my first glimpse of the East was through grey veils of falling water sweeping across the islands that overlook the harbour. They hissed upon the opaque brown water and spattered upon the empty quays and upon the roofs of go-downs.

And since we have now, for better or for worse, arrived in the East, I may as well explain some of these technical terms as I go along. I call them 'technical terms' because using them constantly becomes a kind of 'one-upmanship' on the part of those who have lived for a long time in the East in order to distinguish them from those who have not lived there so long. A 'go-down', then, is a shed or warehouse. The word comes from the Malay *gudang*, which means the same thing.

Under the shelter of the dripping eaves of the go-downs Tamil and Chinese coolies were squatting like scruffy birds, with gunny sacks over their shoulders, chattering and spitting. My fellow-passengers were trooping ashore in the downpour and I watched them from the deck. I was waiting for someone to come and meet me. After all, there was plenty of time.

I came to the East too late to see it in what are still called 'the good old days' by some members of some clubs. Those were the nabob days before the war when every young junior newly arrived from England found himself suddenly a *tuan besar* (literally, 'great lord'), with a house, respectful servants, a high salary and not too much work. And unlimited cricket and 'stengahs'.

The 'stengah' is the drink of the European in Malaya. It is a long, pale, ice-cold whisky and soda. The word comes from the Malay *sa-tengah*, meaning 'a half'. The most blissful moment of the day in Malaya or Singapore is the first mouthful of the first 'stengah' after sunset. All the world is your friend at that moment. The second mouthful is less magical, and thereafter the moments deteriorate slowly in quality. I could only guess what those now vanished nabob days had been like from hearsay and from the sad spectacle of the magnificent houses in which the nabobs had lived. The style of colonial domestic architecture in the parts of the Far East ruled or administered by the British, in Singapore, Malaya or North Borneo, has evolved along gracious and pleasing lines. There are wide balconies made for lounging in bamboo armchairs. The rooms are often open all round so that sweeps of lawn and flowering shrubs can be glimpsed through the shiny leaves of pot plants and hanging orchids. Red roofs of ridge and furrow tiles blend softly with the dark evergreen landscape. But these pleasant houses are things of the past now. Air-conditioning and electricity have killed them, and the universal rectangular concrete boxes are going up everywhere. Many of these old houses are now divided up into flats, their spacious verandas and polished hallways crudely dissected. Others are communal messes, housing the staffs of firms and institutions. The radio plays in them all day long, and torn, thumbed copies of *Life* and *Time* magazines litter the dirty chintzes in the lounge. 'Do come in. I'm afraid it's in rather a mess. Boy! Bring *satu* beer and *satu* gin and tonic *lekas-lekas*.' In the great gardens, full of enormous old trees with ferns in their armpits, the packing-case blocks of flats are going up where in former years many gentle, lazy Indians languidly swept the leaves. Some of these houses still

16

remain and some are quarters for senior Government officers, who pray they will not be called upon to occupy them. For nowadays when you engage a servant he says, 'First I would like to see your house.'

In those spacious colonial days I believe that Asians in Singapore were not allowed into the Botanical Gardens, where they now over-encourage the monkeys on Sunday afternoons, nor into the compound of the handsome Victorian Gothic Cathedral, which they now use as a rendezvous for lovers after dark. No one, of course, could very well prevent them from going into the Raffles and Adelphi Hotels if they wished to. After all, these were public places. But they seldom did for fear of being stared at by all those loud-voiced Europeans in evening dress.

Nevertheless it would be wrong to suppose that those days were less happy than these, for it is always a mistake to judge the past by the standards of the present. Each of these great houses had at the back an array of servants' quarters that almost amounted to a small village. Indeed, the English word 'compound', meaning the grounds of a private house, is derived from the Malay word *kampong*, meaning 'a village'. Here lived a regiment of servants, the houseboys, the cooks, the wash amahs, the baby amahs, the syces, the cleaners, the sweepers, the gardeners, their many wives and still more numerous children in a noisy, chattering, cheerful, amiable throng. They quarrelled and got into debt and brought their troubles to the *Tuan Besar*, and some sort of dependence on him as someone above who was wise and settled disputes and was impartial and fair was the accepted state of affairs. Nowadays the dependence has quite disappeared, but the quarrelling and the debts go on just the same and the *tuans* are much less *besar*.

Great changes are now sweeping over the East, and the old way of life has quite vanished for Europeans. Young men in offices work long hours, and their money buys much less. They have to work hard to keep their jobs because the local ones are much cheaper to employ and almost, though not yet quite, as good. They play hard, too, and I noticed when I first came to Singapore that many of the young commercial gentlemen had a washed-out look, as though they constantly burnt the candle at both ends. Yet, though the position of the white man has radically changed and will continue to do so, it has not necessarily changed for the worse. The time for dominance and rule has gone for ever, but the time for influence and partnership has only just begun. During my years in the East I have often wondered whether the white man will seize the opportunity while it is offered. Presently it may slide unnoticed away. And I have often doubted it very much.

In these days of change the old symbols are being scornfully discarded and new ones assumed, new flags, new stamps, new names, new figureheads. But yet, while cocking snooks all the time at the West, and throwing overboard its symbols and traditions, the East seems to become more and more fascinated by the tricks and gadgets of the West. Their magic spell grows stronger every year. My house in Singapore, when eventually I had one, was built beside, almost on top of, the main road leading to one of the few popular bathing beaches of the island. Thousands of young people of Singapore's several races used to pass by every Sunday. The impact of so much youth was shattering, for half the population of $1\frac{1}{4}$ millions is under the age of twenty-one. Most of these young Sunday crowds were Chinese, some were European. There were fewer Indians and Malays. It was the westernization of the Chinese which somehow seemed formidable, because they seemed to ape without in any way questioning the clothes, the mannerisms, the accent and, one supposed, the values imported from the United States.

Here, for instance, comes an enormous fish-tail sedan in two garish colours with a radio antenna aquiver, half again as high as the roof. The radio is turned full on and, as the great caravan slides past, the mooing sound of an American crooner rises to a crescendo and then fades into the distance. Two brilliant yellow cushions obscure most of the view through the rear window, in the middle of which a celluloid fish dangles on the end of a string. Along the front and rear fenders runs a legend in Chinese characters and in English—'Use Mobiloil'. The car is packed with Chinese. There seems to be a forest of heads inside and there must be about twenty people altogether. The car is parked by the water's edge and most of its passengers get out. The car never seems to stop disgorging them. It is like an enormous gleaming cocoon spewing them forth. All the men wear flowered Hawaiian shirts, brief shorts or jeans and American-style caps with long peaks. The girls wear beach pants, tight round the calves, tight bright shirts, showing the shape of their small pointed breasts, and their hair in pony-tails tied with ribbon. Every face is made into a mask by dark glasses, which young people in the East appear to think be-coming to them, and under the glasses their mouths work rhythmically as they chew. Their manner and bearing are arti-ficially and unnaturally American as though it was all something they had learnt, not very well. Only one passenger remains inside the car, an old lady dressed in the beautiful and dignified costume of the Straits Chinese, a white blouse with two points in front below the waistline and a batik skirt, cut tight but slit in front, down to the ankles. Another radio is unloaded from the car on to the beach; and, while the young people play with a rubber duck on the extreme edge of the tepid, opaque water, the noise never ceases, and the old lady gazes through the window across the Straits of Johore and her face does not betray what she is thinking. Perhaps she is not thinking. When they all get back into their sedan and depart, the radio still blaring, a litter of newspapers, packets and empty tins is left behind. They will lie there for weeks and no one will bother to clear them away.

Now here comes a low-slung, skimming-dish sports car, tearing along at an enormous speed and making the maximum amount of noise. It is bright red and its front is covered with a battery of badges. A triangular pennant flutters from the radio aerial. Three people sit in the driving seat and three, two young men and a girl, are perched on the back, their hair streaming in the wind, a kind of echo of the European sad-gay 'thirties. They ride past twice an hour throughout the Sunday morning, with horns blowing, intoxicated with speed, up and down the long new road and round and round the circuit, just going and going fast but with no destination. A flock of cyclists follows. One of them has a guitar on his back. They all have letters on their T-shirts and pennants streaming. Their backs are bent to the low-slung handle-bars and their long legs work like pistons. Thank heaven, however, they are quite silent and flit past like a flight of birds. Farther away a large party has just disembarked from four lorries and is now being harangued through amplified loud-speakers. This is probably a Communist outing, but the loud-speakers will soon be churning out American tunes. And over there under the sweet-almond trees three Sikhs, who have just been swimming, are combing out their long seaweed-like tresses. Perhaps that spectacle more than any other is symbolic of the changes that are coming over the East.

The reasons for these changes are fairly easy to see. When the Japanese came to Singapore they marched the Europeans, the *tuans*, the masters, in half-naked bedraggled gangs through the streets. Other *tuans* and masters fled to the ships, leaving their servants and the local inhabitants to face the music. The servants and local inhabitants thought it quite in the accepted scheme of things that they should be so left. It never occurred to them that it might be otherwise. But they did not forget The *tuans* could hardly expect to be looked upon with quite the same awe when, after the war when the fighting was all over, they came back again, put on their white drill suits and lifted their feet on to their rattan foot-rests. The cry of 'Boy!' sounded less compelling as it rang out from the veranda. But perhaps a still more powerful force for change is the tide of nationalism which is sweeping over all the formerly dependent countries. This is partly due to education. There is a fever for this heady stuff. It is taken in great undigested dollops with the express purpose of one day fitting the recipient of the mixture for that place, now occupied by a white man, behind that desk with that bell, that telephone and that white blotter. It is also due to the decline in wealth and power of the former imperial Powers and also, one might perhaps add in the case of the British, to a change of heart, a loss of resolution, a doubt, a questioning. 'Ought we to be here? Should we not now hand over the bell and the telephone and the blotter and see what somebody else can do with them?' Then, again, there is the undoubted and bitter fact that America is now Top Nation and is anti-colonial in outlook. Like Mr. Coolidge's preacher she preaches about sin and is against it, though usually it is the sins committed by other people that she is chiefly worried about. In the access of liberalism that overtook America after the Second World War, as after the First, it seemed to good Americans, in their fever for democracy, that the British Empire was almost as much of a menace to peace as the Nazis. The British, however, having lost several empires before, knew the moves and bowed before the wind. It was the Dutch who were the victims of American generosity with what did not belong to them. They lost their rich and splendid East Indies Empire and have never felt quite the same since towards either the Americans or the British. But the Dutch are a small nation, so no one cared. The British, on the other hand, invented the idea of having a Commonwealth instead of an Empire. Characteristically enough, in fact, they turned their empire into a club. Only Burma and the Sudan were caddish enough not to want to belong to it at all. India, Pakistan and Ceylon now belong to it on reduced subscriptions. The Irish were out before the club was formed. Everything has to have a name with a less imperial connotation than formerly, and so, to keep in step, we refer not to the Crown Agents for the Colonies but to the Crown Agents for Oversea Governments and Administrations, to the Commonwealth this and the Commonwealth that. It is all most confusing and makes one feel old. Nowadays, the Americans, their fever having cooled a little in a decent interval of time, observe a vacuum where the British Empire once was, a hole in the ground where a great tree once stood, a glare where there used to a be shade, and desperately try to fill it with more arms all round, more money, more advice and more of those good intentions with which the American hell is paved. The youthful East speeds down towards it in its fish-tail sedans, its radio blaring and its hair streaming out in a pony-tail behind.

Of all the nationalisms, that which is likely to have the most profound effect, not only upon the East but upon the whole world, is the newest of them all, the awakening nationalism of the overseas Chinese. Revolutions always cause reverberations far beyond their borders, and the shock waves of the Chinese Communist revolution are felt wherever there are Chinese communities. For the first time in history these fecund, shrewd and industrious people have awoken to the fact that they are Chinese and that this really means something. Formerly they just worked and lived and reproduced and took this fact for granted, like the fact of being human. Now a great Power is arising in the East, and the farther they are away from it the

greater its virtues, its splendour and its glory. The war in
Korea gave a fillip to these nationalist emotions. The overseas
Chinese felt a pride that took no account of rights and wrongs.
'When China speaks America trembles,' they said. The population of Singapore consists of over seventy per cent Chinese,
and more than half of them are young and ardent and readily
receive powerful injections of the new virus from Communist
sources. No wonder the Federation of Malaya, with already
about fifty per cent Chinese, does not want to join hands with
the turbulent city across the Johore Strait.

It is difficult to imagine the many races which make up the
population of Singapore, ever sinking their identity and merging
into a common Malayan nationalism. Each of them, Chinese,
Indians, Malays and Europeans, is so individual in outlook and
character that it is hard to believe that any symbol could really
unite them. The Union Jack and the Governor driving through
the teeming streets with a gilt crown on the front of his Rolls-
Royce were as good as any others and what they were used to.
The individuality of the various races was always most striking
on the occasion of their festivals, when you saw them gathered
together, celebrating in their own way their own centuries-old
traditions and beliefs. On the Chinese Moon Festival in October
the shops are gay with elaborate paper dragons and lanterns
and round moon-cakes. Children run about the streets with
lighted lanterns in their hands and the explosion of crackers
fills the air with smoke and noise. On the Hindu Festival of
Thaipusam the devotees run and totter through the streets in
a kind of doped shamble with skewers through their tongues
and cheeks and huge *kavadis* of radiating spikes on their
shoulders, the points of the spikes penetrating their flesh. They
mortify the body, and their fellow-Hindus from all over the
city collect in a dusky, odorous crowd to see them do it. On
Hari Raya Puasa, at the end of the fast of Ramadan, the Malays
put on their lovely bright-coloured *sarongs* and *bajus* (long
pyjama-like suits) and walk about in the town, visit one
another and exchange greetings. There is something civilized
about the way the other races stand aside politely when any one
of them is celebrating its own festival. That perhaps is a sign
of an approaching unity. And when the Europeans celebrate
their own Christmas the whole sweltering city is gay with

snow and holly and robins and English things that few of the
inhabitants have ever seen but vaguely take for granted as part
of the European feast day, as we take their moon-cakes, their
kavadis and their long, arduous fast.

The Chinese are the most numerous, the most gifted, the
most pushful and the most difficult of all the races which live
together in this great seething cauldron of human lives and
passions. They have a traditional xenophobia, perhaps born of
many centuries of abuse and suffering at the hands of foreigners.
As a result they are the least amenable and the most intrac-
table of all, and the least easy to govern. The British are good
at governing and on the whole made a success of it in Singapore, and the Chinese tolerated their rule because it brought
law and order, the security necessary for trade and the making
of money. But they have no respect for law and regard laws as
things to be got round by any available means. Also they are
the greatest non-joiners in the world. They do not join police
forces, armies, crusades or movements unless they themselves
think that they will get something tangible out of it. The joiners
are the Malays, who usually join the Police or the Army or the
Navy or the Air Force because these institutions offer jobs
with fair pay and not too much work. The Chinese prefer to
stay out and make money. On the whole they do not trust or
recognize the police force and prefer to rely for their own personal security on gangs and secret societies. Even the clerks
in my office were banded together in gangs and fellowships
for their own personal safety.

The Chinese in Singapore are split by a deep schism. The
young are adopting a somewhat orientalized version of the
American way of life. They learn all about it in the innumerable gigantic cinemas which have spawned all over the city,
glittering temples where the young worship in thousands every
day. Their doors open early in the forenoon, and the shadow
display of sex and violence (Western style) continues until
midnight on week-days. On Saturday nights there is another
show starting at midnight which is immensely popular. The
young pour forth about three o'clock into the cool starlight of
the Sabbath morning doped with transatlantic dream stuff.
Can it be on Sabbath morning that they acquire their reverence
for glittering wrist-watches, fish-tail sedans, elaborate cameras,

speed-boats and pocket radios? But the older generation, and those of the younger who are in love with the new star of China arising in the east, still remain intensely Chinese. Huge ancestor shrines fill the humblest living-rooms. The joss sticks still burn and the gongs sound in the great dragon-decorated and fantastically ornamented temples. They propitiate the old gods, celebrate the Moon Festival, the Feast of Lanterns and the Feast of the Excited Insects. While the young are being married in ice-blue organdie and palm-beach suitings, with a towering cake only one layer of which is edible, with interminable speeches but no champagne, the old are being buried with clashing cymbals, a mile-long procession of mourners dressed in white and mountainous compositions made of frangipani flowers.

The old still cling to the family unit which has been the strength of the Chinese for countless centuries, but the young, in obedience, perhaps, to modern influences, are tending to reject it. Of course, they have nothing to put in its place. Parents have lost control over their children and children have lost respect and even, it seems, affection for their parents. It was a common sight down at the docks to see shiploads of boys and girls leaving for the China of their dreams, leaving their homes and families and parents apparently without a pang. They were surely answering a call far more mysterious and far older than that of the propaganda they had absorbed. The entreaties and tears of their parents, whose mainstay in old age they should be, seemed to mean nothing to them. 'At least I got a watch out of her,' said one boy to a reporter, as he boarded the ship that was to take him away from his mother for ever. Such callousness and lack of humanity, such lack of loving-kindness and loyalty, by no means uncommon in this great city where East meets West, made one think that something dreadful must be happening to the young Chinese.

By about noon the lounge of the big Dutch ship had become quite empty and all the passengers had gone ashore. I was all alone in the first-class lounge, and the rain still slanted pitilessly down. No one had come to meet me, which was most unusual for a newly arrived Government officer. There is usually someone, even if it is only the office-boy. At lunch-time there was only the young Dutch purser in the first-class dining-saloon. He expressed surprise at seeing me still on board. 'I should have thought that you would have gone ashore already,' he said.

About tea-time it became obvious that if I did not want to be carried on to Hong Kong I would have to begin thinking about getting myself off the ship. I would telephone for a taxi. There was no telephone. The ship was not yet connected. All the stewards had meanwhile gone ashore for the afternoon, and my hand-baggage was left standing in a forlorn, solitary pile by the gangway, where it had been since the morning. Its companion heaps of other people's luggage had long ago deserted it, and it now looked lonely and unclaimed, like luggage in a lost property office. As the rain seemed now to have stopped I decided to launch myself upon the Orient and, picking up a suitcase in each hand, tottered down the gangway. Needless to say there was not a taxi in sight, only a long, straight road with warehouses (go-downs), railway lines, high mercury lamps and great ships, all shining in the last of the sun now struggling out from behind the parting clouds. It was a soulless, pitiless dockside landscape, as all such landscapes are. I went up the gangway and came down again with the rest of my hand-luggage. There was no sign of a taxi and no telephone. Telephone booths, I learnt later, are rare in Singapore because the public use them as lavatories and steal the instruments. You have to telephone from hotels, shops or offices. But in order to do that I should have to leave my pile of hand-luggage unguarded while I went in search of a place from which to telephone. For the moment I could think of no answer to this one. But, as is so often the case, the conundrum presently answered itself. One of the figures crouching under a damp gunny sack in the shelter of the warehouse roof uncoiled itself and came to life. It was a small black gnome. It had a bald head and the whites of its eyes were yellow. Its lips and irregular teeth were red with betel juice. It had a barrel-shaped body in a dirty blue shirt and even dirtier blue and white striped shorts, below which a pair of thin, bird-like legs emerged, covered with what looked like fine black wire. This figure of salvation did a little dance before me, making a pantomime to imitate carrying a load on its shoulders. It pointed to itself, nodding its head, to indicate that it was suggesting itself as a porter. Suddenly there were four or five other similar figures hopping about in the road in front of me. And so, leading my baggage train, as on safari in darkest Africa, I set off through the sad twilight landscape of the Singapore docks. It had stopped raining and the clouds had parted, as they do in the evening, and the wet roadways steamed. The heat was like a clammy blanket and I had scarcely gone ten paces before great round drops of sweat began to form on my forehead and dripped off the end of my nose. But at last my caravan and I arrived at a gate marked 'Out'. A very small taxi, driven by a Sikh of somewhat unprepossessing appearance, drove up, and the moment had arrived to settle accounts with my baggage train. I had been looking forward to it with a certain amount of apprehension, foreseeing the kind of undignified argument which I very much dislike and go to great lengths to avoid. But my gnome indicated that he and his fellow gnomes would accept one dollar each for their services. This meant that for being rescued, apparently by a miracle, from a minor but none the less embarrassing predicament I should have to pay the equivalent of about eleven shillings. I thought it extremely cheap at the price.

'Of course, you didn't pay it?'

'I certainly did. I gave them ten dollars between them.' (About 23s. 6d.)

'Good God! You must be mad! They'd have been perfectly happy with thirty cents each.'

'I dare say, but I shouldn't.'

'It's people like you that spoil the market.'

I drove away, leaving five spoilt black gnomes all betel-juice smiles, giving military salutes at the gateway until I was out of sight.

Dusk was falling as my bearded Sikh, driving a ramshackle Ford Anglia, the light of battle in his eye, charged with abandon through the crowded streets of Singapore. Those were the days (they seem like ancient history now) before the new power station had been completed and there was not enough electricity to go round. In those days the city was divided into several sectors, each of which was blacked out for two hours on two evenings a week. At six-thirty all lights went out and all fans and air-conditioners stopped. This, of course, was just as one was changing into whatever one felt one ought to change into to go wherever one was going. I found that if I were struggling into a dinner-jacket ('stengah-shifter') I soaked through at least two sets of underwear and two shirts before I was ready to set out. Street lights and neon signs were equally scarce in those days, and no visitor to the city nowadays, seeing the blaze of light in the streets, would believe what gloom there was a few years ago, nor down what canals of darkness my Sikh seemed to be charging on his mad career. There were no taxi-meters then. When one arrived thankfully at one's destination the driver smiled ingratiatingly and said, 'What you please, *tuan*.' Usually the exhausted passenger was so relieved to have arrived safely that he paid far more than the proper fare.

The principal Indian quarter of the city, Tanjong Pagar, lies immediately outside the dock gates. It was swarming with life at this evening hour and the gloomy chasms of the streets were full of dark-skinned people flitting to and fro in loose garments that made them look as though they were all either going to or coming from a Turkish bath. There were very few women about, possibly because this was the hour of the evening meal and the women were all busy at home. The streets were full of slight, wiry little men who walked holding up the corners of their skirts one in either hand, or looped them up around their waists above their skinny calves. Many of them walked in couples holding hands, their little fingers linked together. This is a universal oriental habit. You see men walking hand in hand among all the races of the Far East and Africa too. At a garden party at Government House, Singapore, I saw two enormous old Sikhs, with quite exceptionally long and bushy beards, wandering about the gardens among the notables and their fashionably dressed wives, with their hands firmly linked together and their shirts outside their trousers. It is a habit which gives a feeling of friendly propinquity and companionship. It has no other significance, such as might attach to it in the West. To orientals, who have not had a non-conformist movement, nor an Oscar Wilde case, nor read the more thunderous parts of the Bible, such an idea would never occur.

Every evening at dusk in the Indian quarter of Singapore the entire population comes out and sits on the ground. None of the other races seems to do this. The Chinese and Malays walk about or go to the pictures or to one of the 'Worlds'—which are a sort of fun fair—or sit at tables in the street eating. But the Tamils sit or squat or lie about on the pavement or on the grass. They are not fussy where it is, but they prefer the grass, even the worn, tired grass in the middle of traffic roundabouts or between traffic lanes. On the ornamental plots in front of the pompous City Hall, in the new Queen Elizabeth garden, and on the wide green expanse of the *padang*—the open space with trees which graces nearly every sizeable town in Malaya—you may see them in hundreds, their coal-black faces and limbs contrasting with the white swathes they wear. Some are playing cards, some are reading their vernacular newspapers, but most of them are engaged in animated and amiable conversation. It is the café habit, but without the tables and chairs, a gregarious social custom developed among a people who in their own homes are accustomed to sit on the floor and do not have chairs or tables. It is like Paris with its kerbside cafés deprived of their tables and chairs and all the clientèle, animatedly talking, or reading, or contemplating the universe seated on the pavement. The evening air at this hour in Singapore is filled with the high-pitched labial sound of the Tamil language, an ancient and beautiful tongue with a noble literature and tradition. It is not easy to learn and has a complicated syntax. To my untutored foreign ear, I am sorry to say, it sounded more like bandarlog talk than anything else.

Most of the people sitting about on the ground in the cool of the evening were dock workers. Tanjong Pagar, through which my Sikh was now charging with loud blasts of his horn, was considered to be a very Red part of the city. Policemen walked in pairs. I must never go there alone after dark, I was told. Of course I did so, and some months later attended a wedding ceremony in the middle of Tanjong Pagar and was given a royal welcome.

Many of the Indians in Singapore are merchants. They own those little shops which never seem to close and seem to sell practically anything and everything. The 'practically anything' they sell is exactly the same in shop after shop all down the street. The proprietor stands at the shop door and lures you inside with honeyed words. If you are a clever shopper, which I am not, you go into one shop after the other and ask for what you want. You end by bargaining for it, starting at half the price quoted in the first shop. But I am not very good at this. I approach the window wanting, say, a tie. A swarthy man in a sarong, for most of the small Indian shopkeepers are Mohammedans, stands in the doorway. There are more swarthy men of all ages, from little boys to patriarchs, his relations, inside the shop. If the shop is rather pretentious the swarthy man wears a smart shirt, tie and well-pressed trousers. But the patter is the same. I am not allowed to contemplate the window unassisted. The heat is turned on me at once.

'Come in, Sair, come in. Like to have a look round? Very nice shirts. I show you something very nice just arrived. Jockey shorts very smart. Very nice. Shoes, ties, handkerchiefs?'

For some reason I am often taken for a member of Her Majesty's Forces, in which case the recital begins, 'Hello, Jack. What you like?'

I am lured inside and presently come out having bought three ties and a dozen handkerchiefs at the first price asked. It is one hundred and fifty per cent too high, of course. Half-way down the street a light dawns. It breaks slowly as a kind of dim suspicion, like the dull suspicion you see in the eyes of an ox when you talk to it across a five-barred gate. 'I could have got that for less. I believe I could.' But it is too late, and the only thing to do is to resolve to bargain more shrewdly next time. But when next time comes I am a push-over once again.

Many of the Indians, on the other hand, are clerks and office workers, for they are quick-brained and intelligent and they compete for the best jobs with the Chinese.

However, it was not these nor the shopkeepers whom I saw taking their ease in hundreds on the ground as I rocketed past behind my Sikh. These were the labouring people, many of whom are not domiciled in Singapore at all. They come over every year in thousands from Southern India. They work as labourers on the roads, in the docks, on land clearances and building sites, and after two years or so they go back to India with the money they have earned. Most of them are Hindus, and on their religious festivals you may see them around their temples in thousands. They are an excitable, volatile people. They frequently have strikes and upsets and often take umbrage, imagining they have been insulted. Almost every day

B

in the newspaper some Tamil spokesman is complaining that something or other is an insult to his race. An affront has been committed, an apology is demanded, drastic action is threatened.

These black excitable people, flitting about in the twilight, seemed to me to be farther from Europeans than any of the other races in this great melting-pot. Their poverty and low standard of living, their way of life so different from ours, even their alien chattering language, seemed to place them far away at the other end of the scale by which we measure our relationships with human beings. More than this, I found during my five years in Singapore that there was a reserve in the attitude of all races, but particularly of Europeans, towards the Indians. Europeans regarded the Chinese, somewhat reluctantly perhaps, as equals or nearly so. One can know them and ask them to dinner. They have an individual and highly sophisticated culture of their own, older and more mature than ours. This the Chinese are well aware of and are without any sense of inferiority towards Europeans. Their wonderful ceramics and paintings can adorn any European home and blend with the products of western taste and culture, which, to tell the truth, are not much in evidence in Singapore anyway. They cultivate an astonishing variety of cuisines which are among the most delicious in the world. Chinese women are attractive and beautifully turned out. Their national dress is a tube-like sheath, slit up the sides enticingly to the knee, called the *cheong-sam*, in which they achieve heights of elegance and chic which European women in the East cannot rival. Both the cuisine and the *cheong-sam* have given rise to a kind of snobbism among Europeans. It is fun to eat Chinese food, to be knowledgeable about it and be adroit with chopsticks, to know how to hold the little bowl close to your mouth and shovel the rice in. It is another form of 'one-upmanship' that shows you have been long in the East. European women, too, adopt the *cheong-sam* and some even look quite well in it, though not many, for most of them are either too overflowing or too bonily angular.

Towards the Malays, on the other hand, Europeans have an affectionate, rather patronizing regard. 'The Malay is a gentleman, but—' with a shrug. The 'but' means that he is also a pretty hopeless sort of a fellow really, charming but lazy and feckless. You cannot, of course, know the Malays in the same way as the

Chinese, except for the few who have become westernized.
Their manners and customs, and their habits of eating, make
social intercourse difficult. They have no very pronounced
culture which will blend with things European. And the same
may be said of the Indians. One never sees a European house in
the East decorated in an Indian style, if such a thing exists,
though often in a Chinese style, and Indian food is too hot and
too messy. One cannot with dignity, and on social occasions,
eat with one's fingers, and scoop up mouthsful of curry with
pieces of *chapati*. Nor, as a rule, have European women taken
with any pleasure to wearing the sari. It is a shade too oriental
and foreign. But, apart from all this, there is a suspicion that
the Indian is a sly and cunning fellow. While remaining un-
alterably oriental, he tunnels and burrows and undermines.
His western appearance is never more than a mask. He seldom
does anything or says anything without an ulterior motive or
without weighing the consequences. And the consequences will,
probably, even at a far remove, be to his advantage. He is by
habit politically minded and forms cabals and cliques, associa-
tions and parties. He constantly aspires to sit in the seats of the
mighty and even entertains ideas about joining European clubs.
Accordingly it is difficult to find Europeans in Singapore who
talk about Indians without expletives. When the expletives have
popped themselves to death, like Chinese crackers, you find that
very few Europeans actually know any Indians at all. They have,
in fact, for the most part carefully avoided doing so. They have
built up for themselves a figure, sly, corrupt, treacherous, the
most subtle of all the beasts in the garden, and they hate it
accordingly. The figure, I think, is largely a false one. My
experience was that Indians are certainly subtle and have a
curious capacity for plotting and intrigue which is a boon to
their lawyers. They are always litigating about apparent trifles.
But they have a strange quality of gentleness and passivity. One
could understand how passive resistance could become a real
force in India rather than in any other country. If rebuked,
Indians are apt disconcertingly to burst into tears. They are
affectionate and extraordinarily hospitable. They love nothing
better than to entice you into their houses and introduce you to
their relatives, their wives, their children, their aunts, their
uncles, their cousins, and their cousins' wives, husbands and

children, all of whom peer at you from around corners and behind doors until you feel that you are a visitor from outer space.

I must confess, after nearly seven years in the East, that I have always found social intercourse between the races difficult and almost impossible to achieve with any degree of success. I have made many pleasant Asian acquaintances, but I do not think I have really made any Asian friends. I have often wondered what the barrier is that still stands between the moderately well-educated Westerner and the moderately well-educated Oriental. It was always there, impalpable, never referred to, unnamed, invisible, but definite and impenetrable, or almost. How well, and with what shame, I recall those many gatherings which began too well, with too much effusiveness, over-jocular conversation and many little introductory bows and nods. Yet soon, after the first few preliminary exchanges, the races had segregated. The Europeans were talking loudly among themselves and over the heads of the Asian guests, all of whom, unless they were particularly assured and able to hold their own, had huddled in a corner and concealed themselves behind the nearest magazine or newspaper. The Asian ladies were wise enough not to try to compete and sat in a row on the sofa in silence, brooding over their glasses of orangeade, which they seldom raised to their lips. They fixed their lustrous eyes in pride and admiration on their husbands. See on what easy terms he is with these Europeans! How he laughs and jokes with them as an equal! Do you hear that confident, easy laugh, Mrs. Ratnam? Of course, he could easily buy up the whole lot of them really. One must suppose there is something overbearing about Europeans when they are gathered together in one place, and this calls for defensive attitudes on the part of non-Europeans. They must be aggressive, the best method of defence being to attack, or they must retreat. If you know you can buy up the whole lot of them you need not retreat, and can be aggressive, laugh as loudly as they, drink 'stengahs' and even crack a familiar joke or two. But if you cannot you feel a deep embarrassment and long for just one thing, to escape, to flee, to get the hell out of it as quickly as possible. If that is not possible then you must erect barriers and throw up defences, the swamping din of the radio, a barricade of magazines, a newspaper, between yourself and these formidable people with their loud voices and incomprehensible talk. But a portion of your attention must be kept poised on the alert, atremble like the antennae of a bright-winged insect perched for a second on an unfamiliar leaf, ready to take instant flight, sensing, feeling, probing. To go forward? To go back? To stay still? Better to stay still, turn another page of *Life* magazine and risk a tiny sip of orangeade.

As for me, I was always looking, in a vague and misdirected way, for some mystical, spiritual East that I had read about somewhere but was never quite sure where. Kipling? Conrad? Herman Melville? Aloysius Horn? Francis Yeats-Brown? Frederic Prokosch? Had they all been leading me up the garden path? Somewhere there must be the world of splendour and colour and mystery I had glimpsed through their pages, the other-worldliness, spirituality and gentleness they hinted at. I found precious little sign of these in Singapore, and none at all in Hong Kong. Gross materialism seemed to prevail everywhere, and nowhere in the world was the Golden Calf more enthusiastically worshipped. Beauty belonged to the past and was everywhere being torn down and destroyed with eager hands by the people who had created it. Yet somehow I felt that the genius of the people must still be there. Often it would reveal itself in small, trivial things, in the way a hawker arranged fruit on his stall, the way the fishermen painted their boats, in the ancient art of cultivating ornamental fishes which the Chinese love, in the elaborate floral creations which decorate every funeral. Sometimes I felt that what I was vaguely seeking was almost within touching distance, and then faded away like a *fata morgana*—a dancer from Bali, a Malay wedding, or the Chinese theatre blossoming suddenly in the village with its colour and lights and noise. At these moments a gateway seemed to open just for a moment and then close again, leaving me with the radio crooning an American sex lament, the snort of a high-powered exhaust, and the bright, hard lights of this troubled, exciting and most moving city.

The taxi stopped. Breathless and battered, but unharmed, I had arrived. 'How much?' I asked limply, in a small voice.

The old Sikh scratched among the hairs at the back of his neck where they were caught up under his unsavoury puggaree.

He smiled a cunning and ingratiating smile and shrugged. The shrug was almost Gallic and full of obvious and unmistakable nuances. It meant that he knew that I knew, and he knew that I knew that he knew.

'What you please, sahib,' he said.

2

Street Scene

The jungle never seems to have quite retreated from Singapore, nor to have been quite subdued by the blocks of flats and offices, the miles of slums and the new building estates. Pockets of resistance remain among the concrete battalions. They seem to belong to that earlier island which Stamford Raffles found when he landed nearly 140 years ago. Thus, the commercial centre of the city is threaded by a black and foetid river, reeking of rotten eggs. Slums mingle with mangrove swamps and squat new bungalows spring up in droves among the coconut palms and mango trees.

It is all an unbridled, undisciplined kind of growth like that of the jungle itself which once covered the island. It has the same sort of vitality, all its components competing with each other to overtop, to choke and to strangle. The sun, beating down upon it all in the forenoon of each sweltering day, is as fierce as the downpour which, from black skies, empties itself upon it every afternoon, purging it and washing it clean. In the evening after sunset the clouds disperse and the moon and stars shine out of a velvet sky upon the neon signs and their fountains of light. Then the ugliness and squalor of the city are hidden, although its strident voice is not hushed for many hours.

In this jungle city survival is to the fittest. It is hard to believe, but it is nevertheless true, that in this modern city the gangster, the secret society and the kidnapper are all part of life, among the Chinese at any rate. Blackmail and protection rackets flourish, or used to when I first went to Singapore, and prostitution is, or was, a highly organized industry, like opium smuggling. None of these things affects the lives of Europeans much and that is why it is hard to imagine that they actually do take place.

Those who make this jungle city their home lead a jungle kind of life in it. Like undergrowth they wrest from the soil whatever sort of living they can. Many climb over their

35

prostrate competitors and reach the daylight above. These are the successful ones who acquire an immense villa built of concrete, lit by mercury lamps ablaze after dark to show the astonished world how splendid it all is and how rich the owner. In case there should be any doubt his name is written on a sign outside the gate. The drive is ornamented with formal urns and concrete lamp standards and leads to a garage housing one or more stupendous motor-cars. But the front door is protected by a heavy sliding grill of steel and windows are strongly barred. For the jungle presses all around, waiting for an unguarded moment.

Between the concrete palaces of the most successful and the slums that house the least fortunate there is now growing up a middle stratum which lives, dreaming of palaces to come, in the long neat rows of new bungalows that go marching out through the coconut palms. Each of these too has its sliding grill and its windows barred.

In the slums themselves, down there in the noisy stews, the shop fronts are open on the arcaded pavements and the washing is hung out on poles from all the upper windows, giving each squalid alleyway and court a gala appearance. Life is fierce and feverish in these warrens, for it is there that the gangs and secret societies work. It is an affair of rackets and protection money down here. The kidnappers and blackmailers operate higher up the scale among the concrete palaces.

In the open shop fronts the people work like beavers all day long, and often far into the night, while the unbreeched children by the hundred play around the wide-open monsoon drains that run down the side of every street and carry away the torrential cleansing rains. At night the rattle of the mah-jong chips goes on into the early morning hours until one by one the tired gamblers lay themselves down to sleep in rows on hard boards, their heads pillowed upon blocks of wood. In these streets are the death houses where families bring their old ones to wait for death. They lie on wooden, shelf-like beds, their glazed eyes open, staring into the gloom, their thin claw hands idle, waiting, ready and measured. Their coffins are ready for them, stacked nearby. When death comes it is easy.

No one takes any notice of you as you walk down these streets. The Chinese have an extraordinary power of concentration, the result, perhaps, of the overcrowding and din in which they live. They never pause or look up from whatever they may be doing or for a moment cease their twanging talk as you pass by. The small two-storied houses with ridge-and-furrow roofs that line these streets are about eighty years old, built in terraces in a classical style of architecture that is distinctly European and certainly not Chinese. I was told, with how much truth I do not know, that the Portuguese brought this style to Malaya. I have seen it nowhere else except in Kuching, capital of Sarawak. Some of these houses are quite handsome with ornate pillars and semicircular fanlights. The older ones have shrubs and plants sprouting from crevices, which gives them an appearance of being even more decrepit than they really are. They are fast disappearing nowadays, which is no doubt just as well, for they must be bug-ridden and quite without sanitation. They are certainly appallingly overcrowded, with twelve or fifteen people living in one small room. Huge blocks of modern apartments are replacing them, hygienic but characterless. The inhabitants hang out their washing on poles from their skyscraper apartment windows just the same and the effect is that the slums have become vertical instead of horizontal. I was told that the inhabitants dislike their hygienic vertical slums and would rather have their lousy, insanitary, horizontal ones in which they do not have to keep climbing stairs and from which they can keep an eye on their children playing in the street. The new ones, anyhow, are far too expensive.

There are miles of these streets and of crowded, noisy alleyways, all very much the same, flanked by vertical signboards bearing Chinese characters and roofed with intimate laundry. They are filled with shouting, swarming life far into the night. Many are lined with food stalls under canvas awnings, lit by paraffin lamps. The Chinese largely eat in the street. There squat the thin men in striped pyjama trousers and singlets, perched on stools like hungry emaciated birds, their feet on the top of the stool and their angular buttocks suspended in space. They hold their rice bowls up to their mouths and scoop the rice in with a shovelling motion of the chopsticks. Or the chopsticks peck into the bowls like beaks.

At the eating stalls the food is stewed in huge copper pans over charcoal braziers. Clouds of steam obscure the lights and an utterly delicious smell fills the air. The food itself is

displayed under the awnings in brightly coloured piles and festoons. Its appearance is perhaps slightly less appetizing than
its smell, for, in addition to the dried, flattened cuttle-fish, the
trussed and naked poultry, the piles of noodles, cockles and
eggs, there hangs from hooks every known form of guts, innards,
lights and offal. Perhaps because they have a history punctuated
by famines and by scarcities due to wars, natural disasters and
pestilences, the Chinese seem to have learnt to eat practically
anything, and no part or organ is too inconsiderable. All are
equally but variously delicious when cooked. Here, glistening
coldly in the lamplight, are veils of tripe, slabs of liver, ropes of
intestines, pancreases, spleens and kidneys. Under the brilliant
lights at each stall, surrounded by auras of rising steam,
accomplished cooks work deftly and with intense concentration,
basting chickens, tossing noodles, adding a little of this, a
pinch of that, chopping, pounding, stirring. And along the main
road at the end of the street the traffic roars by and the crowd
idly saunters and changes endlessly.

A short thoroughfare such as this, filled with eating stalls,
connects two busy main roads. It is called Bugis Street after
the early Malay pirates who frequented the islands across the
Strait and made raids on Singapore before the British came. In
this short street, a channel of light and noise, there are tables
where you may sit and watch the ever-shifting pattern of life
in Singapore. Waiters, in white singlets and shorts, run between the tables shouting orders over their customers' heads in
a high-pitched sing-song chant. You may sit and drink here, if
you wish, until the early hours of the morning, but about four
o'clock they begin putting the tables away and the lights go
out one by one. There will always be a taxi or a trishaw driver
to take you home, or somewhere.

During the early part of the evening the customers at the
tables are almost all Chinese. Many large family parties arrive
with their numerous children. They choose one of the many
circular tables and take a long time deciding what they will
have. They eat with great gusto, all helping themselves with
chopsticks from a dish or dishes in the middle of the table,
dipping each morsel they pinch up with the chopsticks into
little bowls containing sauce. Beggars drift to and fro with
expressions of woe appropriate to their calling, pointing into

their mouths and holding out tins for contributions. The customers, as a rule, take no notice of them. Later in the evening the Europeans begin to appear, the respectable and the not so respectable, the drunk and the sober, the quiet and the noisy. It is quite the thing, after a show or a party, to go down to Bugis Street. Men loosen their ties and women kick off their tight shoes under the table. The noisy get noisier and the drunk more drunk as the small hours after midnight draw on. The whores arrive, the same ones every night, and the beggars become more numerous and more insistent. I used to sit there and think that Bugis Street must be one of the most beautiful streets in the world in its own way, because of the lights and the ever-changing crowds and because of its irrepressible vitality. It is civilized because of its merciful, uncritical tolerance. Nothing matters, and the chief sins are not to smile and not to pay. All this is displeasing to authority, and many attempts have been made to do away with Bugis Street on one pretext or another, but somehow it survives. Perhaps these attempts have succeeded by now.

As I sit there and let time drift past like a river a little girl, heavily made-up and looking many years older than her age, comes to my table and sings a song in a Chinese dialect. She has a slight, true, reedy little voice. Her eyes are never still for a moment and wander all over the tables as she sings. She never looks at the customer she is singing for. I give her twenty cents before she has got half-way through her song, which is the same every night, and she breaks off abruptly and runs away. This is Patsy, a pretty little thing with the very sharply slanted eyes and eyebrows which I love. They said she was being trained to be a whore, but she disappeared and Bugis Street knew her no more. Probably some Welfare Committee got hold of her and she is now being given a useless education and made to wear hideous clothes.

An old woman comes next with a child on her back. The boy is well able to walk, of course, and gives the show away by clamouring to be let down, kicking the old woman's sides with his legs as though spurring a horse. She found it profitable to carry him around thus four or five years ago when he was a tiny baby asleep on her back. Now he has become part of her stock-in-trade, a sort of stage property, but he has become so heavy that she has to lean forward to support his weight and his legs hang down on either side of her nearly to the ground.

Two children appear and place a screw of paper on my table. There are two metal bottle-tops inside it. It is a token which I am supposed to buy by giving them whatever I may think such a gift may be worth. It removes from the children the loss of face which outright begging would entail.

Little shoe-shine boys, organized in gangs, impish and *gamin*, little thugs in miniature, crawl under my chair and seize me by the ankles.

'Soo sine? Soo sine? Soo sine? Gimmy ten *sen!*'

I have to be fierce, otherwise they become a terrible nuisance and will not let me alone.

Two young Indians willow in and out among the tables. They wear sarongs and carry in front of them trays of cheap nonsense for sale, cigarette-lighters, cigarette-cases, propelling-pencils. They seem to sell very little and one seldom sees any-one buy from their trays. Sometimes I saw horrible exhibitions of rudeness on the part of Europeans. But I never saw either of them become in the least discomfited or show any sign of loss of temper.

'Hallo, my friend. How's business?'

'Very poor biznis make no biznis very bad. You buy lighter for you special price.'

He runs all his words together into a sing-song which sounds like Welsh.

'I bought a lighter from you yesterday and one from your friend last week. I don't think I want any more lighters, especially as I don't smoke.'

'You buy very nice pencil very cheap?'

Perhaps I settle for a propelling-pencil, which I shall almost certainly lose. But if even that will not tempt me he makes the curious rotatory gesture which Indians make with the open hand, a long, thin hand in this case that might belong to an artist. Perhaps it does. Who knows? The gesture means much the same thing and is used in much the same way as the French shrug. It means, 'Perhaps, yes. Perhaps, no. But who cares anyway?'

'No biznis very bad biznis perhaps you come tomorrow make biznis.'

He glides away laughing, with no business but with laughter. Which is perhaps just as good in the end.

A tall, thin old woman stands at my table, silent, statuesque. She is paper-thin, and the dirt of centuries seems to be encrusted in every wrinkle of her leathery integument. She is dressed in a black nondescript garment that seems to be disintegrating with age and dirt, and she leans upon a stick with a hand on which the skin seems to be stretched so tight that you can see the bones. She wears a fixed, motionless smile like that of a skull. She is like a bad conscience and will not go away. But I hate her and will not give her anything.

'Go away. I won't give you anything.'

She does not move.

'I said—"Go away!" I'm not giving you anything.'

She still stands immovable, holding out a claw. Sometimes she wins by sheer persistence and I reluctantly give her ten cents. She raises her skinny claw as though to bless me and moves off to haunt another table and intimidate somebody else with her menacing presence and her silence. At other times I am obdurate and will not yield no matter how much she persecutes me. She is like something from the grave, surrounded by an aura of cerements and ashes. She exhales death. I shoo her away. At long last, when it becomes obvious to her that she is wasting time, that the centuries are passing and nothing gained, she begins slowly to turn away. She still smiles, but only the skin around her jaw is stretched into a grin. Her eyes do not smile. She curses me, still smiling, raising her stick to point at me in emphasis. May the bones of my ancestors be dishonoured. May my seed fall to the ground. May my mother mourn the day she bore me. As she moves off she pauses now and again to give me another baleful glance and mutter another imprecation, as though she had just thought up a new one.

The girls, who have been sitting at tables together in the background for quite a long time, waiting for the street to fill up, now get up one by one as and when they think the moment appropriate, and saunter up and down in front of the tables so that everyone can see them. They all have English names which hide their true identity, and I do not suppose that any European knows what their true names are.

Some are Chinese, some are Malays and some are evidently Eurasians. You can tell the Eurasian ones by their ladylike demeanour and because they love to tell you about their respectable white relations and forebears. Unfortunately they sometimes forget and tell different stories about their forebears to the same person. But they are all friendly, easygoing, amiable.

Rosie is not in the least ladylike, but very friendly. She smiles all the time and is short and plump, for a Chinese. She wears a *cheong-sam* made of some shiny material, with its skirt slit up the sides to more than half-way up her thighs, and so tight that every movement of her behind is revealed. She could scarcely look more unclothed if she were stark naked. She always goes through the pretence of looking for someone, glancing over the heads of the seated people as if expecting to recognize an acquaintance several tables away. Although she does not look at your table the search for her imaginary acquaintance brings her nearer and nearer. Now she sits in the chair by your side, if there is one, as if by the merest accident, her eyes still questing in the middle distance. She crosses her plump little legs so that, by the merest chance, one thigh is visible almost as far as where it is no longer a thigh at all.

'Hallo, Rosie. Looking for someone?'

'Me? Oh, I thought . . .' She gives a little laugh. 'But never mind. It does not matter.'

'Have a coffee?'

'Yes, thank you.'

For a moment the quest is forgotten. But soon her eyes begin to rove and search once more. She falls silent and seems preoccupied. Presently she rises, perhaps even before she has finished her coffee, and goes once more in search of her imaginary acquaintance. The search is taking her, I notice, in the direction of two merchant sailors, but they are too drunk to observe her as yet. It will probably be all right when they do, though.

Julia is a Malay. She is a large, fine-looking, handsome girl dressed in the Malay style with flared blouse and tight brightcoloured hobble skirt. Her good looks are rather spoilt by two gold teeth in front and too much make-up carelessly splashed on. She is covered with glittering things, ear-rings, bracelets, necklaces and rings, that flash and wink as she moves. She has a superb carriage and might be a queen the way she sails majestically up and down the rows of tables. She speaks English well but, having learnt most of it from Her Majesty's Forces, she loads it with unfortunate expletives of which she does not know the true meaning. But she does not drift away when she finds you do not mean business and she sits relaxed at your table for a while. You may buy her half a fried chicken if you wish, on which she will fall to with gusto and not speak until she has picked every bone clean and licked her fingers with loud smacking noises. Then she thanks you with a flash of her gold teeth, wiping her fingers on a paper napkin.

'*Terima banyak kaseh*. That was bloody good. Bye-bye.'

She rises and goes her royal way, her splendid breasts sparkling with glass beads. You think of a great ship in full sail.

Auntie is a Malay too, but she is very different. She is an elderly lady and very motherly. She looks exceedingly respectable, safe and understanding, as no doubt she is. Lonely men like to confide in her, and you often see small, insignificant-looking chaps talking to her earnestly. They are pouring out their troubles over their beer. This little man is repeating to her what the Chief Engineer said when he complained about the Third being late on watch night after night. The man with the bald head is telling her about life at 47 Rosemont Avenue, Bradpool-on-Tyne. Auntie is not listening, though she appears to be. In any case the little men are too wrapped up in themselves and their troubles to be aware of the divided attention of their confidante. One is mentally back on board the *Esso Cavalier* now lying at Pulau Bukom, the oil island across the harbour. The other is thinking of his wife who is all right in her way, 'but keeps on so'. Auntie is wondering which of the little men is going to get drunk first and whether his companion will be too far gone to get a taxi by himself. It is a nuisance coping with drunk gentlemen. Perhaps she had better move on. Suddenly the little man finds there is no one there. He shrugs, pours out some more beer, spilling most of it on the tablecloth, folds his arms on the table and lets his head sink on to them.

Lily is a fine girl too, perhaps the most magnificent of them all. She is Chinese, but very large and tall, yet graceful. Like Rosie she stands with a nonchalant air apparently looking for someone or for a suitable vacant place, in an elegant pose in front of the tables so that everybody can see her. Her favourite pose is the one with her hip jutting out and a long cigarette holder held aloft to show her lovely arm and wrist. She is always beautifully dressed in a somewhat startling style, with very bright colours and lots of heavy costume jewellery. She is said to be employed by a film company and wears a thick theatrical make-up with her jet black hair differently arranged every day. Her technique is that of the sulky beauty, not at all on-coming like the other girls. It is hard to say exactly what the difference is between Lily and the others, but her aloofness and goddess-like detachment seem to be main points. She takes no notice of anyone and does not associate with the rest. She seldom speaks and hardly ever smiles, always choosing an empty table if possible. If anyone sits at her table she ignores him. Without a glance round, after she has seated herself, she opens her compact and touches up her generous vermilion lips in the chalk-white face and is brought a coffee without ordering it. She seems to be quite removed and far above the hurly-burly of Bugis Street. But she gets her man.

And now here comes Maisie, tall and graceful too, but perhaps a trifle over-slim and flat-chested. She wears a smart, black, sheath-like *cheong-sam* with little jet beads sewn in patterns. They shimmer as she walks. She has long black drop ear-rings to match and carries a crimson fan. Her smooth hair is cut short and trim and sleek. But there is something not quite right about her feet. They are a shade too large. I will tell you a secret about Maisie. No one is supposed to know it, but it is surprising how many do. She is not a girl at all. She is a boy. Sometimes clients have been known to make quite a scene when they discover their mistake, and Maisie has sometimes had to stay away from Bugis Street for a day or two nursing a black eye. But not for long. Nothing daunted, she will be back again in a day or two with a new *cheong-sam* and some new ear-rings.

The girls, indeed, are by no means without competition.

Two little Malay boys walk down the rows of tables hand in hand. They keep stopping to giggle and ogle and pretend to take great interest in a punch-ball in one of the open shop fronts. This is a great favourite with young servicemen who crowd round it, wearing horrible shirts, showing off their strength. You punch the ball and a hand registers on a dial. If you punch hard enough a bell rings and you get your money back. The possibility, even probability, that the thing may be rigged never seems to worry the contestants. The two boys stand and watch for a little while, still holding hands. They wear very brief shorts, hung low on their hips, and their hair is trained into an elaborate series of undulations and turns up in a duck's tail behind. Inside the punch-ball shop there is a juke-box giving out blasts of rock-'n'-roll, and inside the juke-box there is a mirror. The two boys place themselves in front of this and produce combs from the hip pockets of their shorts. For two or three minutes combing operations as careful and elaborate as the sweeps of a cat's tongue occupy all their attention. They comb with devotion and concentration as though nothing mattered so much in the world as the arrangement of those gleaming black tresses. Perhaps nothing does.

One of the soldiers at the punch-ball looks at them with amused contempt. 'Ow, Claude! 'Ow nice!' he says in a voice of mincing mockery. The boys turn and bow gravely, as though at a great compliment, and continue on their way, not in the least discomposed.

Every evening the city is invaded by a horde of frustrated, lonely and bored young servicemen, like the ones at the punch-ball. They come from barracks, from camps and from ships. They drift aimlessly into cinemas and into bars, hoping to forget and drown in alcohol and noise their loneliness and homesickness, and to build up defences against the strangeness of their environment. Many clubs and institutions exist, of course, established by well-intentioned authority, for the purpose of helping these young men to forget these familiar aches of youth. The authorities aim to keep them off the streets, out of the bars and away from the fatal attractions of the city, and as much as possible out of contact with the local inhabitants. Accordingly an enormous Naafi has arisen opposite

Raffles Hotel. It has its own dance-room and swimming-pool and an interior that seems to wear an air of perpetual, slightly strained brightness, like an anxious air hostess. Select entertainments are constantly being arranged here which begin by being very respectable, but somehow seem to come unstuck as the evening goes on. There is a Union Jack Club and several hostels for seamen, while every air-field, barracks and naval camp has its welfare arrangements, its cinemas and its club rooms with bright chintzes, torn magazines and uncomfortable arm-chairs. But none of these things really keeps the boys away from the bars, although, in the R.A.F. especially, there is a growing addiction to expensive photographic apparatus, ice-cream and young ladies. For in bars you can assert your virility in so many ways. You can make the juke-box obey you and everyone present must drown in the noise of your choosing or get out. You can shout and sing or pick a fight. The little bar girls, who are also hostesses, have just the right mixture of aloofness and friendly accessibility to flatter the male ego. Each male ego thinks that, among all the other egos present, he has just what it takes to break down that air of hard-to-get which is so expertly worn. It is all a question of charm and personality, of course. Technique, my boy! Watch me! Until at last the heat and noise turn to a chill between the shoulder-blades and the male ego vomits itself up in the lavatory. But none of this is quite possible among the chintzes and the potted palms, the masters of ceremony and the small gins-and-oranges of the base or barracks club.

But in Bugis Street everything is possible, and after midnight male egos in their hundreds drift there. Perhaps this ego is just the one that Rosie is looking for. You can tell Auntie all about it and try to get a smile out of Lily. Buy a fried chicken for Julia and laugh at her terrible language. 'What for you always laugh when I speak, you silly bugger?' Or you can just sit there, as I used to, and let time slide past like a dark river, flowing out of nowhere into nowhere, bearing to your feet upon its flood driftwood and frail blossoms. They spin at your feet and glide on again. The stars are kind and look down blandly upon our poor humanity.

3

Portrait

At certain seasons of the year, about the turn of the monsoon around May, I seem to remember, enormous black-and-white butterflies appear in Singapore. They have wings the size of the palm of your hand and they look like pieces of printed notepaper fluttering aimlessly through the air. They often appear in the middle of the city, volplaning about among the traffic. They flop in at your open window and sit spread out on your furniture, their wide, frail wings stirring gently as they breathe. One night several of these soft papery creatures, no doubt attracted by the bright lights, arrived in Bugis Street. They fluttered, as though borne by perverse and varying winds, among the stalls and the tables, up to the roof tops and down again among the lights. Nobody took any notice of these visitors or even appeared to see them. Perhaps, I thought, they were familiars which only I could see. Then one of them parachuted slowly and deliberately downwards and came to rest in the middle of the roadway, under the feet of the drifting crowd, under the wheels of the trishaws and taxis. There it lay like an open book, its dark body marking the place, its antennae poised as though about to write. The passers-by then seemed suddenly to become aware of it. It was an alien presence, something they wished to destroy. It aroused their hostility. It was too strange, too foreign, too beautiful to be there. It was something to be feared, as are all things out of place, and its very paper-like frailty was a challenge. That inexplicable itch to destroy something delicate and ephemeral seemed to come uppermost in the minds of many of those present. One often sees this tendency in human beings and it is not edifying. A man put his foot out and tried to crush the butterfly. It flopped a few paces farther off, and as it moved people started back in alarm as though it were vicious and would sting. Its helpless, limp movements seemed to many to be more like the strike of a snake. I thought how far divorced from nature these people must have become to regard with terror and suspicion the homely creatures of their own island. A boy, greatly daring, advanced upon the insect with a brick and hurled it from a safe distance. It missed the butterfly, but the silly creature only moved away a foot or two and would not get up off the ground. It continued to sit there with its wings spread in the middle of the road, now surrounded by quite a large hostile crowd. Another boy picked up the brick and advanced into the middle of the circle of people in order to attack the butterfly, but I decided it was time to act. I must save the stupid thing. Nature must be spared the consequences of her own folly. But I soon wished I had let the old girl mismanage her own affairs. She always dislikes being interfered with anyway. I got up from my seat and advanced into the circle in a self-confident manner, my hands cupped to capture the waiting insect, and bear it to safety. But it rose and fluttered a few feet farther off, scorning my good intentions. Then a ridiculous chase began among the feet of the bystanders, among the food stalls and the tables, myself in pursuit of the butterfly. I blush to recall it even now. Every time I advanced upon the insect and thought I had really got it, it arose in front of me in a tired and leisurely manner and fluttered on a foot or two. But, having begun the chase, I was loath to admit defeat and give it up. It led me on like a 'will-o'-the-wisp' among the tables and I was soon sweating profusely. We might have gone on all night like this, the butterfly and I, had not my quarry come to rest on a man's shoulder. He slowly put up one finger to it and the butterfly, hesitatingly and with every mental reserve, climbed on to it with its long thin legs and was gently lowered to the table. It sat on his hand for a while and the man gazed down at it like God gazing down upon His creation on the first day. I sat down beside the man, wiping the sweat off my forehead and neck.

'Phew!' I said. 'I never was much of a one for collecting butterflies.'

'Quite a chase you had an' all,' the man replied with a Yorkshire accent.

'I wonder why they all wanted to kill the poor beast.'

'Because they were scared of it, I suppose. And they were

48

scared of it because they didn't know what it was. We're all afraid of the unknown. Ay, and because it's defenceless and easily destroyed. Fair asking to be destroyed, I reckon.'

And suddenly the butterfly, as though now rested and refreshed, rose into the air like a spirit released. It sailed up beyond the lights and the clouds of steam, like a leaf borne aloft by the wind, and soared above the crooked roofs of the houses. Soon it was a blacker smut against the indigo sky and the stars. It vanished out of our lives and Bugis Street forgot it.

The man and I sat on at the table with a kind of vacuum between us. He was eating a large plate of noodles, using chopsticks in an expert manner. Obviously he was not a serviceman, for very few of them care for Chinese food, which they regard with suspicion. Presently the Yorkshireman spoke to the waiter in a Chinese language. This, too, is rare in Singapore, for if Europeans are fluent in any of the vernacular languages it is almost always Malay.

When the Yorkshireman had finished speaking the waiter burst out laughing and went back to his food stall still chuckling. Whatever the joke was it seemed to have a great appeal, for he repeated it to the man behind the stall, who passed it to the man juggling with the cooking-pan over the brazier. Soon a whole gallery of grinning Chinese faces was peering at us through the rising steam, from behind the festoons of flattened cuttle-fish and trussed chickens, through the ropes of intestines and over the piles of cockles. This, too, was a rare sight for Singapore, for the Chinese seem to be a people who, as a rule, seldom laugh outright.

'What did you say that amused him so much?' I asked.

'I don't think I know you well enough to tell you that,' the man said. He forked up a coil of noodles expertly with his chopsticks. 'They like a ripe joke, do these folks.'

'You speak the language very well. You must have been out here a long time.'

'Seventeen years altogether, including three in the bag.' 'In the bag' in Malaya means 'inside a Japanese prison camp'.

'You seem to know the people well. You obviously like them too, which is something. Knowing the language helps, I suppose.'

'I ought to, considering my job.'

'What's that?'

'I'm a Resettlement Officer. I couldn't do that job unless I could talk their language. I speak Hokkien and Malay. The Malays are rather different, but you can never hope to get on really with the Chinese unless you can speak their language—or one of their languages. You're simply a red-haired foreign devil else. By the way my name's Alf. What's yours?'

Europeans are known to the Chinese as 'red-haired devils' —devils because they are foreign and therefore not the sons of Heaven, and red-haired because they are frequently not black-haired. It is a manifestation of the xenophobia which is probably more pronounced among the Chinese than any other race.

In those days a Resettlement Officer's job was not a very enviable one. It called for great tact and patience, under-standing and sympathy. Many Resettlement Officers had these qualities, but some had not. They were the officials recruited since the beginning of the Malayan emergency to oversee and manage the carrying out of Templer's plan for countering the menace of the Communist terrorists who lurked in the jungle and drew support in the form of food and arms from the straggling country villages. In essence the plan was a simple one. It consisted of uprooting whole populations and re-settling them behind barbed wire so that they could no longer make contact with the bandits, nor the bandits with them, nor communicate with them in any way.

The Malayan countryside, except around Malacca and along the east coast, must be among the saddest and most forlorn in the world. It has a gloomy, haunted look, and the heavy clouds that cover it seem to weigh it down. For hundreds of square miles it consists of angular hills, often sculptured and moulded into strange knobs and monoliths, covered by a dense mat of evergreen jungle. Huge trees, the *Dipterocarps*, tower above their fellows, raising gaunt arms above the general level of the green canopy around them, as though trying to claw down the rain clouds which weep perpetually upon the jungle and are the reason for its existence. Beneath the main roof of the jungle is a tangle of lesser growth with thorny, strangling festoons of lianes. It is a dark, gloomy, dripping world, unadorned by blossoms, the home of monkeys, snakes and giant leeches. It is loud with the shriek of cicadas, an evasive clamour which is always there or there, but never here. This is where the brave, tough and desperate men and women lived who made themselves the enemies of the State.

Many square miles of the Malayan countryside have been cleared of jungle. Over some areas a secondary jungle has been allowed to grow up, among which lie the dead trunks of the primary jungle like the corpses of a smitten army. But over still greater areas the jungle has been cleared altogether and rubber trees planted. The roads drive straight on in pencil-like perspectives through miles and miles of rubber trees, all planted in rows so that the long aisles of them spin like the spokes of a wheel as you drive past. The eyes ache from this endless rotation. Some are old trees with overarching branches, making long arcades like those of a gigantic railway station. There is no sound in them but the pop and flop of nuts as they split and fall. Others are smaller, young trees, delicate and feathery, and others again are tiny saplings. Where they grow the landscape opens out, and beyond their long lines you can see the rolling, dark hills, covered with still more ranks of rubber trees. The bark of every tree is carved into V-shaped grooves, and every smooth trunk wears, like a phylactery, a little metal cup to catch the latex that bleeds from these wounds.

In the tin-mining areas great clay-coloured lakes have been scooped out of the face of the earth, and conical artificial mounds of tin-washings rise beside them. It is mostly in the tin-mining areas, especially around Ipoh, that the low mountains assume strange shapes, like stooping, hooded figures turned to stone in the midst of some act of devotion, but long, long ago, so that forests have grown as a mantle upon their backs.

The villages straggle through this countryside for miles —or used to—without form and void. A few rows of Chinese terrace shop-houses, in the familiar style, form a sort of centre. Here are the cafés with the juke-boxes, the pin-table saloons, the mercury lights. Perhaps a brilliantly lit shop or so, full of cheap rings and wrist-watches, glows in the surrounding darkness. The Chinese wait behind their counters like spiders in their webs. But away from these nuclei of light and noise the villages stretch out as long tentacles of wooden shacks up to the jungle's edge among the banana palms and the sweet-almond trees. The shacks are roofed with palm thatch and corrugated iron. Flattened kerosene tins help to eke out the walls. Here and there the ground has been cleared and a bright, gleaming new bungalow has been built by some well-to-do Chinese. But mostly the villages are—or were—just miles of unrelieved poverty unadorned by any civilized touch. They reach out towards the jungle and the jungle creeps towards them.

It was from these tentacles, where the jungle and the village meet and marry, that the bandits were able to get support, food and even arms. Their methods were terror, kidnapping, blackmail and murder. The villages were too diffuse and shapeless to be adequately patrolled or watched.

Templer's plan was to eliminate these tentacles, to cut them off as though they were the arms of an octopus. That often meant eliminating whole villages, for in many cases a whole village was a tentacle. Accordingly the inhabitants of these straggling, miserable settlements were dislodged and re-housed elsewhere, away from the jungle and behind barbed wire. Entire populations were sometimes uprooted and placed within a perimeter fence in this way. At sunset the gates of the fence where shut and no one could get in or out until daylight.

You can see the resettlement villages on the long, straight road from Johore Bahru, just across the causeway from Singapore, to Kuala Lumpur. The road comes to a police post with wide gates in a barbed-wire fence. The chunky little Malay policemen have agreeable faces and wave you through. There are a few British soldiers about in their jungle-green uniforms and perhaps some Gurkhas. The resettled village has been grouped around the wide main street of shop-houses and climbs up the hill behind them. Part of the apparently endless rubber plantation has been cut down to make room for the rows of new little wooden houses, brightly painted, their cor-rugated-iron roofs gleaming hotly in the sun. There are many compact rows of them covering the hillside, each with a small square of ground in which some tapioca is growing, some sweet potatoes and some papaya trees. There are ducks and chickens about. It is not beautiful, but it is not bad, and better than the leaky, low-lying, insanitary shack town which it replaces. Or so one would have thought. The whole compact, trim, hygienic-looking block of hutments is surrounded by a high perimeter fence of barbed wire, with police posts at intervals. It climbs up the hill and away behind and back again down to the main road. You pass out of the gate at the other side and on down the long straight road through the rubber trees to the next village. And then some more rubber trees, and then perhaps the jungle, never very far off and often pressing forward and down upon the road as though it wished to strangle it.

Every householder thus transplanted was given a sum of money with which he had to buy the timber, supplied by the Resettlement authorities, to build or cause to be built his own house on a site chosen for him within the perimeter fence. Needless to say, since human beings are what they are, the whole operation was apt to be regarded with resentment and loathing by the poor and illiterate populations affected by it. They were mostly Chinese and Malay smallholders, Tamil rubber-tappers and labourers. No matter how mean and miserable, leaking or insanitary his old house, no one wanted to turn out at the order of an impersonal authority and move into a new one. The new one was never as good as the old. The new plot of land would not grow such good sweet potatoes, paw-paws or tapioca as the old one. It sloped south instead of north, or north instead of south. It was too high up or too low down. There was too much sun or not enough. And that was where the tact and sympathy of the Resettlement Officer, if he had any, came in.

The authorities were not always very clever about this operation or very intelligent in the choice of sites for new villages. Alf had just been posted to a new one near Muar on the west coast of Johore. It had been decided to transplant the inhabitants of a long winding colony of wretched shacks that followed the course of a stream. Farther down the valley, about two miles away, the stream joined the great, green, greasy, Muar River, all set about with mangrove trees, winding through its swamps to the Malacca Strait. The authorities—that is, Alf's predecessor—had chosen as a site for the new settlement a patch of low-lying but fertile alluvial ground near the junction of the stream and the river. Alf's predecessor meant well enough. The land was good farming land. But what he did not know, and no one, naturally, had told him, was that in the January rains the river habitually rose and covered the ground at this point to a depth of four or five feet. In a few months, therefore, the inhabitants found themselves sitting on their corrugated-iron roofs to escape the turbid flood that swirled around their wooden shacks, washing away their crops and their possessions.

Alf's predecessor was one of those who believed in standing no nonsense. You had to let the people see who was the master, and that when you said a thing you meant it. They respected you much more if you did that, right from the start.

'Don't listen to their moans, you know. Never does any good. Try anything if they think they can get away with it. Show 'em who's the boss from the word "go".'

The result of showing them was that all sorts of strange things kept happening. The boss's villa, a new three-roomed bungalow built by the Government, was on a hill overlooking the new village inside the perimeter fence. At the height of the flooding, when the boss was away ordering people about and standing no nonsense from anyone, somebody pushed his car out of its garage and let it run down the hill into the flood-water. Nobody knew who had done it or saw it happen. Once the tyres were slashed and once something uncomplimentary was scratched on the boot with a stone. Wires around the bungalow were occasionally cut and once a window was broken, but again nobody knew anything about it. However, worse things than that have happened to other Resettlement Officers, and more than one has been brutally murdered in the course of his duty by the people whose interests he was trying to serve.

After the floods the village was resited higher up the hill out of reach of the flood-water, and the Resettlement Officer, having demonstrated beyond doubt who was the boss, was transferred. Alf took his place and it was a sullen, resentful flock which he inherited. The Chinese met him with blank impassivity. The Indians fawned and lied and avoided him.

The Malays looked the other way. But Alf had two advantages, perhaps three. Firstly, he did not wish to show the people who was the boss but only that he was ready to help them, a fact which broke very slowly through the defensive crust which they had formed. Secondly, he spoke the language of most of them and did not have to convey his meaning by shouting in bad bazaar Malay. Thirdly, he liked them. And lastly, perhaps, it was an advantage that, instead of having reached the exalted rank of captain in a non-combatant unit during the war, as had his predecessor, he had spent most of the war in a Japanese prison camp, having started it as an Army cook. One of the earliest signs of a change of attitude on the part of the flock was that several of them offered to keep Alf's Morris Minor clean for him. Boys in the East seem to love cleaning motor-cars—it gives them a sense of accomplishing something if they can make those rounded surfaces shine. But they love driving them much more. That gives a sense of importance and power. Alf did not drive himself. 'Enough lunatics on the road as it is,' he said. 'Don't want to add to their number.' But now he was able every month or so to be driven down the long straight road between the rubber trees into Singapore. Since he did not drive himself he was quite unaware that this was a dice with death, because the young man who drove him never let the speedometer get much below 65 m.p.h. However, he almost always arrived safely and almost always, though not quite, without mishap. He came to see what he called 'a bit of life'. Anything was a relief from the drab resettlement village. He nearly always rang me up on these occasions and said, 'Well, here we are. Let's go and have some Chinese chow.' So we would go round the town together, and it was astonishing to see what a difference a knowledge of the language would make in the conduct and bearing of all the Chinese we met. The sound of it on a 'red-haired devil's' tongue seemed to cause open-mouthed amazement and delight. Golden faces, hitherto closed and blank, broke into smiles and often the almond eyes opened wide with incredulity. Whenever Alf stopped to talk to a stall vendor or entered a shop a crowd of men, boys and children, all in singlets and striped shorts, collected to listen and observe this phenomenon, a red-haired devil who could talk.

One evening we encountered an old Chinese woman at a street corner. Like thousands of others she wore a black cotton tunic and trousers. Her hair was screwed into a knob at the back of her head and had been thus treated for so many years that much of it had come out by the roots, so that she was now, like me, but artificially, balding. Her feet had been bound when she was young so that they were now tiny and deformed and like small hooves. There was a little boy with her, her grandson perhaps, clad in a vest and striped shorts, watching the old lady busying herself with something on the pavement in the angle between two walls. Here, oblivious of the jostling crowd of passers-by, she had made a little humble shrine upon the ground with some coloured paper, a piece of mirror, and three joss-sticks stuck in a cigarette-tin. Thin spirals of blue smoke wound up into the air. Now she was laying neatly upon the ground beside the tin an orange, a banana, a few red peppers and a small bunch of lichees.

Alf spoke to her, and she started and turned round. Then she laughed and showed a mouth with one old warrior tooth that had long outlived its fellows. Her face was wizened like a shrunken apple, and her skin, which had the texture of a gourd, was etched with innumerable creases. Centuries looked out from that ancient face. It belonged to a civilization different from ours and older, and it spoke of an approach to life and death, and an acceptance of both of them, far removed from that of any Westerner.

'Something pleasant once happened to her here in this spot,' Alf explained. 'She is making a thank-offering. These are presents for the kind spirits. When she has gone the kind spirits will come and take them.'

What could have happened in the angle between two walls on a public street that was worthy of the thank-offering? Some meeting, perhaps, or reunion years ago? Perhaps this was where love first sprang up and clutched the heart, once young and beating fast, but now frail and feeble beneath the black cotton tunic. Perhaps the touch of a hand or glance of an eye, or some soft word, began something long ago that was not yet ended when now she lit her joss-sticks there years afterwards, though the hand, the eyes and the voice had long vanished. One often sees these humble votive offerings on the ground in the most unlikely places in Singapore, hallowing the grimy, odorous corners of the roaring city. There burns the gratitude of some citizen for a small favour given, sending up thin spirals like prayers for a touch of God's cool finger among the rattle, the stink and the clamour.

'But won't the kids steal them?'

'Of course. But that'll be the same thing. It will be the spirits acting through the children.'

Alf spoke to the old lady and bowed to her. She bowed in return. As we moved away the little boy, who had been gazing up at us open-mouthed from his squatting position, said something to her. Alf laughed.

'What did he say?' I asked.

'He said—"The devil talks",' he explained.

That was the old China. At the very moment when we left the old lady and her little boy on the corner the new China came roaring down upon us. One behind the other heavy lorries full of youths and girls came charging down the long neon-lit street and halted at the traffic lights. The boys and girls stood up in their lorries shouting and singing. The neon lights glinted on their spectacles. Most of them wore white shirts and white or blue shorts, or white blouses and white or blue skirts. Many of the girls had their hair done up in the inevitable pony-tail behind. They all sang, swaying to the motion of the lorries, with a kind of grim, humourless determination as though daring the passers-by to contradict or shout something in opposition. No one did so. The crowd on the pavement looked at them with indifference, so they sang more loudly and doggedly. A youth in the one of the lorries, seeing Alf and me standing on the pavement, raised a clenched fist and shouted something.

'What did he say?' I asked again. I was constantly asking this when with Alf.

'Something very rude. Come on! Let's follow them and see where they are going.'

We drove in Alf's Morris Minor to the western outskirts of the town, where the Hock Lee Bus Company had its headquarters.

The Hock Lee Bus Company operated its big single-decker Diesel buses over a network of routes mostly to the north and west of the city. Their buses ran first past expensive houses standing in their own grounds, then past lines of Chinese shop-houses and rows of wooden shacks roofed with palm thatch, out to the low-cost housing estates that the Government was busily running up with feverish haste to keep abreast of the city's steadily increasing millions. Finally they ran out beyond even these to the fern-covered hills of the island, as yet virgin but already marked for doom, where at present you can see the Straits of Johore gleaming like a scimitar and a great prospect of rolling landscape and billowing cloud, marred only by the hideous works of man. Nowhere in the world, I should think, are the works of man so generally offensive to the eye as they are in Malaya and Singapore.

Just now the Hock Lee Bus Company was having a little trouble, and many of its big red buses were not running. Some of their men had formed a splinter or 'yellow' trade union to which the original union, which comprised the majority of the employees, strongly objected. They wanted the Company to withhold recognition from it, and, when the Company refused, they came out on strike. But the members of the new union continued to work and drove their buses in and out of the garage as usual. Pickets tried to stop them, and the buses were stoned as they drove about the town. Seats were slashed and intending passengers were intimidated and persuaded, by forcible and easily understood arguments, not to travel. Then the strikers shut the gates of the garage and encamped in front of them so that the non-striking members of the new union could not take their buses out. But this, of course, was illegal picketing, preventing citizens from going about their lawful occupations. So the police intervened and tried to persuade the pickets to move away from the gates so as to let the buses out. The pickets refused. They erected shelters and made beds in front of the gates and prepared for a siege. The police tried to remove them by force and turned fire hoses on them, but the men resisted with desperate determination. They clung to the railings, and even the fire-hoses could not move them. Feelings became more and more bitter, and the great city held its breath while passions rose.

It was at this point, as always, that the Communists joined in. It was just the kind of situation they were waiting for.

They arrived on the scene by the hundred, both boys and girls, in hired lorries. They almost all came from the Chinese schools, but there was always a leavening of party members whose job it was to direct operations and stoke the fires. They held meetings outside the Hock Lee Garage and made violent speeches, distributing food and cigarettes to the strikers. They sang songs and did turns which were supposed to entertain them and keep up their fighting spirit.

Discipline in Chinese schools, one must assume, must be practically non-existent. There seems to be no control over the pupils either by the masters or the parents. One of the most striking things one notices about Chinese children in Singapore is that they never seem to think it necessary to consider their parents at all and will stay out late at night or away from home almost indefinitely without ever bothering to tell their parents where they are or what they are doing. And the parents seem to take all that as a matter of course. In the present circumstances there seemed to be nothing to prevent whole schools from simply absenting themselves from their classes for as long as they chose. Masters and parents seemed powerless to intervene. Both the masters and the younger boys were terrified of the older boys, many of whom had been set back in their education by the Japanese occupation and were in fact far too old by now to be at school at all. Many of them were no more schoolboys than I am, but thugs, nearer twenty-five than twenty. It was they who were the moving spirits behind most of the trouble.

Chinese schoolboys are a strange lot altogether, in Singapore at any rate. They have almost become a race apart. They have been so much in the news and been given so much notice, out of all proportion to their importance, that a kind of unnatural glow seems to have settled around them. They wear the appellation 'Chinese schoolboy' as though it were a kind of title, as though there were something clever and special about being one.

'Guess what I am,' they say. And when you can't imagine, they say with the air of someone revealing a proud secret— 'I am a Chinese schoolboy.' In the same way one might say 'I am a doctor of science or a ship's captain,' in circumstances where you would not expect to meet one.

As for the girls, they always reminded me of those young women, their English counterparts, who show an exaggerated and somewhat desperate enthusiasm for rugger. You see them cheering frantically at Twickenham and sporting enormous rosettes, shouting shrilly above their male companions. Afterwards they are present at the beery jollity that follows, their presence not really perceived by their boy friends, but somehow necessary. Only a difference in upbringing and tradition made these pony-tailed bespectacled young Chinese females cheer themselves hoarse about Communism instead of about rugger. They followed the boys to the strikers' picket posts, into riot and into battle, for much the same unacknowledged reason that makes their English sisters follow their males to Twickenham.

When we arrived in Alf's Morris I could hardly imagine a more suitable place for a riot than the somewhat soul-destroying district around the Hock Lee Garage. I should be in a constant state of near-riot if I lived there. It was not a slum. On the contrary it was a bright, mercury-lit, geometrical, hygienic twentieth-century subtopia. I have no doubt the drains were excellent and all the plugs pulled—or did originally. There was, originally, the right number of cubic feet of air to every inhabitant. No roofs leaked. Rediffusion was laid on to every house. There was electricity. You had only to press a button, turn a switch, push a knob. No wonder there were riots there, for there was nothing else to do.

This was a low-cost housing area where blocks of flats like incubators stretched away into the distance, their self-consciously modern fronts aching under the interminable diminishing perspectives of the daylight street lamps. There was row upon row and quadrangle upon quadrangle. There were also modern factories ablaze with neon lights where radios and electrical things were made. Yonder the blocks were still going up among the older wooden and thatch shanties, where I had a sneaking feeling the people were probably far happier. In the rioting that was soon to follow, the local residents of this subtopia, so the police complained afterwards, did not co-operate with the forces of law and order. They saw nothing and heard nothing. They would not give information and would not help to incriminate rioters.

They concealed fugitives and helped them to dodge away through the modernistic quadrangles and alleys. This was surely ungrateful conduct on the part of the inhabitants of this bright new housing estate. They should have risen against any disturbance of their illuminated, concrete peace and helped to throw the intruders out. Instead they looked on with stony indifference while the battle swirled around them.

The place was swarming with people when we arrived. We were doing something of which I really rather strongly disapprove, for I think that anyone who is present as a spectator when storms of this sort are brewing deserves little sympathy for anything that may happen to him. He adds by a fraction to the difficulties of the hard-pressed policemen. But it was Alf's idea and I just went along. A huge but quite orderly crowd filled the long straight road, which had two traffic ways divided by a line of mercury lamps stretching for ever into the distance. The crowd centred chiefly on the double gates of metal and wire which were now closed upon the main yard of the garage. The yard was filled with idle red buses bearing their destination plates. They seemed to stand bunched together behind the gates in an expectant manner as though about to rush forward like huge pigs waiting to be fed. The gates were a brilliant focus of light around which the crowd swirled and eddied. The strikers, all Chinese, in their very unsmart and shapeless khaki drivers' and conductors' uniforms, were sitting, squatting or lying on mattresses and on bunks up against the closed gates and up against the long wire fence, on which they had rigged up canvas shelters supported by poles. Hurricane lamps hung from the poles and from the wire mesh of the fence and made a white glare over everything, on the men's disordered possessions on the ground where food and fruit were piled in readiness for a siege, on their faces and their hair and their stony eyes. Some of them were lying with their eyes staring vacantly at the lamps and the insects that circled round them. Others sat or squatted, reading Chinese paper-backs or playing cards with long cardboard strips carrying Chinese characters. Food stalls and peanut vendors, sensing business, had set up pitches nearby, and the dark-skinned crowd milled round. It all had the air of a fair-ground, and it was obvious that nearly all

61 c

the people were simply there to enjoy themselves. That they were doing so on other people's unhappiness was, of course, neither here nor there.

In places the crowd had gathered in knots and circles, ever shifting and varying in size and position, round groups of schoolboys and girls who had dismounted from the lorries. More lorries kept driving up and discharging more young Communists, who gathered crowds around themselves. In the middle of one circle a youth was playing a mouth-organ. In another there was community singing, Communist songs one presumed, the girls adding their high voices to those of the boys. Another group was being harangued by a spectacled boy who kept wagging an admonitory finger at his audience. He was talking in one of Singapore's many Chinese languages and, since Alf said he could not understand it, it was probably Cantonese. His impassive audience gave no clue as to what he was saying. There was neither laughter nor comment, and the circle he was addressing kept crumbling at the edges and reforming elsewhere like a patch of froth on the surface of a stream. Other boys and girls moved up and down the fence with cigarettes and trays of sweets like attendants at a cinema. All this was supposed to amuse and encourage the strikers and give them heart for the workers' struggle. But it seemed, in fact, to have very little effect on anyone, and no one paid a great deal of attention. The fairground atmosphere persisted, and the crowd stood around the performers with blank impassivity, registering no emotion. Policemen stood about in twos and threes, armed and steel-helmeted, and police cars moved up and down the long straight road under the mercury lamps. It was difficult to picture them in the role of the oppressors of the workers for which they had obviously been cast by the gesticulating speakers, who kept pointing at them over the heads of the crowd.

We seemed to be the only Europeans in that vast company. No one took any notice of us. Sometimes, when we joined a group or a circle to see what was going on, faces would turn and stare at us. If we spoke the sound of English would attract attention and people would turn in our direction and look at us for a moment. Once or twice a member of the crowd smiled as one might at seeing a stranger at some ceremony which must be foreign and incomprehensible to him. Indeed it was astonishing that the whole great gathering, which the next day was to be a scene of bloodshed and disorder, gave no sign whatever of any hostility to us as Europeans. People in the crowd frequently made way for us and sometimes guided us forward with a hand on the arm so that we could see better the antics of some youth capering in the middle of an impassive circle.

I had thought we were the only Europeans among the throng, but I was mistaken. Near the gate a tarpaulin, supported on poles, made a kind of tent, illuminated by hanging hurricane lamps. It was surrounded by a crowd of Chinese, who seemed to be eagerly pressing around to see what was happening in the tent. We stood among them. No one took any notice of us, for all were too intent on what was going on inside. There were a table and some chairs under the hurricane lamps, and a sort of committee meeting was being held around the table. Several Chinese, whom I took to be union officials, were sitting round the table, and the crowd pressed up against their backs, often leaning over to interject remarks. In the centre of the circle an Englishman sat in the attitude of Rodin's *Penseur*, his chin on his hand. It was the British Assistant Labour Commissioner. One of the Chinese was leaning across the table talking eloquently to him in a Chinese dialect, both hands stretched out across the table to illustrate what he was saying. Others around the table from time to time interrupted with remarks of their own. They were pouring out their troubles to this young Englishman, who sat in their midst, wise, patient, sympathetic and without fear, in the tradition of British administrators. The lamp had not yet gone out, I thought.

The lamp went out next day. The Communists extinguished it. The following evening they saw to it that the crowd was infiltrated by an army of several hundred whose business it was to make trouble. Leavened by these and whipped up by the lorry-loads of schoolboys and girls, the crowd was in an ugly mood by sunset. Cars were set on fire, several policemen were killed and many people injured. A young American journalist, anxious to get a story, hastened to the scene by taxi and was battered to death by an infuriated mob. One of the Communist schoolboys was mortally wounded. His comrades carried him, bleeding to death, through the streets of Singapore, showing him to the people as a victim of a cruel and oppressive colonialism. He was dead when they brought him to the hospital.

4

A Military Occasion

Very long ago, in the legendary kingdom of Ayodhya in India, there ruled an aged king named Dasarath. He wished to hand over the reins of government to his eldest son, Ram Chandra, but his favourite wife had other ideas and planned to place her own son on the throne. She persuaded the old king to banish Ram Chandra from the kingdom for fourteen years. Accordingly Ram, with his wife, Sita Devi, and his younger brother, Lakshmanan, went to live in a small hut in the jungle of Chitra Kut.

Now it happened that Rawan, the King of Ceylon, coveted Sita Devi, the beautiful wife of the exiled Ram. He had already been an unsuccessful suitor whom the lady had rejected in favour of Ram. One day, when Ram and his brother were out hunting, Rawan disguised himself, lured Sita away from her house and carried her off to his kingdom.

For many years and in many battles Ram and his brother fought against Rawan, but were unable to defeat him. In his bitter discouragement Ram prayed to Danga, the Goddess of War, and vowed to fast for eight days if she would give him victory. He fasted and on the eighth day celebrated the end of his fast with a great feast. Next day he went out and gave battle to Rawan and slew him and many of his followers, and regained the beautiful Sita.

This Hindu legend is celebrated every year by the most famous mercenary soldiers in the world, the Gurkhas of Nepal. It is a kind of Gurkha Christmas and is known as 'Dashera'. They send their friends cards, which are the universal oriental pink colour, the colour of rejoicing, wishing a happy Dashera just as we send Christmas-cards wishing a happy Christmas. They, however, do not have holly or bells. The celebrations last for two days, and there are feasts and games, football matches, sports and jollities and that feeling of good-will and diffused benignity which Christmas also brings. On the first day there is a feast and dances to commemorate those with which Ram Chandra celebrated the end of his eight days' fast. But the second day is the real celebration, when the great victory of Ram Chandra over Rawan is commemorated in blood. The Gurkhas love blood and do not seem able to have enough of it. On this day they publicly chop the heads off hundreds of ducks, chickens and goats to symbolize the casualties in Rawan's army. Finally they behead an ox with one blow of a long, curved Gurkha knife, or *kukri*, symbolizing the slaying of King Rawan himself.

Sometimes Alf and I used to go up to the Sergeants' Mess at one of the Army barracks and drink beer on Sunday mornings. The room was full of red-faced men and tobacco smoke, loud laughter and stories. The women sat about at tables sipping sherries or small gins-and-limes and made unsuccessful attempts to control their children. It was at one of these gatherings that a sergeant invited me to the Gurkhas' Dashera ceremony which was to take place at their transit camp during the coming week.

'The wife and I usually go to the dances on the first day,' said the Sergeant, 'but the wife doesn't care about the second day, when they do all the chopping. But it might interest you to go along, just for the experience like. I'll send you a ticket and we'll meet there, eight o'clock Tuesday evening. Rum idea of religion some folks have, I must say.'

The transit camp was some way out of town beyond the last housing estate, where the newly gashed earth showed like red wounds. It was among those fern-covered uplands that lie behind Singapore, where great distances surprisingly unfold. Here, on a hillside, were row upon row of Nissen huts, lorry-parks, gun-parks, car-parks and a square parade-ground, all enclosed by a perimeter fence. Stocky little brown sentries stood on guard at the entrance.

I arrived, wearing my white tuxedo, a little after eight, which was the time stated on my invitation card. There seemed to be no one about and certainly no sign of the Sergeant who was to be my host. The car-park was empty, but I could see that the parade-ground had been arranged for an occasion. It was surrounded by flags, and along one side of it there was a spectators' stand with rows of chairs, several large important comfortable ones in the centre of the front row, and larger and more numerous flags. As I got out of my car and walked towards the stand I seemed to be the only guest and to be embarrassingly early.

A soldierly figure led me to a seat in the middle of the front row of chairs on the covered stand and, clicking his heels smartly, left me there in solitary state. I moved guiltily a few chairs away from the centre and waited. It would be terrible to be found sitting in the seats of the mighty when the mighty arrived and to be obliged to begin with shame to take a lower place. Soon I felt the tide of guilt and apprehension rising again. I furtively moved back into the second row and went on waiting. For hours, it seemed, nothing happened, and there was no sign of my host.

Then at last I saw that something was happening. In the velvet darkness at one end of the parade-ground I could just make out what looked like a bright herbaceous border which had suddenly come into flower. It moved as though a wind blew through it. Then I saw, straining my eyes in the gloom, that the bright flower border was in fact several rows of Indian ladies sitting on the ground in their bright saris. I could hear the sibilance of their talk, and the continuous move-ment of their hands made the border ripple as though in a gentle breeze. Their babies ran in and out among them like large butterflies, were reproved continually and slapped, and went on tumbling on the edge of the arena. These were the wives and children of the soldiers who would take part in the dances, which, if one were to believe one's invitation card, should by now have been in progress for a good three-quarters of an hour.

I reminded myself, however, that this was the timeless East and waited patiently, wondering whether I were going to be the only guest on the stand. But soon people in evening dress began to arrive in twos and threes, and there was the sound of loud conversation. It was officer-like conversation, which made me feel like a being from another planet—as, indeed, I was. People slowly drifted, talking the while, into the rows of seats facing the parade-ground, round the edge of which a great murmurous crowd had now gathered in the darkness. About half a dozen seats in the centre of the front row were left empty, and I felt waves of guilty horror overwhelming me again. I sidled into the third row.

'Excuse me. Are you alone, sir?'

'Well, yes. I am, as a matter of fact. My host and hostess this evening don't seem to be going to turn up. They said eight o'clock, but I don't see any sign of them.'

'Really? Very odd. May we introduce ourselves? My name is B——, Captain, 10th ——.' He named a famous regiment then stationed in Singapore. 'And this is Sally, my wife.'

Sally was a pretty and charming English blonde. I also introduced myself and explained, rather apologetically as one always does for some strange reason, that I was a civilian. I believe I was actually cowardly enough to say 'a mere civilian.'

However, the Captain and his wife did not seem to be in the least put out by my lack of service status and indicated an empty seat between them in the front. I began to enjoy the evening and quite forgot about my absent friends. My new-found ones were delightful, and I was grateful for their hospitality. We made easy small-talk and I flattered myself that they were as pleased with the chance encounter as I was.

Suddenly floodlights reached out long pale arms from above each corner of the parade-ground, turning it into a pale carpet of light. I saw now that while I had been talking to my new acquaintances the six vacant chairs in the middle of the front row had been occupied. The Colonel and his party had arrived. I saw the backs of balding heads and greying feminine coiffures. Cigar smoke curled into the air.

On the far side of the ground was an illuminated dais where a small party of Gurkha musicians had taken their places.

The entertainment began with a prayer which the typed programme we had been given stated was 'A Prayer to the Goddess with a Happy Heart'. I presumed the Goddess was the Goddess of War to whom indeed these little brown men dedicate their lives. Unfortunately I have quite forgotten it and only remember the long procession of swaying, tripping Hindu maidens that filed on to the parade-ground in two long sinuous lines after the prayer was over. They converged from opposite corners of the parade-ground, formed complicated figures and squares in front of the spectators' stand, repeatedly advancing and retreating. Each girl was dressed in a long flowing robe and carried a half-hoop of twined flowers which she lifted above her head, swept down to the ground or held at arm's length, moving with well-drilled but slow and graceful precision. They moved with a tripping, *chassée* step, swaying their bodies from side to side to the monotonous chanting music of the musicians on the dais. As the lines of swaying dancers wound and intertwined they drew nearer to the officers' stand. They moved and swayed with unaffected beauty and grace, their eyes half closed and downcast as though in a trance, their long plaited hair hanging down their backs. There was warm applause.

'Charming!' I said, clapping enthusiastically.

'Don't get too excited,' said the Captain's wife. 'Look at their feet.'

I looked and saw what I hadn't noticed before. As the maidens drew near the stand I could see large white gym shoes twinkling in and out beneath the long flowing robes. The maidens were Gurkha soldiers. The womenfolk never take part in these dances, and, as was once the case in our own theatre, all female parts are taken by men. These fierce little soldiers were impersonating Hindu maidens with perfect, unaffected natural ease and grace. No one thought it in the least extraordinary.

The front line of dancers now moved up towards the officers' stand. Each dancer chose a member of the audience in the front row. With the last chords of the music she laid her garland of flowers about the neck of an officer or his lady. For a second a wide brown face, eyes half closed as though in a trance, was close to mine. Hands lightly touched my shoulders, and a rope of entwined frangipani flowers, orange and cream, and yellow trumpets of Allamanda lay round my neck. The air was full of the heavy scent of them. I placed my palms together in the Hindu greeting. The maiden placed hers together, bowed and retreated. The floodlights went out and she was swallowed up by the darkness. The lines of dancers wound away with tripping, swaying steps into the shadows.

The dances, interspersed with items obligingly labelled 'Comic' in the programme, in case there should be any doubt, seemed to go on for hours. A curious listless melancholy seemed to underlie the whole entertainment, even though this was supposedly a most joyous celebration by a people renowned for their martial ardour. The same melancholy, indeed, seems to inform all Hindu ceremonies. The turns which were labelled 'Comic' took place on the illuminated dais on the far side of the ground. They all consisted of long gabbled dialogues between two characters called Chota Sahib, which I took to mean 'great Lord', and Juthe. But they were all in the Gurkha language, so I am afraid the humour escaped me. Ripples of restrained laughter occasionally broke out from the audience around the edges of the arena but there was no sign of amusement from the Gurkhas' own officers around me on the stand. I gathered that the Gurkhas (like the English) have a sense of humour of their own not easily appreciated by foreigners.

One of the dances was very striking. It was called the 'Shankar' dance. On the lighted dais a small boy sat cross-legged and quite alone. He wore a yellow robe and a yellow turban. He sat there for a while quite motionless, like a small image. A musician in the darkness twanged out a monotonous rhythm on a stringed instrument, but still the image did not move. It sat with its little brown face looking down at the ground, its arms folded. An attendant placed a garland of flowers round its neck, and suddenly the image came to life. Still without moving from his cross-legged sitting position the boy swayed his body from side to side while his hands flickered round and over him like dark insects against the yellow robe. He was a small flame, burning alone and briefly on the ground before an altar. The music, which accompanied the swaying curving movements of his body, outraged the senses. He was a flower taken by the wind beside a mountain road. He was innocence and sensuality at the same time, purity and lust. But suddenly the music stopped, without apparently reaching any real end. The boy bowed down, touching the ground with his forehead. The lights on the dais went out and he too was gone, swallowed up in the darkness. So you touch beauty only for an instant and instantly it is gone and you cannot recapture it.

'What about a drink?' said the young Captain.

'An excellent idea,' I replied and, rising from my seat,

turned round to find my Sergeant host and his wife standing a few paces behind my chair.

'Oh, there you are!' I said. 'I'd quite given you up. Thought you weren't coming.'

I turned to the Captain and his wife. 'Er—may I introduce—?'

A mask had descended upon the Captain's face. But it was nothing to the opaque blankness that had come over the English freshness of his wife's.

'I think, my dear, we ought to go and talk to the Andersons. I see them over there. Will you excuse us, please?'

They pointedly moved away to the far end of the stand and I never had an opportunity to speak to either of them again, though I saw them engaged in animated and intense conversation in the distance. If I happened to come near them during the remainder of the evening they drifted away, as though accidentally, still animatedly talking. It was as though I had suddenly become a leper white as snow. I had really. For the Captain and his wife had suddenly and simultaneously, and with a profound shock, discovered that they had been entertaining someone who all the time was really the guest of a non-commissioned officer. They had been nurturing a viper in their bosoms. As for me, I had broken the rules of caste, which, it seemed, still held in the little world in which my Captain moved. Unhappy man! A gulf yawned at his feet.

I suddenly felt that the evening was over for me. The dances anyhow would go on for hours. There were at least four more 'Comic' ones to come, and so, feeling upset and unequal to the strain, I excused myself to the Sergeant and his wife and left for the more egalitarian atmosphere of Bugis Street.

However, I went back for the second day's celebrations, drawn by curiosity of a rather morbid sort. The parade-ground ached under the hot forenoon sun. On the spectators' stand from which I had witnessed the dances the night before a small number of British N.C.O.s with their wives and children had already arrived. The children were scrapping with one another for front seats and the women were talking chattily together about this and that as though they were in Lyons' Corner House. I thought it was surely an odd sort of entertainment to choose for one's children on a fine morning. Already the birds and beasts that were shortly to be done to death were being marshalled on the other side of the ground. A British regimental band was drawn up there too, sweating in their tight-collared white tunics and peaked caps. Their round plough-boys' faces glowed red.

'Look at the dear little quack-quacks, Johnnie! And here come the nannie-goats!'

The chickens went to their doom in a state of furious female indignation, protesting against the outrage to their dignity, but the ducks took a calm view of the proceedings. They walked in file, their feet going like little wheels, and their heads turning in unison from side to side to give now the audience and now the band a cool, humorous, appraising once-over with their bright, beady eyes. They made little contented duck noises as they walked. The procession was guided gently by a soldier to a group of other soldiers, who grasped the birds one by one by the wings and unceremoniously and swiftly chopped their heads off. Each chicken or duck had only time for one protesting squawk or quack before its head joined one pile and its body another. It was all so impersonal and matter-of-fact that I do not think the children really noticed what was going on.

The goats were rather different. They were led on to the parade-ground in strings of three or four, mincing along on their silly little hooves, bleating apprehensively and pulling this way and that. They were led to another group of soldiers. The soldiers repeatedly raised their *kukris*. A flash! A flick! There was another head, still bleating soundlessly on the sand. A little blood spurted, once, twice, thrice, from the severed neck. Flick! There was another! Thus silently the army of Rawan perished.

'Look at the nannie-goats, Mummy! They can't say baa with no body, can they?'

'No darling. Of course not.'

Children must be much tougher nowadays than in my young days, I thought.

This mechanical slaughter went on for some time, while the stand slowly filled up. Presently the Colonel arrived again and took his central chair. There were no women in his party, I noticed. The sweating bandsmen began to play familiar and martial airs. Chickens, ducks and goats continued to be decapitated to the strains of *Blue Bells of Scotland* and *Men of Harlech*. While this drowned the bleating and quacking of Rawan's army our attention was drawn to the entrance of the King himself, who was now, with great difficulty, being pulled by ropes from in front and pushed by poles from behind slowly and cumbrously towards his place of execution.

A sturdy upright pole stood in the earth between us and the bandsmen. At its foot lay a grotesque shape which had puzzled me for some time. Now I saw that it was a model of the head of an ox, fashioned out of earth, brutally ugly and unskilful, but barbaric and terrible. The snout and half-open mouth were towards the spectators' stand while the horns curved back on either side of the base of the pole.

King Rawan moved slowly and unwillingly towards the pole. He was a big battleship-grey water-buffalo. The mud from the cool wallow where he had last lain was still caked upon his leathery flanks. Two ropes, each pulled by four or five soldiers hauling backwards with grunts and shouts, formed a halter round his head. Poles levered him under his stern, pushed by other grunting soldiers. He knew something was up. All this pulling and shoving and shouting, he knew, boded ill for him. Something dreadful, he dimly felt, was coming, but how could one possibly know what it was? One could only dig one's hooves in and keep on resisting, refuse to take a single voluntary step forward or do anything these shouting, shoving, pulling little humans wanted. There was a dull fear in the eyes of the King. His head went down and his legs splayed out forward. The soldiers shouted and heaved.

'Look at the moo-cow, duckie! Johnnie, move over and let Doris see the big moo-cow.'

The children laughed and jostled one another to see better.

'He doesn't want to go much, does he, Mummy? Mummy, why doesn't he want to go?'

Slowly, foot by foot, wounding the red earth of the parade-ground with his reluctant hooves, the King was dragged to the execution pole. He was tied now with his head down to the base of the pole and his forefeet splayed out before him. The band had stopped playing. The bandsmens' faces shone and glistened under their peaked caps.

From the door of a hut near the execution pole a big Gurkha

soldier stepped into the sunlight. His paunchy torso was clad in a white singlet and shorts, and he wore a cloth round his head like a turban. A huge curved knife, an outsize *kukri*, gleamed in his right hand. He raised it in a salute and stepped forward towards the taut neck of the King.

The executioner for this occasion is carefully and specially chosen and for weeks beforehand undergoes a rigorous course of training, with special dieting and special prayers. For the King's head must be struck off at one blow of the great heavy *kukri*. Failure to achieve this brings bad luck and is a dishonour. The executioner is chosen for his strength and skill.

There was a roll of drums. The executioner lifted his knife and down it flashed—almost right through at one blow. Almost, but not quite. As the head fell away and the body rolled over sideways, there was still some connecting skin and tissue which took a few sawing movements of the knife to get through. Some blood, but not very much, gushed out on to the earth. The head was hauled away by the horns. It was just a head, that was all. King Rawan was dead.

I turned to see how the children had taken this rather gruesome spectacle. Astonishingly, they seemed to be totally unaffected by it and certainly much less so than I, who felt slightly ill.

'Will they eat him now, Mummy?' said Johnnie.

The executioner stepped up to the Colonel, who, rising from his seat, placed a garland of flowers about the executioner's neck. But he, his knife still red and dripping in his hand, was in tears. It had not been a single blow.

5

Quiet Wedding

When I first arrived in Singapore the research project, which was to carry out the exploration of the seas to the east and west of the Malay peninsula, existed only on paper. The lists of figures had to be translated into action, a ship had to be acquired and a laboratory built. I had to set the wheels in motion to acquire the ship and build the building. Like the mills of God, the wheels revolved exceeding slowly and for months and months my 'organization', as it was officially called, consisted only of Jim, my Tamil stenographer, and myself. The two of us occupied a table in the Singapore Government Fisheries Office.

The Fisheries Office, as in all the Colonies, was concerned with the administration and development of the fishing industry. It issued licences to fishermen for the operation of boats or traps, helped them with money to install engines or buy fishing gear and tried, with varying success, to do something to lessen the grip of the middleman. It facilitated the marketing, handling and transport of fish, tried to regulate prices and quantities and employed a corps of inspectors who collected and recorded the statistics of catches. In fact it did its best to father the fishing industry along and to protect fishermen from too chill economic winds and from the consequences of their own improvidence and folly. At the same time it tried to promote the supply of cheap fish to the many-mouthed public. All these efforts are attended by varying success in different colonies and it is uphill work in all of them. Most Fisheries Officers feel like the thief whom Theseus threw over the cliff, but who hung suspended in mid-air because neither the sea nor the land would have him.

The Singapore Fisheries Office, in which I had my table, the nerve centre of my as yet unborn project, was a large rectangular go-down made of corrugated galvanized-iron sheeting, one of three in a row on the waterfront. One side of it faced the anchorage and the mole and the open straits beyond. In the distance was the blue line of what used to be known as the Dutch Islands, now part of Indonesia. Here was the quay where the Japanese-built trawlers and the Hong Kong long-liners lay. Here they unloaded their catches, took on fuel and ice and made and mended their gear. The other side of the go-down faced a large tidal basin which was usually chock-full of wooden lighters, each with an eye painted on each side of its prow. They nudged and jostled one another in the swell that crept into the entrance. The Tamil lighter-men slept and ate on their barges under straw-matting shelters. Often they lay or squatted on their hams up against the cor-rugated-iron sides of our go-down or perched in the squatting posture like black birds of prey on the iron bollards along the edges of the wharf. Like birds in a rookery they jabbered in-cessantly, and one believed that knives were to be drawn at any moment. In fact they were only passing the time of day. After a while Jim would get up from his table with the air of an imperious mama about to reprimand her tiresome children and, going outside on to the wharf, would jabber something in his turn. I gathered he was telling these inferior beings to cease their low clamour as they were causing disturbance and inconvenience to the boss. This always had the desired effect, and the skinny black men would drift away and begin again farther off. I never told Jim to do this or gave any indication, so far as I knew, that I was particularly disturbed, but he always did it and with such a grand air of authority that they never questioned it. I have no idea what we should have done if one of them had invited the boss to go and fry his face, especially as I was not in fact the boss at all. But that still does not quite happen in the East—not yet.

The go-down was not perhaps an ideal place in which to grapple with administrative problems involving the drawing up of estimates, the working out of columns of figures showing other people's salaries for years to come, and the writing out of those endless drafts. They still, I suppose, exist some-where in Singapore, those masterpieces, in files bound with the pink tape I tied round them sorrowfully on my last day some five years later. For, in addition to the incessant clamour from outside, the go-down was extremely hot. The corrugated iron trapped and held a great stagnant pool of heated air, so that every day about three o'clock in the afternoon my organization ran on whatever momentum it had acquired before lunch, while its head and brain sat with its mouth open gazing into space. Sweat dripped off the forehead of the head which contained the brain and dripped on to the minutes as I wrote them. Above us in the roof rows of squeakily revolving fans maintained a gentle rain of smuts and dust over everything, so that any papers left lying about became grey after a day or two. From time to time, in moments when for a second one's vigilance relaxed, letters, minutes and memoranda took off from one's desk and parachuted down to the floor like weary butterflies. Whenever it rained heavily, which in the south-west monsoon season was very often, all work in the Fisheries Office came to a standstill. Water dripped through the roof in a thousand thin vertical streams on to files, minutes, type-writers, records, cash-books. Large sheets of cardboard were kept specially for covering them, and as soon as the drumming assault of the rain began on the roof all desks and tables were covered up and work stopped until the storm was over.

The go-down housed a small army of clerks, mostly Chinese with Malay and Tamil office-boys. They issued licences, recorded statistics and typed out the minutes which the Fisheries Officer indefatigably wrote. 'I do wish he wouldn't,' a Government official said to me. 'It only means we have to read them.'

'Be careful,' said one of the Chinese clerks when I first arrived. 'Never leave your fountain-pen or your watch lying about. These Malay boys . . .'

'Always keep your car locked,' said my Malay driver. 'Many Chinese no good. *Penchuri*—steal. . . .'

The Fisheries Officer, the head and general-in-command of this little army, wrote the minutes complained of in a sort of enclosure made of book-shelves arranged around a desk so as to give the appearance of a separate room. A fan overhead reserved all the dust it showered down especially for him. Here, in this sanctum, Tom worked remorselessly, his face pale and shiny with sweat on hot afternoons, a growing pile of cigarette butts filling a glass ashtray in front of him.

No gazing into space for him. His glass-topped desk was littered with the horrid paraphernalia of a Government executive, the disordered mountain of shabby files, the semi-circular hand-blotter, the rubber stamps, the paper-weights, the 'In' and 'Out' and 'Pending' trays, the dog-eared copies of estimates, regulations and standing orders. All this I acquired myself in due course, beginning with a rubber stamp bearing the word 'Director', above which I proudly signed my name dozens of times a day.

Tom was a man of great energy and real ability in the middle thirties. He had been in Singapore for three years, and in that time, by sheer driving and hammering, by ceaseless churning out memoranda, he had succeeded in building up an organization the value of which was known and recognized by the fishermen themselves. There can hardly be a greater tribute than that, for fishermen as a rule are apt to despise and resent anything in the nature of Government control or interference. But when Tom's contract came to an end after three years the fishermen sent a petition to the Governor expressing their appreciation of all that he had done and begging for his services to be retained. The full measure of this success can only be appreciated by anyone who has worked for Governments in the tropics, where the pace at which the great machine moves is even slower than in more invigorating climates. There are times when a black despair descends upon one. Things will never get a move on, and the reluctant creaks and groans with which the mechanism works when at last the penny drops make a mock of all enthusiasm and dampen all hope. Tom sweated and cursed but would not be bullied or frightened or stone-walled. Nor would he be put off by what we came to know as the 'bottomless pillar-box technique'.

Under him the little army toiled and sweated willingly. It is indeed a remarkable fact, and one that of course must never be mentioned, that Asians work better for a European whom they like and respect than for one of their own people. One sees this again and again. It is because the European as a rule knows what he is doing, makes decisions—even if they may be wrong ones—and stands by them. Asians, on the other hand, when in official positions, often have the utmost horror of arriving at any kind of decision and go to almost any length of procrastination and delay and 'buck-passing' to avoid doing so. A Chinese Government official once said to me, 'Why should I decide anything? If I make a wrong decision I get a black mark and may even endanger my pension. If I make a right one, it won't be I who will get the credit.' This, you may say, is one of the evil effects of the colonial system, which has kept Asians in the background so long and given them a dependent habit of mind. That may be so, but it has a paralysing effect on the machine. But Asians also seem to distrust each other, perhaps because they know the workings of each others' minds too well. The workings of the European mind are less familiar and less easy to interpret and therefore less suspect. Anyhow Tom's little army in the tin shed worked with remarkable devotion and was very often still all hard at it long after half-past four, the regulation closing time for Government offices.

One of the reasons for this was that the army felt that it was marching somewhere. An army always likes to feel that it is being led forward. In spite of all obstacles the outfit was growing and progress was obvious for all to see. From being quartered in an office on the fourth floor of a building on Collyer Quay, the army had expanded and moved into half of this salubrious tin go-down. Then it expanded further and took in the whole of the go-down. Then a detachment of the Customs came and encamped in the go-down, after protracted negotiations, in order to provide a quicker Customs clearance for fishing-boats. Then arrangements were made for tanker-lorries to refuel the fishing-boats alongside the wharf so as to provide them with a quicker turn-round in port. Then an exhibition of small-boat engines and fishing-gear was set up in the go-down, and many other innovations, tirelessly conceived and brought to fruition over the mounting pile of cigarette butts on the boss's desk, gave the impression of inexorable forward movement. The army was on the march.

So far as I was concerned, however, I found only one of the many innovations of direct benefit to myself personally. It did not spring from the fertile brain of the Boss at all but from the ruthless, unsleeping commercial enterprise of the Chinese clerks. This was a soft drinks service which one of them started. He arranged for a large selection of ten-cent bottles of Malaya's national drinks, Coca-cola and synthetic fruit-juice, to be delivered daily and to be kept in an ice-box near the door at the end of the go-down behind a discreet screen. As in a private bar in England one could drink and not be seen drinking.

About eleven o'clock in the morning I would pause in whatever I was doing. 'Enclosed please find a statement of estimated Capital and Recurrent Expenditure for the quarter ending June 30th, 1953,' and then I would sign it above the rubber-stamped word 'Director' and toss it with a sigh of relief into my 'Out' basket, hoping that I had not forgotten some vital item whose absence would wreck the whole edifice. I usually had. But for the moment it was time to relax and I would get up and walk the whole length of the go-down between the files, the ledgers and the typewriters. The clerks looked up from these and bowed and smiled as I passed. At the end of the long room was the screen behind which was the ice-box. When I was within reach of it Rajoo, one of the Tamil messengers, ran forward with the air of a coachman letting down a step for a duchess. He opened the lid, pulled out a bottle of orangeade, prized off the top with an opener that hung on a string, wiped the top of the bottle with a not very clean cloth (but who cared?) and presented the bottle to me with both hands and with a bow that was grander than that of any major-domo.

These are the little childish things that I shall remember about the East, and that will be for me the East as I shall remember it when, in ten years' time, I am growing my sweet peas in Surrey, or dozing on winter evenings over *The Times*. No doubt by then its middle page will have announced in small print the last British withdrawal from the last outpost in Asia, and the British Empire that I was born heir to will by then consist of the Maldives and the Chagos Archipelago, which will probably have become a problem and be battling for independence. But I shall still be able to remember Rajoo running forward to give me a 'Coke' with a courtly bow, the clerks smiling and bowing over their ledgers and Jim, with matronly solicitude, shooing away the Tamils and upbraiding them for disturbing the Boss.

Sipping my cold sweet drink, which was like the elixir of life to me, through a straw, I would stand in the door of the go-down and pause awhile in my feverish activity to look out southward across the shimmering strait.

Beyond the tiny, chunky trawlers lying at the jetty, so small that they scarcely overtopped its edge even at high tide, and beyond the crowd of lighters which nosed and nudged each other, there were strange high-chested steamers riding at anchor, their winches rattling, surrounded by clusters of sampans. They were built for the Borneo traffic, all the passenger accommodation piled above the decks for coolness, and the bridge built very far forward, almost over the bows, for navigating winding, swirling Borneo rivers. Sampans moved slowly among all the anchored ships, each paddled by a thin Chinese in a plate-like conical hat, standing up and facing forward to row in the Chinese manner, pushing instead of pulling, the oars crossed in front of him. The Malays do not row like this but pull on the oars or scull over the stern. Farther off across the floor of shining water a great liner was coming proudly in to her berth. Beyond her the sky was already blackening above the Indonesian Islands, and the silver oil tanks crowded on one of them shone white against the dark clouds. Towards the zenith the black mass flowered into white and yellow mushrooms and cauliflowers. You could pick out the faces of old men and animals in them, and as the clouds writhed and contorted ever upwards they changed, became blurred and grotesque and finally melted away. But good heavens! What am I doing mooning here? It is twenty minutes past eleven and I must get back to work. 'The following is a list of the staff which it is envisaged will have been engaged by 1961, together with a statement of their personal emoluments. It is hoped . . .'

The Malays live in little wooden houses with palm-thatched roofs. The colonies of them huddle together and shrink away under the trees, as though frightened by the advancing ranks of brick and concrete which stretch out tentacles to surround and engulf them. Many of the little houses stand on legs with their feet in the water along the margins of creeks, along the sea-shore and on sandy spits, on promontories and on islands. The Malay villages, many of them surrounded by the modern sprawl of the city, islanded by the advancing tide of the twentieth century, are very much the same as they were when Stamford Raffles first landed a hundred and fifty years ago. The houses are still built of wood because it is cheap, now as then, and they stand among the trees because it is cooler in the shade. Let the Chinese and the Europeans swelter in concrete boxes laid by the mile in the open sun. The Malay houses stand with their feet in the water because, in the first place, such a situation does away with the necessity for expensive sanitary arrangements and, secondly, because many of the Malays earn their living on the water as fishermen, sailors or boatmen. And, thirdly, for the best of all reasons, namely that they have always stood there and were there when the foreshore and the muddy banks of creeks were the only places free of jungle where human habitations could find a foothold.

On the islands which lie to the south of Singapore, separated from the clamour of the city by stretches of water, the Malay villages crowd along the foreshore as though the rickety, crazy houses on their spindle legs were trying to jostle one another off the land into the water. Most of these villages are inhabited by fishermen who earn a precarious living by putting down fish-traps of various sizes and shapes on the coral reefs around the islands. The largest Malay village, however, is the little wooden shanty town that huddles along the shore of the island of Pulau Brani ('Island of the Brave') across the channel from the deep-water quays where the ocean liners lie. This is sailors' town. Nearly all the Malay sailors in Singapore live on this island, and the village looks today very much as it must have looked a hundred and fifty years ago. It is not your idea of a sailors' town. There are no bars or waterfront cafés or boisterous night-life. There are no bright eyes or enticing voices. It is dirty and smelly and happy and quiet—or was before every sailor had his wireless and played it full blast for all his neighbours to hear. You walk between the houses along narrow wooden plankways. Breechless babies peep at you round innumerable corners and scuttle away up innumerable wooden side-alleys. The women washing at the pump pause for a moment, but do not smile. There are no young men, for they are all away at sea.

This lucky village has piped water, but the other villages on the hot sandy islands scattered farther out in the Singapore Strait are not so lucky. They have no water at all. One of the benefactions which Tom introduced was the free carriage of water in drums by launch to the island villages. Until then the inhabitants had to pay for their water to be delivered and stored on their islands.

The boat that carried out this useful weekly service did little else, but occasionally she took parties of students out to the islands and their surrounding coral reefs, and sometimes she took people like me around on sightseeing trips. She was called the *Pukat*, which is the Malay word for a net, but she seldom had much to do with nets. At night she lay at Pulau Brani, where all her crew lived, and she chugged her way across to the go-down every morning. Sharp at four-thirty every afternoon she chugged bravely home again. You could tell the time by her departure. When she was not taking weekly trips round the islands she mostly lay at the quayside, on the landward side of the go-down, in the basin where the lighters nudged each other in the murky swell. The Malay crew polished things, squatted on their haunches, smiled and made a lovely smell of cooking. Their thin, melancholy cook pounded the spices which he mixed in their curry on a worn piece of granite which lay in the stern of the boat where the nets would come in, if they ever did. They never did. The rest of the crew mostly squatted on their haunches and watched the cook, with something handy nearby to start polishing if a *tuan* happened to look that way. It was the life for them.

When I first arrived in Singapore I thought I ought to go round the coast sightseeing. 'I think you should tour,' wrote the Colonial Office. I toured. I do not quite know what I expected to see, but Tom agreed that I ought to go round the islands and, to my great pleasure, decided to come with me. Accordingly the *Pukat* was made ready for a voyage. The preparations consisted in placing two comfortable wicker chairs under the awning on the after-deck, one for each *tuan*, and laying in a supply of soft drinks. At a moment convenient to ourselves we took our seats in the wicker armchairs and were each handed a bottle of orangeade and a glass with a large rock of ice in it. One of the crew opened the bottle and poured out the yellow liquid, bowing as he handed it to us. Thus, being in all respects ready for sea and prepared to engage whatever enemy there might be, the *Pukat* glided away from the go-down, and the tall commercial buildings behind it began to diminish.

The islands are sinking. Some are little better than sand or mud banks topped by a few mangroves and surrounded by a coral reef. At low tide the sea lays bare a wide expanse of slimy mud within the limits of the encircling reef, and in this vast flat circle things wriggle and crawl and slither and pop, and if you stop to listen a tiny crepitation, an oozy whisper, comes up from the ground everywhere. The enormous black clouds tower up and fling down barbed lightning upon the far-distant white city. Sometimes you plunge in suddenly knee-deep and bring your leg out with a sucking noise, covered with a dark grey, shiny boot of slime. But the island of Sudom, unlike many of its half-drowned companions, still has its head well above water. It is a whaleback of sand covered with tall coconut trees which, seen from a distance, look as though they were growing in the water. At one end of the whaleback a village of little wooden houses huddles on a narrow sand-spit. The houses crowd along the shore on spidery legs, their feet in the water, into which the ones behind seem to be trying to push the ones in front. The tall, slender palms tower above them and bend over them while the mangroves creep along underneath, pushing up their aerial roots like fingers in the shallows.

The day was blindingly hot and the water glassy calm. Lightning flickered in the distance. Deep water came right close in to the houses and we were almost beneath them before I could see the sandy bottom under the boat. The crew put a pram over the side. Every one of the houses used the sea beneath it as its only sanitary receptacle so that the smell along the foreshore, under the photogenic forest of spindly legs, was almost tangible, but would not come out in any photograph. One day, perhaps, cameras will be invented which will include smells in the snapshots they take and then there will be a slump in pictures of the glamorous East in photographic exhibitions all over the world. I wondered, as I stepped ashore, how the inhabitants stood it, but obviously nobody minded. The village stood along two sides of a sandy spit and thus had a V-shape with the whaleback in the apex of the V. You waded ashore between the legs of the houses and climbed on to the ridge of sand where the stems of the great palm trees leaned this way and that. Among them the ground was pegged out with hundreds of little granite posts like large tent-pegs. This was the village burial-ground and here the rude forefathers sat out eternity waiting for the Last Trump, each with a bowl of rice on his knees. For the Malays bury their dead in the sitting position, which takes up less space than lying down, and the bowl of rice provides refreshment on the journey through the shades. The Chinese also bury their dead in the sitting position, but the monuments marking their graves are always circular to signify infinity. After a term of years the dear departed is dug up and his bones placed in an urn which is returned to the family grave. Generation after generation can thus rest in the same place.

The apex of the V-shaped sandy spit formed an open triangle, where I presently joined Tom, who was surrounded by most of the male inhabitants. The female inhabitants, as is usual, retreated into their houses and kept away, but could be seen shyly peering from doors and verandas. Occasionally one or two of the more daring would make a dart from one house to another as though a torrential downpour were in progress.

The women were dressed in loose brightly coloured garments with skirts down to their ankles, but their husbands, sons and lovers, most of whom were now gathered round us on the triangle of sand, were much more exiguously dressed, usually only in a pair of shorts. Most of the small boys under the age of about ten, of whom there seemed to be a very large number, were stark naked. They rushed about, showing off and chasing one another among the dear departed like little hairless brown puppies. One figure, however, wore a sarong and the Malay cap or *songkok*, a tall, thin, dignified old man who was the *Penghulu* or headman of the village.

Tom had been talking to a young man who was making a large polygonal fish-trap out of wire netting. It had two funnel-like entrances, and, when he had finished making it, he and two or three others would take it out to the edge of the coral reef, or perhaps to Sirene Shoal to the north, and lower it in seven or eight fathoms. They would leave it there for about a week, its position quite unmarked. They had no means, other than their local knowledge, of remembering where they had placed it. After about a week they would return to the place and find their trap by trailing a three-pronged hook or grapnel over the spot. On the east coast of Malaya the fishermen insure against having their traps stolen or lifted by their rivals by running a wire from the trap to the shore, fixed to a rock or large stone in shallow water. When the owners come to pick up their trap they dive for the wire in the shallows and then follow the wire along to the trap. If the young men of Sudom were lucky their trap, after lying on the bottom for a week, would capture perhaps 20 lb. of fish. Not much, but the old Chinese man in the village will buy it and perhaps let them have enough money to buy wire to make another trap. The fish which find their way into the traps are those which habitually seek the shelter of coral growths and rock crannies—parrot fishes, wrasses, groupers and so on. They swim easily enough into the funnel-shaped entrances of the trap, thinking—if fish think at all—that they are entering a grove of coral or a cavern among rocks, but they cannot find their way out.

Presently the *Penghulu* led us to the only shop in the village, that kept by the only Chinese, who was the local middleman. He loaned the money to make the fish-traps and bought the meagre catch. He lived quite happily and obviously on terms of the closest friendship among his Malay clientele and was happily owed money by all of them. He happily owned the souls of the entire village; their debts, their careful wives, their children and their sins were laid upon his thin shoulders. He was an old man, thin to the point of emaciation, with a thin white goatee beard and a mole from which four long white lucky hairs hung down nearly to his chest. He bowed to us and led us into his overcrowded, suffocatingly hot little wooden shop room where two or three young Chinese boys were lying on bunks listening to the radio, which, at the top of its pitch, was playing a Chinese opera interspersed with the deafening clash of gongs. They rose from their bunks and gave us orange-ade from the only refrigerator in Sudom. When we had drunk our orangeade and shouted a few remarks above the gongs, which no one made any attempt to turn down, we yelled that we really ought to be going. We shook hands and bowed in dumb show. It was no use attempting to say anything. A small crowd of brown-skinned smiling people followed us down to the beach and waved as the pram took Tom and me back to the *Pukat*. The men waded out into the warm unsavoury water and the little boys swam alongside the pram like little brown frogs. The woman stood in the back-ground and stared but did not smile. One or two of them made a quick scurry from one house to another through the imaginary downpour.

It was a few weeks after this that one of the Malay sailors on board the *Pukat* got married. He was a small, neat little man, named Idris, always smiling a gold-toothed smile. The little island town of Pulau Brani where he lived was *en fête* for the occasion of the wedding, and all the staff of the Fisheries Office were invited, including me. The bright pink invitation card, in its bright pink envelope, the colour of thanksgiving and rejoicing, was something of a puzzle at first and I had to make discreet inquiries to find out where it came from, and from whom.

We sailed to the ceremony in the *Pukat*, which was once more made ready for a voyage—a gala one this time. She was gay with flags, and her paint and brasswork shone with several days of assiduous pre-nuptial polishing. A table was placed on the after-deck with quite a battery of wicker chairs, and here some of the Chinese clerks improved the festive occasion by sitting all day long, wedding or no wedding, playing mah-jong. We heard the rattle of the chips as we congratu-lated the bridegroom. Let those who care for birth, marriage and death, and all those unimportant milestones in life, get on with them. There were more important things to attend to.

The little sailors' town was hung with flags and palm

fronds, and one house in particular, that of the bridegroom's parents, was the centre of all the activity, aflutter with palm fronds, bunting and paper flowers. Inside the women were noisily preparing the wedding feast.

At a Malay wedding the bridegroom's friends assemble at his parent's house and eat an enormous curry meal, after which the bridegroom is escorted by his friends and family to the house of the bride's parents, where he and the bride are enthroned and hold court, receiving the congratulations of all their friends. Meanwhile in the house of the bride's parents another feast is taking place.

Idris was marrying the daughter of a soldier who lived in the Army Malay lines about a quarter of a mile away, and already the population of sailors' town, mostly women, were gathering along the route between the little houses and across the football ground, and were crowding at doorways and windows to see the procession pass by. All the inhabitants of the town were dressed in the charming, flowing bright coloured clothes which the Malays wear on ceremonial occasions both grave and gay. For the women this consists mainly of a loose shirt blouse over an ankle-length embroidered skirt. Frangipani and hibiscus flowers glow in their blue-black hair. They whiten their faces to an unearthly pallor. For the men the principal features of their costume are the silk embroidered shirt and trousers and the brightly coloured sarong wrapped round the hips, the velvet *songkok* on their heads.

The wedding feast was being laid out on the floor of the main room of the little house, and there was a great female commotion in the back parts of the house which overhung the water. This increased in intensity as the guests, including ourselves, arrived. We could hear the clatter of plates and smell a wonderful smell that tickled the palate even at ten o'clock in the morning. The girls kept running in and setting down bowls full of curry and rice in the middle of the floor. As we mounted the steps of the veranda, under the palm fronds and the paper flowers, the bridegroom's father came forward and greeted us all with great courtesy, but, rather to my disappointment, it appeared that we Europeans, Tom and I, and those of the Chinese clerks who could tear themselves away from the mah-jong game on board the *Pukat*, were to be given special treatment. We were not expected to lower ourselves by sitting on the floor and eating curry with our hands among the other guests. I would not have considered that I was lowering myself by doing this at all, but I felt that I could not explain and must do as was expected of me. A table had been spread with a cloth on the veranda. There were even spoons and forks. Here we sat like royalty in a kind of stuffy aloofness from the other guests, many of whom gathered in a bunch at one end of the veranda and goggled at us as though they hoped we would give some sort of performance. The bridegroom's father kept coming in and filling up our glasses with warm beer. We decided to make unconcerned conversation, pretending like royalty not to notice the audience watching our every movement with rapt attention. Every remark fell like a stone into a silent pool and seemed to leave widening rings round itself.

I said I thought it was hotter than yesterday and wiped what was largely the sweat of embarrassment from my forehead.

Tom said he thought it would cool down later on, because the sky was already clouding over.

Three little Malay boys in purple sarongs, clutching tambourines, huddled a little closer together and waited for the next pearl of wisdom.

However, soon there was a movement into the principal room where the feast began. All the male guests, but none of the women, sat down on the floor and helped themselves to curry with their right hands in the Muslim manner. How do I know they did if I was sitting on the veranda? Because I got up and stared at them in my turn and even took photographs, which caused much coy laughter and made the little boys with their tambourines huddle still closer together.

This odd sensation of being a sort of minor royalty is something you get used to in the East. Perhaps it is one which will be experienced less and less frequently by Europeans in the future, for it is a hangover from the nabob days. It gives me the feeling, which royal personages must have, that one never sees things as they really are or people behaving as they really behave. Everything always seems to be specially arranged, organized and laid on. Buildings and streets are always half hidden by flags and lined by crowds—metaphorically anyway. Things are tidier and more polished than is normal, and everybody is especially well behaved and well dressed. They rush forward and bob and bow and give you flowers. The only difference is that for royalty the flags and curtsies are real, for me they are imaginary.

But the curry we shovelled in with our spoons was the same as they were eating in the main room with their hands and was delicious and very hot. The little boys with the tambourines laughed to see the sweat streaming down my face and my shirt, wet through, sticking to my back. Huge snow-white mountains of rice went with the curry, and soon I began to get that inflated feeling as though I should rise up to the ceiling and stay there, like the man in H. G. Wells's story. This was followed by a feeling of great weight and drowsiness as though I should never be able to get up from the chair at all. My eyelids suddenly seemed to be made of lead. Conversation on the veranda languished and the audience began to melt away. Even the two little boys with the tambourines rose and walked away.

Meanwhile there was no sign of the bridegroom. The proceedings seemed to have reached a sort of static condition and there appeared to be no reason why they should ever change. We should still be sitting there in a week's time.

Now a crowd of men and boys was gathering outside the house, evidently waiting for something or someone. There were more little boys with tambourines and others carrying long wands at the ends of which were what looked like sprays of pink almond-blossom made of paper. Suddenly there was a shout and a clamour. All the male guests ran out into the alleyway between the houses. The bridegroom had appeared and was waiting to be escorted to his bride. One could hardly recognize the little Malay sailor in the splendid figure who now stood in the midst of those who knew and loved him and showed it in their fashion. With downcast eyes and his hands clasped before him he stood in front of his father's house. No prince in an oriental fairy-tale could have been more richly dressed. He was wearing the beautiful and ancient ceremonial robes of his family which were handed down from generation to generation. His father had worn them when he had married Idris's mother, and his grandfather had worn them before him. His elder brother had worn them for his wedding, and his small brother, who now hopped around and made a joyful sound with his tambourine, would wear them when his turn came.

On his head Idris wore a cloth-of-gold turban decorated with flowers. A long, richly embroidered robe of crimson and gold, with puffed sleeves caught at the wrist with silver bracelets, covered him from the neck to the ankles. The fingers of both his square sailor's hands, which were clasped before him holding a nosegay of flowers, were covered with rings. Only slightly detracting from his appearance of grave and princely dignity were the heavy square-toed Army boots which were visible beneath the robe.

The *cortège* formed up in the narrow alleyway. The bridegroom, his mother and father on either side of him, walked in the middle with slow, measured tread, his eyes downcast and fixed upon the little bunch of flowers he held in front of him in his clasped hands. He could not have looked more solemn if he had been going to a funeral. All around him the friends of his now dead bachelor past, his young brothers and nephews and all the men and boys of the village, made a ragged, jovial procession, carrying their wands of imitation blossom, the little boys running in and out clashing their tambourines. They laughed and joked and shouted in Malay, and only the bridegroom looked as though this day were the end of life. For they were trying to make him laugh, but he must not do so, for if he were to give way and let even the suspicion of a smile at their ribaldries cross his face it would be an evil omen. It would mean an unhappy and perhaps childless marriage. So, as we walked along the path which led out of the village and across the football field to the Army lines, the men and boys laughed and joked, and the jokes became broader and broader. I believe that on these occasions the jokes may become very broad indeed, but since they were all in Malay their point escaped me. Idris, however, remained less amused than Queen Victoria, and not a trace of a smile relieved the gloom beneath the gilt, flowered turban.

The bride's parents lived in one of a row of small apartments

built in the red-brick prison style of Army quarters before
World War I. The long one-storey block had a continuous
veranda on to which all the doors in the row opened. One
door was the centre of another gay throng, for here the bride's
parents had been giving a feast, and the bride taking leave of
the friends of her youth while awaiting the coming of her
bridegroom.

On the balcony outside the front door a gorgeous double
throne had been set up. Two chairs stood on a dais, draped
and backed with embroidered cloth and paper flowers and
festoons of coloured electric lights. Here Idris and his bride
were enthroned in state. The bride too was regally dressed
in her family ancestral robes, an embroidered gown and a
high crown of silver ornaments and flowers on her head,
long silver ear-rings and a heavy collar of Malay beaten silver
round her neck. Her face was a white mask of heavy make-up
and her expression one of unutterable woe. Judging by their
forlorn and woebegone appearance the young couple had many
years of happy married life ahead of them.

Since that day when for a few hours Idris was a royal
prince upon a throne receiving the homage of his friends
nearly six years have now passed. The next day he was the
little Malay sailor again, naked to the waist and bare-footed
squatting on his hams and often smiling. A few months afterwards his little wooden house in Pulau Brani collapsed in
a severe 'sumatra', or line squall, and we sent the hat round
to collect money to rebuild it. A reporter from the local
Malay vernacular newspaper called on me to ask what my
organization, as a Government body, intended to do about
Idris's house. I said, 'Nothing,' but we were subscribing
to a fund. Did I not think I ought to be taking some official
action about Idris's house? I said I could hardly go to the
Treasury about that and mentally composed a minute: 'It is
felt very strongly'—a cliché meaning 'I think'—'that the cost
of rebuilding this dwelling should be charged against the
estimates of the Scheme for the year 1953-4, Sub-head B
Recurrent Expenditure, Item 3 (b) IV. Maintenance and
Repair of Buildings. Approval is accordingly sought'. I wondered what the reaction would be in the air-conditioned office
guarded by the non-air-conditioned secretaries. But Idris

rebuilt his house himself and there are now, I think, five brown babies running about in and out of it stark naked and happy as kings. And if Idris is not richer in worldly wealth than on the day of his enthronement he is rich beyond counting in the things not of this earth.

On the deck of the *Pukat* all that day the mah-jong chips rattled ceaselessly, and some of the Chinese clerks grew a little richer in the things very much of this earth, and others poorer. Life, birth, death, marrying and giving in marriage—it was all the same to them.

6

My Village

Changi village lies in an enclave of territory ruled over by the R.A.F. on the easternmost tip of the diamond which is Singapore Island. There are several of these enclaves where the paternal rule of one or other of the armed forces affects the lives of the native inhabitants far more closely than the remote goings-on in Government offices in Singapore. A huge slice of land on the north coast of the island overlooking Johore Strait is held by the Navy, a large green island bordering the harbour of Singapore is occupied by the Army and flourishes under a Military Government, and there are several large aerodromes where the R.A.F. command is law.

Changi aerodrome, on the easternmost point of the island, was originally built by the Japanese during their occupation, one of their more lasting and useful memorials. A huge drydock which they built in the jungle on the south-west coast was bombed by the Americans at the end of the war and is now merely a ruinous haunt of bats and snakes. A pompous victory obelisk which they put up, somewhat prematurely, at Bukit Timah was blown up when the British returned, like its fellow on the top of the mountain at Hong Kong. Both were believed to have a Samurai sword and what-not concealed in the foundations.

The main road from Singapore runs past Changi gaol, where the Japanese imprisoned all the Europeans during the war. It looks forbidding and implacable enough and every inch a gaol. Then the main road passes the runway and ends up in the village itself. The immediate surroundings are pleasant and green. Barracks, mess rooms, married quarters and labourers' lines stand about on sweeps of smooth grassland amid casuarinas, bamboos and frangipani trees. But the village itself, of course, like all villages in Malaya and Singapore, is quite deplorable and regrettable. It has no redeeming feature except its own blousy charm.

On either side of its wide main street stands a row of large drooping dragon's-blood trees, with leaves of August green like lime trees in late English summer. With their overarching branches they must have once made a fine avenue, but nowadays the street is flanked on each side by a line of shanty shops, built of wood with corrugated-iron roofs, dazzlingly lit by mercury strip-lights, with gaudily painted and neon-lit signs on the outside. Here we have the Sincere Store, the Good Luck Café, the Old School Tailor and the Fashionable Bar. There are the brightly lit caverns full of rings, fountain-pens and wrist-watches, the new symbols of status that the young of all races covet, presided over by smooth Chinese with faces like masks. The shanty shops stand back from the road behind the trunks of the dragon's-blood trees, leaving wide strips of mud and puddles uncared for on either side of the road where cars park and big red buses come to roost, and the Chinese fruit-vendors pile up their glowing pyramids and drape their luscious festoons under the hurricane lamps. They fashion little boats out of melons and paw-paws with sails made of their skins. They make arcades and triumphal arches out of bundles of furry lichees and perch sweet pine-apples on top of mountains of oranges.

Some of the trees on either side of the road have become casualties before the invaders, and there are gaps in the ranks. Others have been chopped about and mutilated wherever their branches might obscure a signboard or overhang a roof, for no such thing as a tree was ever allowed to get in the way of business in Singapore. Now the City Council, not to be outdone, has arrived with enormous electric standards which cast a pallid, sickly glare over everything at night. But Changi is really so endearingly ugly that there is little that even a City Council could do to make it worse.

In the fullness of time Changi was destined to become my village and my home town. I look back upon it now with a nostalgic ache and hear running through my head the warring refrains of its many juke-boxes booming from the cafés (the Good Luck, the Cheeroh and the Europe) where the R.A.F. ate their sausages and mashed, and from the Chinese food shops with less pretentious names where the bus drivers and conductors sat on narrow benches shovelling rice into their mouths from little bowls.

A spit of sand, covered with mangroves, tussocky grass and thorny scrub, lay between the village and the shore of the Johore Strait and was separated from the village itself by a very smelly creek where there was a jetty from which you could hire a launch to cross over to the islands and equally smelly creeks on the other side of the strait.

The foreshore, where this sandy spit sloped gently into the warm, murky waters of the Johore Strait, was the only bathing-beach worthy of the name on Singapore Island. On Saturdays and Sundays it was thronged with people of all the island's many races, and bodies, white, golden, brown and black, smooth or hairy, bulbous or trim, bobbed and splashed in the turbid shallows. People undressed, made love and made water among the bushes and draped a strange variety of garments on them to dry in the sun. It was on this spit of sand that one day my temple of science was destined to arise.

Tom took me to see the place within a few days of my arrival in Singapore and called upon me to say whether or not I thought it would do. There was only one alternative site, on the other side of the island, but it was at that time occupied by a squatters' village, a happy but insanitary collection of shacks which had just grown there. No one knew when the squatters could be dispossessed. Evicting squatters was a ticklish problem in Singapore which the authorities approached cautiously, as with tongs. For not only had the squatters nowhere else to go, but they had votes. Accordingly no one was prepared to say when I would be able to get possession of the alternative site if I were to reject Changi. Stepping over the prostrate bodies of lovers I said I thought the place seemed a bit remote from the centre of things, but I supposed it would do.

For months after that my temple of science came slowly into existence on paper, and about once a fortnight, when I felt like a change from sitting in the go-down, I would drive out down the long east-coast road that led to my village in order to see if my dream palace were beginning to take shape on the sand-spit. But for month after month the hot tranquillity of the place remained undisturbed, and I could only admire the lovely, uninterrupted views of nameless terrorist-ridden hills on the other side of the strait. Then I went to England to look for a ship, found one and returned to Singapore bursting with pride. But still nothing had happened on the sand-spit. Surely these must be the very same couples that I had seen there before I left, lying in a hot, gritty embrace under the bushes. I wrote a minute, marked 'Urgent', and requested that the matter might be accorded some measure of priority in view of the now protracted delay, etc. I thought that was rather well put, and in language horrible enough to ring a bell in the most air-conditioned quarters. It did, but it was the wrong bell.

'The final paragraph of your minute,' said the reply which came back after the usual fortnight, 'suggests that the delay is not the responsibility of your department. Any suggestion that the blame lies with this department is resented.'

I thought of innumerable ripostes to this—witty, cutting, patronizing, reproachful, self-justificatory. But I did not send any of them. Instead I drove out to my village and sat in a soft-drinks stall kept by an Indian and listened to passages from the Koran being bellowed from amplified loud-speakers outside a shack marked 'Welfare Centre'. Elvis Presley was competing from a juke-box in the Splendid Café and Restaurant, which was another shack just across the road. From another juke-box a little farther along an Indian lady throbbed out what sounded like a hysterical lament in a minor key. Hens with bare behinds pecked and scratched in the sand around my feet. The young Indian leant on his counter, his chin in one hand, and picked his teeth, staring fixedly at me with luminous eyes. He found the spectacle of me drinking warm orangeade infinitely diverting.

When the Japanese built Changi aerodrome they also began to build a road along the coast towards the sand-spit. But they did not have time to finish it. Long after what the inhabitants of Singapore, as an unwitting compliment, still call the 'Liberation', the beginnings of the Japanese road remained as a long, sinuous red gash in the island's earth. In due course the British built a fine motor-road along the coast, ending at the sand-spit, along which the skimming dishes and the fish-tail sedans and the lorries full of Communist boys and girls raced to the bathing-beach on Sundays. But instead of using the track already marked out by the Japanese the new British motor-road followed a majestic course of its own a few yards to seaward. The Japanese road now approached and now diverged from the new one, now accompanied it for a little distance and now swerved off among the coarse grass and sick-looking coconut palms. But there was one place where the Japanese road ran for a few hundred yards alongside and contiguous with the new road. Here, on sites as bald and innocent of soil as the palm of your hand, three little white houses like little white pillboxes eventually arose for myself and my staff. They seemed to vibrate in the heat.

As a matter of fact the houses arrived a little before the new road itself, which, just at this point, was raised up on an embankment about four feet high. The riders to the sea in the fish-tail limousines and the skimming dishes, as they went shooting past, could therefore look down upon me for a fraction of a second as I sat at supper in my dining-recess under the languidly revolving electric fans. A fleeting second of time in my life, like a still from a movie, could be preserved for each of them as I reached for another potato or rang for the boy to clear away the remains of the lamb chop.

The motor-road along which my privileged public whizzed was named Nicoll Drive, after the Governor during whose tenure of office the building of the road was begun. Our little white houses were known as 'Nicoll's Nests' because the same Governor, at the beginning of his reign, laid down that all future houses to be built for Government Officers were to be the same little three-roomed boxes of this severe austerity pattern. They were good enough little houses, modelled for the tropical subtopia to which all the newly independent lands aspire. Mine suited me well enough even though my every movement was plainly visible from the motor-road.

'But everything I do can be seen from the road!' I protested to the architect.

'Then you must do it upstairs, old boy, or not at all,' he said.

From my sitting-room I could look right through the sitting-room of the house next door into that of the third house in the row. I was a goldfish in a bowl, but on the whole I was a fairly contented fish and was happy in my bowl.

As a bowl it was extremely stereotyped, moulded to a pattern to fit extremely orthodox fish. From the furniture, supplied by the Public Works Department, you could envisage exactly the kind of people the Government assumed its expatriate employees to be, and judge the type of life the Government assumed they would lead. Thus the hypothetical inhabitants of any small Government quarter would, of course, be a married couple, but would sleep in separate beds. The climate of Singapore is against prolonged uxorious pleasures. They would perhaps have two children, who would not be too old to need separate rooms but would also sleep in separate beds in the one extra bedroom. There was a dressing-table in the main bedroom with a long mirror at which Mrs. Younghusband could sit with a light conveniently above her head when dressing for dinner with the Deputy Director and his wife. Downstairs there was a sitting-room with a dining-recess, which could of course be screened off, and a dining table and chairs for four. The invitation of the Deputy Director and his wife could therefore be returned, but any other guests would make rather a squash. There was a sideboard, which was convenient for the cups which John had won at London University, and there were drawers for the fish knives and forks which were a wedding present. Near the sofa in the sitting-room was a low, round coffee-table and beside each of the four easy chairs a small unstable round object which could be very easily overturned and was listed as a 'pahit table'. During the whole of my stay in Singapore I never heard of anyone drinking a 'pahit' and am still not clear what it is, but gather it is the drink of Deputy Directors. There was a table especially for the radio and another for the bridge which would be played after dinner. And the Government judged entirely rightly. Indeed, so appropriate were all these accoutrements for the pattern of life that was led in most of these pretty bowls that in most of them the curtains were left undrawn evening after evening. The passing world could look in and see, brilliantly illuminated as in an aquarium tank, young domestic life as it should be with the children safe in bed.

As for me, my curtains were drawn every evening at sunset.

'Don't you ever feel rather lonely, my dear fellow?' asked the Deputy Director.

'Practically never,' I replied.

Life ran easily and smoothly, because in my village there were so many people who were willing to do things for me. The grocery store that supplied my household needs called every morning. I wrote down what I wanted and it arrived in the afternoon. If it did not I drove round to the village when the sun was going down behind the casuarinas. In the store the stout Chinese manager, with a smile full of gold, was sure to be sitting at his desk flanked by shelf upon shelf of tins up to the tin roof, and surrounded by show-cases full of novelties and sweets with which the memsahibs silenced their offspring when they came in sweatily in the afternoon heat. The manager was usually busy with his abacus.

'Towky, you no send bottle whisky. Me nothing to drink, very thirsty.' I don't know why one tended to talk this kind of pidgin English when shopping. It was a kind of infectious disease.

'I'm terribly sorry, Tuan Doctor,' said the manager, in perfect English, looking up from his accounting. 'An oversight perhaps. Francis, the Doctor's whisky.'

A bright and spry little Chinese youth ran out from the back regions.

'One minute, I fetch,' he said, and darted away across the road. The towky went on with his abacus. ('Towky' is a Chinese word—though what dialect I do not know—for a proprietor or landlord.)

Presently Francis returned all smiles from the Café Europe across the road, clutching the bottle.

'There, Doctor. I'm sorry you have disappointed me.'

'On the contrary, it is you who disappointed me.'

'Of course, yes, I should say. Please excuse.'

These pleasant exchanges took place in every shop. In the Wellcome [*sic*] Store a graceful Indian lady in a bronze or blue or saffron-coloured sari presided with majestic and aloof charm behind banks of cosmetics, stationery, sweets and contraceptives. In the Sincere Store a young Indian with a glittering wrist-watch and a hair-do held sway over banks of much the same things in reverse order. Next door was the book-shop, where the young Sikh in charge seemed to have read every book. *How to Be an Expert Photographer*, *The Diesel Engine*, *English in Twelve Easy Lessons* and *Manual of Electricity and Magnetism*—they were all the same to him. 'Very good book, fifteen dollars.' But he was not in the least disappointed if I walked out with three who-dunnits instead. Next door was the Chinese radio-shop with stacks of records to suit every height of brow. Judging by the blanketing noise that came from the shop all day long one gathered that brows were worn pretty low in Changi. A friend of mine staying with me for a week-end visited the shop and after he had left the little Chinese behind the counter were enjoying a giggling joke. I asked what was the matter and what was so funny anyway.

'Your fliend,' said one of the assistants. 'I sell him Chinese opela.' This was held to be ludicrous beyond words, for the addiction of Europeans to anything Chinese, furniture, ceramics, paintings or music, is considered to be an odd and slightly dotty quirk, especially now that all Chinese are striving desperately to achieve a westernization. I found the opera less of a joke as I had to leave the house whenever it was played.

There were several shops along the street that dealt in cameras, mostly Japanese. They were nearly always filled with young R.A.F. men, examining cameras with an air of expert knowledge which the results would almost certainly belie. The appetite for bad photography is insatiable nowadays, and the more elaborately foolproof the cameras become, the more built-in exposure meters and filters, the more self-winding and self-timing, the lower the general standard of the products. Cameras have become status symbols like wrist-watches, motor-cars and sun-glasses.

In the Café Europe and the Good Luck Café the R.A.F. boys, having wandered from the radio-shop to the photography-shop and to the shops where they sold elephants crossing bridges and figurines made of bone pretending to be ivory and other horrors made of bamboo, came finally to roost over eggs and bacon and the comforting wail and machine-like pounding of a gigantic illuminated juke-box.

There they would sit for an idle hour or so, saying nothing but jerking their bodies and stamping their feet in time to the anaesthetizing Negro rhythm. I was often depressed by this spectacle, not only in Changi but everywhere in Singapore (or anywhere else) where the forces (or anyone else) forgathered. It seemed to argue a frightening mindlessness and vacuity. But the youngish colonel of an infantry regiment, homeward bound for England after service in the Malayan jungle, had comforting words to say at a farewell barbecue given in his regiment's honour. I sat next to him over a steak which I had somehow grilled myself.

'The lads are very young and lonely and homesick and in a strange city,' he said. 'Their appalling shirts and hair-dos are a form of revolt against having to wear uniform all day. But the stuff is there all right. I've seen it.'

When our nests were being built I often went to Changi to observe the progress of the work and talked to the old Indian foreman, who always carried a black umbrella and wore a huge sola topee. The nest that I was to occupy was being built, I noticed, right in the middle of the excavated bed of the old Japanese road. There was no earth but only red compacted sand as hard as brick. One day I saw that under the foreman's eye some Chinese labourers were busy carrying buckets of dry sand and scattering handfuls of it on the hard red foundation. In this light covering they were planting some sad little tufts of dead-looking grass in widely spaced rows.

'We must give you some nice earth, isn't it?' said the old Indian, poking at the sand with his umbrella. 'So now you can beautify, sir. Beautify with some nice cherry trees.'

I did my best during my two years in the house but not with much success, for almost everything died of sheer inanition. I made a fine pink Bougainvillaea trail over the roof of the veranda (in which two people could just sit side by side) and I planted some oleanders. I also had some beautiful reed-like plants with crimson bells called *Juncaea* on which little golden sun-birds used to come and perch upside down while they sucked at the flowers with their long, curved beaks. But the tufts of grass which the old Indian so thoughtfully caused to be put in never really made a lawn, and nothing could prevent the Japanese road from breaking through in patches.

About three weeks after my arrival Raman took charge of my plot of sand and did all my beautifying for me. When I came home after work in the evening I would go round de-beautifying. His idea, like that of all Indian gardeners, was never to allow anything to grow or fall naturally, but to tie up all stray branches and tendrils in inextricable tortured knots, to scrape and tidy ruthlessly, piling up the sand in a tall cone round the base of every plant. All gardeners in Malaya behave as though the plants and flowers under their charge were implacable and ferocious enemies which, if not firmly dealt with and kept in check, would soon get the upper hand and arise to choke and strangle. I often wondered, watching Raman battling with a frail oleander bush that I had just put in, or dealing summarily with my Bougainvillaea's single hopeful shoot, whether his zeal were not the result of a kind of ancestral race memory, left from the time when the encompassing jungle was in fact a real live enemy that pressed hard upon the village settlement won from the valley and had to be fought constantly. After his gardening operations, anyhow, my half-acre plot looked as though it had had a crew-cut, and there was not much I could do about it except go round loosening tortured branches and pulling down banked-up earth.

After a few weeks it appeared that Raman was really the head of quite a large syndicate which battled with the jungle in the sand-patches of a number of my neighbours. As time went on Raman, as the head and brains of the syndicate, began to turn up less and less often and at last only about three times a month, one of the dates on which he never failed being the first of the month, when the wages were due. On other days the junior members of the organization carried on the unending battle against the encroaching jungle.

Raman himself was a good-looking Tamil with iron-grey hair and mouth permanently stained bright red with betel juice. In the early half of the day he worked for the R.A.F. and was what he called a 'pumping engineer'. I never found out just what a pumping engineer did, but I gathered that he was a labourer, and so, like all labourers employed by the

Government or the forces, he worked from about seven o'clock in the morning to midday, after which he was free to take other employment or cultivate his own land. The rest of the syndicate consisted of Raman's three sons, aged seventeen, fourteen and eight, a married nephew who lived with the family in their two-roomed labourers' quarters in Changi village, and several friends who turned up at odd times. An army of seven or eight altogether did battle with nature in my garden plot.

Imagine, then, the astonishment of Jakob, the Malay caretaker of the Government rest-house across the way, when, leaning over his fence with a clean sarong and his pipe in the evening, he observed the Tuan hard at it with a mowing-machine, drenched, of course, from head to foot in sweat.

'But has the Tuan no *kebun*,' he asked.

(*Kebun* is the Malay word for a garden, but Europeans use it to signify 'gardener', pronouncing it 'kaboon'. This is considered to be just another rude habit of a rude race, for one should really say '*Tekong kebun*', which means 'one who is skilled in the garden', though I was always rather doubtful whether that title could really be awarded to my syndicate. However, no one really likes to be called just plain 'garden'.)

'I have indeed, Jakob,' I would reply, the sweat running off me in rivulets. 'I have seven.'

The member of the syndicate who rendered the most faithful and constant service was the most junior of all, Gopala-swamy, aged eight. When I returned almost every evening I would find his diminutive, half-naked figure staggering about with buckets of water and watering-can nearly as big as himself. These watering operations always took place in the evening. No sooner had I sat down on my veranda than the barrage of pot-plants, which had served no particular purpose all day but now concealed their owner from the public gaze, was removed and dotted about the lawn. The plants were then dowsed with water with much clanking and staggering to and fro with buckets. After a while the little boy, after several preliminary questioning glances, would put the bucket down and begin to talk, in a high, chirruping voice like a bird, using excellent English taught at the English

school a few hundred yards down the road. Auntie was one
of the problems of this small life and it was usually some item
of information about Auntie with which the conversation
opened when he put down his bucket. She lived in the house
with the family and was a great trial to everyone, it appeared.
She had cast spells upon all the family in turn. Govindaswamy,
the eldest brother, had applied for a job in the Customs Department, but owing to the spells cast by Auntie he had been
unsuccessful, his application had been rejected, and he must
now go on working in the Immigration Department, where he
wasn't at all happy. Pillai, the middle brother, aged fourteen,
had come only tenth in his class exam, which was also, of
course, entirely due to Auntie's machinations, because everyone knew that Pillai was much cleverer than the other boys
and ought to have been top of the class. Now Raman, his
father, had fallen down on his way back from the toddy-shop
and hurt his arm and would be unable to come to work for
at least two weeks. And all because of the spells worked by
Auntie, who hated his mother. She made little clay images of
all the members of the family and stuck them full of pins and
then buried them in the earth. Oh, she was a bad woman and
wicked. Yesterday the Hindu priest from the temple came
and prayed against the spells in the house, and this, of course,
cost the family a lot of money. They were all now praying
that the prayers would work. But he didn't mind, not he.
Tomorrow he was going hunting with some friends. Oh,
just some of the other fellows in the gang. Would I like to
come too? I thought not, but next morning I would see the
pack go by in full cry, with catapults at the ready, and thought
that boys are much the same all the world over. The gentle
doves, that were their intended prey, crooned in the hot noon
among the coconut palms and casuarinas. Knowing that they
were quite safe I waved the gang 'Good hunting' from behind
my pot-plants.

When there was anything rather more complicated than
watering to do, like torturing bushes into less uncontrolled
shapes or clipping the hedge that marked out my drive, it
was Pillai who came and did it. He was less talkative than
his younger brother, slower and not so bright. He had a
languid manner and spent hours at work without accomplishing

very much. Occasionally he had conversational bursts. These he preceded by gazing at me in a solemn manner over the hedge he was cutting or the bush he was wrestling with. One day he straightened himself from battling with a recalcitrant Allamanda bush and, after gazing at me earnestly for some time, said:

'Sir, where are your wife and children?'

'In England,' I said untruthfully. He was silent for some minutes, gazing at me reproachfully over the top of the bush.

'Sir, I think you are lying.'

'Oh,—and why shouldn't they be in England?'

'Because they say that you have no wife, but two sons in England. And, sir, it is known to us that you have twice had a new motor-car since you came to live in Changi. The old ones you have surely given to your sons, isn't it? But your sons are not here. We never see them. Therefore they must be in England. It is said in the village that your wife is dead and that you mourn for her. But soon you will have ended mourning and then, I think, you will take a woman to live with you in this house.'

Thus, I became aware, my affairs were settled in the village along accepted lines.

'Sir,' said Pillai one day towards the end of my stay in Singapore. 'It is said that you are leaving.'

'Yes, Pillai. I think so.'

'Why, sir?'

'Well, most Europeans in the Government are leaving now, you know. Singapore will soon be ruled by its own people. That is Merdeka.'

'I do not understand why you must go.'

'We are all going, Pillai.'

'But, sir, you are a good man.'

Later he said, 'Sir, when do you go to Hong Kong?'

I had said nothing to anyone about Hong Kong so far as I knew.

'Now how on earth do you know I'm going to Hong Kong?'

'It is known, sir. They say it in the village. Some people are sad.'

When there was heavy work such as mowing to be done the nephew, who was married and lived with the family, or, at week-ends, the biggest brother, Govindaswamy, came and did it. Nephew seemed to be afflicted with a permanent melancholy and seldom spoke and only occasionally smiled. But Govindaswamy was very lively. He was a well-built young man and much darker than his brothers, almost black, with flashing white teeth. During the week he worked in the Immigration Department and lived with relations in Singapore, so that I only saw him on Saturdays or on the many and various public holidays which punctuate the calendar in Singapore. Like his brothers he spoke excellent English, but very rapidly and with a rising inflexion which gave him what sounded like a Welsh accent. You had to be tough in the Immigration Department, he said, because both the Chinese and the Malay boys were gunning for the Indian boys, and fights frequently broke out. But he was strong, and on the whole they left him alone.

Sometimes several weeks would pass during which I would see nothing of Govindaswamy. Then he would send me a note by Pillai or Gopal.

'Sir,' Pillai would say, handing me an envelope addressed in large copper-plate handwriting to 'Tuan Doctor', 'my brother Govindaswamy has written you a letter.'

Govindaswamy wrote a very beautiful copy-book hand, far better than anything I have ever been able to accomplish.

'Honoured Sir,' he wrote, 'I write to say how sad I am that I have not worked in your garden for many weeks. This is because I have twisted my foot at the Badmin Ton and was forced not to walk very much, but it is now better, though for three days I was not able to go to work. I pray that God will make you happy and grant you long life. Please remember me affectionately to all your friends and to your family when you write home to England. Yours ever respectfully, Govindaswamy. I would very much like a Badmin Ton rackett. I saw a nice one in a shop for $35.00 Perhaps one day I will be able to afford this. Who knows?'

'Dear Govindaswamy,' I replied, 'Thank you for your note. I am very sorry to hear about your foot and hope it will soon be better. When you are able to get about again we will see what can be done about that badminton racket. Yours very sincerely.'

I had a badminton racket, a relic of the war, which I had restrung and cleaned up so that it was as good as new. Govindaswamy was delighted with it, smiled a flashing smile and made passes with it about the lawn for the rest of the afternoon until after sunset, when he went home, having mown only a very small section of my lawn. But after that I saw nothing of him again for some time and, when I did at length see him again, he was curiously silent about the badminton racket. In fact he never again mentioned it, and I developed a sort of mental block which prevented me from speaking of it too. It was Gopal, on one of his chirruping days, who let the cat out of the bag.

'My brother Govindaswamy very silly,' he said. 'Ha, ha, ha!' and he hopped with joy and did a hand-spring beside the watering-can. 'The day you give him bat he hit it against the door-post of our house. All broken in pieces, finish, no good. Ha, ha, ha! He say he punch me if I tell.'

So I never mentioned it to Govindaswamy, and so great, I suppose, was the loss of face involved that he never mentioned it to me.

When I left Singapore the syndicate formed a deputation and came to say good-bye, Raman at their head bearing a great basket of fruit. Govindaswamy gave me a downcast smile, but said nothing about the badminton racket.

'Sir,' said Pillai. 'We are sad that you must go.'

I do not believe that the days when Europeans can win faithful and devoted service are finished in the East. I have seen too many examples of the contrary for that. But the days when they could employ great retinues of native servants are certainly over. In the years since the end of the Japanese occupation the wages of servants in Singapore have been rising steadily and are now very high. It is not unusual to pay a cook-houseboy $180 a month (£4 10s. a week) with quarters. Europeans of modest means, therefore, cannot afford many servants at these rates. A married couple with two or three children will usually have a cook-houseboy with his wife to do the washing. There will probably be a baby-amah for the children. Well-to-do Europeans may have a cook and a houseboy as well, with the wife of one or the other to do the washing. The baby-amah, whose job must be a highly specialized and unenviable one nowadays, usually has to be specially re-cruited. Nowadays you have to register your servants and pay a weekly contribution towards their insurance. Every house-servant claims at least one evening free in the week, and large presents are expected and received during the Chinese New Year Festival, which falls in February when most families are just recovering from Christmas.

All these improvements in the lot of house-servants are, of course, excellent and unexceptionable. But a point is now being reached where European families sometimes decide to do without servants altogether. Now that the inhabitants of Subtopia are arriving in the Far East in increasing numbers and setting up tropical Subtopias for themselves one often hears British housewives say: 'Well, I've never had servants before and I don't see why I should start having them now. More trouble than they're worth, if you ask me. I'll do all the work myself.' But they reckon without the Singapore climate, that sweaty, steamy fug that saps the energy and destroys the will-power. Women who start out by trying to do all their own housework seldom keep it up for long. They either engage a native servant after all, or pack up altogether and go home.

But servants themselves are becoming scarcer and good ones increasingly difficult to find. They are very 'choosy' and will not take the job if they do not like the look of your house or if it is too far from town. No one can really blame them for this. Some Europeans live, not by choice by but force of circumstances, in large, rambling old houses built in the days when an army of servants was the usual thing. The cavernous, echoing kitchen, grimy with the smoke of genera-tions of cooks and half a century of charcoal fires, is often far from the living parts of the house. There are acres of wooden stairways, balconies and passages all needing to be constantly polished. The servants' quarters are hot, mosquito-ridden cells built in a row at the bottom of the compound. But the memsahib, with her dinner-parties and bridge-parties, expects everything to be as polished and spick-and-span as when there were four or five houseboys instead of only one. Dinners plough through the inevitable sequence of soup, fish, entrée, sweet and dessert even though the cook-boy and his wife are still entrenched behind a mountain of unwashed dishes long after midnight.

In Singapore Chinese servants are generally acknowledged to be the best, and the Cantonese women, who wear the white tunic and black silk trousers (known as 'black and white amahs' in Singapore), are the best of all. But the religious life of the Taoist community in Singapore seems nowadays to be entirely in the hands of these humble, diligent and gentle women. They tend and care for the temples and are constantly hurrying off to take offerings and attend ceremonies, so that they are very unwilling to stay in any work which is a long way from their favourite temples. Malay servants are said to be lazy and dirty though much 'nicer', whatever that may mean, than the Chinese. Some friends of mine in Singapore, however, refused to employ any but Indian servants and insisted in calling them 'bearers', which was felt to be terribly 'pukka', but what other advantages resulted from having Indian servants I do not know.

'Of course, you'll never get a servant out at Changi,' I was told. 'Too far away.'

'Of course, they'll swindle you out of house and home. A single man is always fair game.'

'Of course, you'll have to pay the earth. The R.A.F. have got all the best ones out there anyway.'

But in fact these gloomy prognostications turned out to be quite wrong, as do so many know-all statements about the East.

The best way to find a servant is through those of your friends. Agencies exist, but their books are usually full of the unsuccessful and the throw-outs. A bush telegraph system seems to exist among the servants of one's friends and the fact that you are in the market is known long before you really realize it yourself.

Before I moved into my nest I confided in one of the room-boys at the hotel where I was staying. He already knew all about it. I had no need to worry—everything was already fixed up. The result was Ah Fat and his wife, who was called Ah Chuen. The prefix 'Ah' is a familiar expression used by those of the servant or menial social level when speaking of themselves to those whom they consider to be of a higher social level. It is, I suppose, a symptom of a caste feeling which is deeply ingrained in the Chinese as in all oriental peoples. More than the phrases of politicians will be required to eradicate it from this generation at least.

Ah Fat came to see me in the hotel, and his name suited him, for he was a Buddha-like figure, and his oblique eyes, small and sly, were almost slits in the general pudginess of his face. He spoke very little English, but through the house-boy of the hotel he intimated that he would be willing to come to me as cook-houseboy, with his wife to do my washing, for a total wage of $240 a month, about £7 a week. Believing, as I had been told, that no servant would go as far out as Changi, and that all the local ones had been snapped up by the R.A.F., I fell a fairly easy victim. 'But first,' said the hotel boy, 'Ah Fat want to see your house.' I drove him out to Changi to view the nest, and he duly approved.

Ah Fat made me comfortable enough, though the language difficulty was acute at times. He never understood anything he did not want to understand, but over matters connected with work or money his comprehension was surprisingly crystal-clear. I never noticed that he over-exerted himself, and as time went on he became lazier and lazier. He resented my having guests and would draw me aside to inquire threat-eningly how long they were intending to stay. If I had people in to a meal he would get very impatient if we lingered over our preliminary drinks and, after a certain time which he considered reasonable, would walk round the table rattling knives and forks and bumping the chairs on the floor. The longer we tarried the more peremptory and challenging these movements became. As time went on Ah Fat did less and less and Ah Chuen did more and more until, after he had been with me for some months, an excellent state of affairs had come about whereby he would sit for hours, con-templating the infinite, on a small kitchen chair in the garden behind the house, his great backside and stout, smooth, golden thighs bulging over the chair like a great pudding and his belly hanging down between them.

Ah Chuen was a pretty little thing, much younger than Ah Fat. I often wondered if she were really his wife at all. When they first came to work for me she had a blue-black bell of

straight hair with a square window in the front of it framing
a round, golden face with dark, upslanting eyes both piquant
and mischievous. She wore a pair of blue, flowered pyjamas
about the house and yellow wooden-soled sandals with red
tops. Her back view was, if anything, even more piquant
than her front view, and the clip-clop of her sandals around the
tiled kitchen and the back parts of the house seemed to convey
at once a challenge and an invitation. Or so, in the feverish
climate of Singapore, I imagined. But as time went on Ah
Chuen began to become rather grand. She became grander
and grander. Her lovely smooth casque of blue-black hair
gave way to a terrible hair-do, all frizzed and crinkled, sticking
out nearly at right angles to her head. Presently she acquired
a wrist-watch, which, one could see, was a status symbol.
Some ear-rings depended like fruits beneath the hair-do, and
with the appearance of a mother-of-pearl compact an unaccustomed and exotic fragrance began to make itself felt in
my dining-recess. I had no objection to these signs of improving
status, but unfortunately as the status improved the work
suffered. Soon she too took to sitting on a chair in the garden,
and I would find them both there side by side when I came
back from work in the evening. Then I discovered that she
was no longer doing my washing herself but arranging for
the laundry to collect it and paying for it out of her wages.
I began to feel that my establishment was a trifle over-staffed.
And at the beginning of each month I began to feel that I
was underpaid. I went on leave about nine months after moving
into my nest and decided that when I returned a change of
régime was called for.

The next deity who presided over my domestic life was a
dear man called Wong. His sister was a wash-amah to some
friends of mine in Singapore and she was a 'black and white'
amah. She was a handsome, stout woman with hair screwed
back into a tight bun at the back of her head. Like many of
her kind she was a wonderful needlewoman. Her meticulous
neatness and tidiness, the skill and delicacy which she used
in her work, could have only come from the centuries of
civilization which stood behind her and of which she was,
of course, quite unaware. Her brother, Wong, was a tubby
little man with a charming, amiable face. He remained with

me for the rest of my stay in Singapore and, though he did not have his sister's neatness and delicacy, he was a very good servant, and when I left Singapore I said good-bye to him with tears.

Not without sorrow, too, I took leave of my neighbours at last. Across the road opposite to my nest was a big, unwieldy old mansion, built in the old colonial style, now used as a Government rest-house where tired civil servants and their families came to relax for a week-end or a week or two at a time, to take the air, their files and minutes laid aside. This they did by sitting under the casuarina trees with bottles of beer, gazing across the sea at the mountains of Johore. The long row of servants' quarters faced the road in front of my house and was inhabited by the rest-house staff, nearly all Malays, and their unbelievably numerous families. The long, low building was divided into small, two-roomed dwellings, and it was hard to imagine how so many people and babies could possibly squeeze into the building. The walls seemed to bulge with the cheerful, brown, swarming throng which they enclosed. The head and chief of this delightful tribe was Jakob, the caretaker of the rest-house. He was an ex-soldier of the Malay Regiment, a handsome, elderly man with a thin, lined face and extremely courtly manners. One got the impression that to him all desires were known, and certainly from him very few secrets were hid. He arranged. He fixed. In the evening he put on a clean sarong and leaned on the gate of the rest-house garden, puffing his pipe, while the babies, his own and those of the other rest-house servants, rolled and tumbled on the sandy ground. Sometimes when the babies yelled and the women yapped and the radios boomed, I would be moved to make a protest and would cross the road to find Jakob. In the midst of the din he would be leaning on the gate puffing his pipe.

'What a row!' I would say. 'Can't you do anything about it?'

'It is terrible, Tuan. Terrible—sometimes I think I shall go mad,' and he went on placidly puffing his pipe while the noise surged round him like a sea. 'But tomorrow the school opens again, so we shall be quieter.'

A Government primary English school had been built along a side-lane behind my house, long, low open buildings along two sides of a sandy playground. Hundreds of little brown boys and girls came trooping past at half past seven every morning and went trooping back again at six in the evening. Each little girl wore a blue gym tunic with a white blouse, and each little boy a white shirt and blue shorts. They were all spotlessly clean with brown or golden or coal-black but shining morning faces, their black hair carefully brushed and their satchels bobbing on their backs. Their voices filled the air like the voices of birds. They were the children of poor working parents, mostly Malays and Indians but also some Chinese, and many came on foot in twos and threes and in little groups, some from a long way off, from the labourers' lines near the gaol and from the little Malay *kampong* of Ayer Gurong—'Roaring Water'—in the valley over the hill. Others came in ramshackle motor-cars and others in special buses. They laughed and chattered together, their arms round each other or hand in hand, the Malay, the Indian and the Chinese together without distinction of race or colour. They had in common the fleeting gift of youth and the morning sunshine. They were, let us hope, the new Asia, the new world.

One day things began to happen on the sand-spit. I drove out from the go-down to find that a large space had been cleared among the bushes. A few days later lorries arrived and a large wooden shed was run up. A notice proclaimed 'Projected Marine Research Station for the Singapore Government.' The work began of driving piles down into the sand for the building to stand upon. When they were finished the building took shape slowly upon them, and it was eighteen months before the prospect of the blue hills of Johore was blocked from the village and from the Indian shop, where I drank my warm orangeade, by two gaunt, concrete, red-roofed buildings. One was the laboratory itself and the other the junior staff quarters. These I recognized, rather unwillingly, as bearing a distinct but somehow unfamiliar resemblance to the elegant architects' drawings which had idyllic, slim bathers faintly suggested near the seaward aspect, palm trees that never were or could be and the ghost of a grand limousine—the Deputy Director's?—arriving at the front porch, which was surrounded by improbable ornamental flowers.

The work went slowly because the sub-contractors found
t very difficult to get labour to come as far afield as Changi.
There had always been a good deal of head-shaking over the
ite, which seemed to be generally regarded as much too
ar away. A similar building in the Antarctic, surely, could
carcely have presented thornier problems of labour and
ransport. Since there was a building boom in Singapore it
vas easier not only for the skilled labour, the carpenters,
oiners and plumbers, but also for the unskilled casual labour
—those stocky, sturdy, ugly, red-bonneted Hakka women—
o get work in the town, and much more profitable since they
lid not have to pay a bus fare to get to their work and back.
As a rule, therefore, when I drove out to see how my building
vas getting on, I would find very little difference from the
ast time and only one old man and two small boys working
on it. Nevertheless, it arose and was finished at last, and we
moved into it, my two young scientists and I. We looked around
it our Temple of Science with considerable pride, especially
who had watched it grow from a mere typewritten figure
on paper. I had filled files full of letters and minutes about it,
ttended meetings about it, walked round its skeleton with
groups of chaps giving my opinion (for what it was worth),
ointing and waving my arms. I had even got into a row with
he Treasury about it and been called upon for immediate
xplanations. These, when forthcoming, had been held to
e somewhat unsatisfactory. Now here it was at last, shining
nd white and new. As the Sikh *jaga* (watchman) went from
oom to room unlocking doors, it seemed like a fairy dream-
alace of my own creation. It was air-conditioned throughout
nd of course, electrically lit. There were electric pumps which
vould draw sea water through a long hose with its end buoyed
n the Johore Strait into a settling tank in the foundations. From
his the sea-water would be raised to a gravity tank in the
oof and thence would run down through the aquarium tanks
or the delectation of our collection of submarine monsters,
nd then back to the settling tank. There was a septic tank in
he compound which would be evacuated by an automatic
lectric pump into the smelly creek. There was another tank
or the noxious and terribly toxic chemicals we would be
ound to use in what were mystically referred to always as

115

our 'experiments'. There was an electric oven, even more mysterious, and a fume chamber from which the foul gases from our concoctions could be exhausted by an electric fan. The only snag was that there was no electricity, and not likely to be for an unspecified period to come.

Alas! My Temple of Science stands gaunt and forlorn and empty today, surrounded by the oleanders and casuarina trees which I planted with my own hands, the only part of all our plans to come to fruition.

Part Two

SEASCAPE

7

Fishing

The Malay Peninsula divides the outer marches of two oceans, the Indian and the Pacific. Two monsoon winds blow across it from directly opposite directions, dividing the year between them roughly in half.

The south-west monsoon blows from April to October. Hot and damp from its long journey across the tropical Indian Ocean it drops a large part of its moisture on the high rampart of Sumatra, which stands like a bulwark between the Malay Peninsula and the Indian Ocean to the south-west. During these months in Singapore the sky blackens frequently westward and about noon there is a sense of foreboding in the sultry air. Presently all hell is let loose for an hour or so, a very wet kind of hell in which the whole world seems to become a grey mass of flying water. This is a line squall, known locally as a 'sumatra'. The rain streams down as though emptied from a gigantic celestial bucket, slanting in the fierce but evanescent wind. Sampans jostle one another in the tidal basins and ships tug at their moorings like animals on a leash. Coolies run for shelter and the Tamil lightermen shout and jabber as they pole their barges off from one another. The water spouts and gurgles in the city's monsoon drains, those broad and perilous troughs that run along the sides of all the streets between the pavement and the roadway. One sees, as one huddles in the shelter of the overhanging arcaded shop-fronts and watches the swirling torrent, how necessary these ditches are. But all is soon over. After an hour or so the sun comes out and the steam rises from roofs and road surfaces. At night the stars shine innocent and bright and low down as though no such turmoil could ever have been possible.

The north-east monsoon blows from November to March and comes from central China. On its way it gets warmed up over Indo-China and the rice-bowl of Siam and picks up moisture over the South China Sea, an enclave of the Pacific

Ocean between Borneo and the Gulf of Siam. Much of this it deposits with dreary persistence on Malaya and Borneo. During December and January the rains are almost continuous. They pound without ceasing for days together as the low, slug-like swollen clouds ride up from the north-east trailing their grey veils across the sodden land. Traffic in the streets moves hub-deep through lakes and rivers that were once roads. Squatters get out and sit on the roofs of their huts, and the muddy, swollen rivers race out to sea carrying away the soft laterite soil of Malaya. On the west coast the turbid rivers drop their burden of soft mud close inshore so that for miles along the Straits of Malacca the land merges with the sea as a fringe of mud flats and mangrove swamps and it is difficult to know just where the land ends and the sea begins. At low tide the sea runs out over the oozy foreshore, which sucks and bubbles with tiny crabs, and almost disappears out of sight. At high tide the warm waves never reach above the knees of the old men who fish for prawns.

But along the east coast of the Malay Peninsula a swift current runs from north to south under the influence of the north-east monsoon and from south to north under the influence of the south-west monsoon. The mud which the rivers bring down does not get a chance to settle, so that most of the coast consists of sandy beaches with long lines of palm trees among which stand the native houses and the fishermen's nets hung up to dry. The monsoon rattles in the palm fronds, and one recognizes the ageless tropical landscape.

On the west coast, along the Straits of Malacca, the fisher-folk are mostly Chinese and live in villages of houses huddled together on stilts above the mud flats. One walks on plank-ways through a multiplicity of stenches, rotting fish and sewage and pungent cooking all contributing. On the east coast the fisherfolk are mostly Malays and live in wooden, steep-gabled thatched houses among the palm trees. They laugh and wear bright clothes. They are feckless and charming and improvident. They will not save money or form co-operatives or trade unions or take thought for the morrow or count their chickens before they are hatched. They will not play properly at being a Welfare State and they drive the Government mad. They remain poor, happy and handsome.

I do not know—I was once told but have forgotten—how
many different ways there are of catching fish along the
shallow, muddy west coast and the sandy east coast of Malaya.
There are over twenty different ways on the east coast alone.
As is the case everywhere along tropical shores the fishing
is what is known as 'on a subsistence level'. That is to say, it
is made up of thousands of individual fishermen, or small
groups of fishermen, using hand-operated, often primitive
gear with one or two boats each. They fish for their own
breakfasts. That is to say, they take small catches and sell
them to middlemen for their own profit. And meagre enough
the profit is, for, again as everywhere in the tropics, individual
catches are very small and the middleman takes most of what
they fetch. This formidable figure, the middleman, presides
over the destinies of the poor and humble fishermen everywhere
in Asia and Africa. He is usually an Indian in countries where
there are no Chinese, or a Chinese in countries where there
are no Indians. He knows nothing and cares less about fishing
or the sea, but the fishermen are in debt to him all their lives
and never pay him off. He supplies their nets and gear and
buys their catch at his prices. But he runs the risk, and takes
the knock if prices are poor or there is a slump in prices.
Because of the middleman the fisherman can never get himself
up by the bootstraps out of his poverty, but on the other hand
he and his family are assured of enough to eat and a roof over
their heads, and, when they want it, enough to drink. Nowhere in tropical countries is there a heavily capitalized and
mechanized fishing industry such as we find in Europe, America
or Japan. Nothing compares with our trawler industry with
its costly ships, long voyages to distant waters and elaborate
marketing organization. And since fishing gear and nets are
very expensive and the middleman must get his whack and
catches are usually meagre, the price of local fish in tropical
countries is ridiculously high. Frozen fish, imported from
Europe, Canada or Japan, is nearly always much cheaper
than fish caught in local waters and sold in the markets.

Native fishermen of tropical countries seldom go far out
to sea for their catches. In the first place there are few offshore, deep-water fishing grounds. But even if such grounds
existed, or were discovered, a heavy outlay of capital would

be needed to provide the ships and equip them to fish there
But more than that, the seafaring tradition, with all that it
implies of hard work, endurance and long voyages away from
home, does not exist among the humble, individualistic
fishermen of tropical shores. Only the improvidence, the habit
of living from hand to mouth and the deep-rooted conser-
vatism are common to fisherfolk of all lands under the sun.

The methods of fishing in tropical seas, therefore, are all
designed to catch the fish populations of inshore shallow waters
of the mud flats and tidal beaches, the swirling, turbid estuaries
or the glittering coral reefs. They are all ancient and ingenious
well-founded upon an unwritten lore which embraces a knowledge of the coast, the currents, the tides, the nature of the
bottom, the weather and the natural history of the fish themselves. This lore, which the fishermen know and will not impart
to strangers, makes impossible the jobs of so-called experts
who come out from Europe to teach native fishermen how to
fish. They find themselves learning instead of teaching. The
wizened old fisherman, with eyes yellow from gazing at far
horizons, knows and has forgotten far more about fishing
than the young man with his B.Sc. and his enthusiasm will
ever find out. 'Who is this baby?' an old African headman
once said of a new young Fisheries Officer. 'Has he ever had
a woman?'

In general there are two principal ways of catching fish
You can go after them with nets or lines, or you can wait
for them to come to you. In the first of these two general
methods of attack you encircle or scoop up the fish with a
bag of netting called a 'trawl' or 'seine', or you pull a line
along with a lure on it which you hope the fish will be silly
enough to pursue and snap at. Nine times out of ten you are
right. Sporting fishing may really be said to be the art of
catching big fish with inadequate gear. In the second method
of fishing you simply set your nets where the fish will swim
into them, or dangle your line where the fish will snap at
the baited hook.

In tropical countries the first way of fishing is exemplified by the seine net, probably one of mankind's oldest hunting
instruments. It is known to have been used by the ancient
Egyptians and in its simplest form is merely a bag of netting

—as its name, from *sagena*, a bag, implies. One end of the bag is anchored on the beach and the other end is carried out in a great arc through the shallows and back to the beach again. Then the net is slowly hauled in with much chanting and singing and cheerful hubbub, and a few handfuls of flickering silver treasure are yielded up. Whenever one watches tropical fishermen seine-netting one is astonished at the smallness of the reward of their labours.

In Singapore the seine-net fishermen work their nets mostly along the south coast of the island, where there are flat expanses of mud. When the tide is high you can see them go by in the hot pastel morning, paddling their long canoes with slow strokes, each of which leaves a scar upon the polished surface. In the evening after dark, when the sea is filled with fierce stars, you can see them returning with their catch, their day's labour finished. You can just make out their conical hats and hear their voices talking across the still, dark water. They are the immemorial East, and you look upon them across measureless gulfs of time. They seem to be mostly Tamils and Madras Indians, stringy black men with loin-cloths or *dhotis* tucked up around their skinny shanks. They chant a monosyllabic song as they pull in their long, sinuous nets. Sometimes they catch in them more than they bargain for, and I once saw them drag up on the beach a huge black-and-white Manta ray, twelve feet across from wing-tip to wing-tip. It was alive, but so overpowered by its own weight that it could not move and lay on the beach, an inert mass, suffering itself to be cut up piecemeal without being able to do anything by way of protest. Yet so great is the surface area of these creatures, compared with their volume, that they are active and graceful in the water. They can volplane about and fling themselves high into the air to strike the surface again with a noise like a thunderclap.

The second way of fishing, by waiting for the fish to come and be caught, is exemplified by the big stationary fish-traps, or *kelongs*, which are a feature of the coastal scene all round Singapore island, Malaya and the islands of Indonesia. By day they look like a community of huts on legs in the sea, but after sunset the shallow sea all round the islands is lit by their hundreds of lights. They burn steadily all night, each

one at the head of the shimmering column of its own re
flexion. You can see them far down the coast and out to se
like another city afloat upon the water.

This is perhaps the most ingenious of all the ways of en
ticing fish, as opposed to actively going and catching them
It is a method ideally suited to shallow coasts with a fairl
strong, but not too strong, tide. Each trap consists primaril
of a long row of upright poles. Each row is several hundre
yards in length, and the poles, made of the stems of the *nibon*
palm, are set in the mud about two feet part. They stand i
a row, obliquely to the tide, and therefore more or less a
right-angles to the shore, extending from the shallows int
a depth of about seven fathoms. At the end of each row is
triangular enclosure, built of vertical poles, with a floor o
netting which can be raised by ropes attached to its edge:
wound up over rollers on the platform above.

Small fishes, in shoals or solitary, swim against the tid
or drift with it. When they encounter the row of poles the
cannot pass it, no matter how small they may be and eve
though the poles are spaced two feet apart. The reason fo
this is not understood. It may perhaps have something to d
with the strength and direction of the eddies round the pole
themselves. But, whatever the reason may be, the fish ar
guided by some unexplained force along the row from pol
to pole into the triangular enclosure above the floor of netting
Here hangs a powerful kerosene lamp, and it is these lamp:
hanging in hundreds of fish-traps all along the coast, whic
we can see burning far down the straits at night. The ligh
brings the fishes together over the middle of the net. Ever
three or four hours or so the little Chinese boys, who liv
in the hut on the platform beside the enclosure, run out an
wind up the ropes over the wooden rollers, pulling up the ne
Most of the fishes which come up in the lifted net are sma
anchovies, sardines, moon fishes and 'soapies', like sma
silver coins. Most of these are sold as cattle-food or fertilize:
but the anchovies are sorted out and boiled in brine befor
being sold salted to the food stalls in Singapore. This
done in a cauldron kept perpetually stirred by an old man i
striped shorts. He is the headman of the fish-trap, and i
a position of authority over the boys.

A Hindu devotee at the festival of Thaipusam, Singapore

Singapore River

Singapore street scene

The death of Rawan, Dashera 1955, Singapo

alay village, Pulau Sudom, Singapore

*A Malay wedding at Pulau Brani, Singapore. The bridegroom and his parents
at the start of the procession to the bride's house*

Stationary fish trap or kelong, *Singapore Strait*

Mackerel fishing station, Pangkor Island, Mala

'Manihine', Singapore, 1955

The policeman of
Pulau Aur

The old Japan

The new Japan

ht-seeing, Kamakura

A Hong Kong street scene

Aberdeen fishing harbour, Hong Kong

'Alister Hardy'

The Fisheries Department in Singapore was on friendly terms with many of the fish-traps around the coast, and occasionally we visited those which were within easy reach of the harbour. Sometimes we made an outing of this and took along fried chicken and rice, which we bought beforehand at a food stall, and made a picnic in the hut on its platform out over the sea. The little boys were delighted with this and, if the old man in striped shorts did not exactly welcome us as we climbed up the stilts of his house on to his platform, at least he showed no signs of open hostility. In fact he took not the slightest notice of us but went on stirring his cauldron as though we did not exist. But the boys hopped about and spread mats for us to sit on, and giggled and stared. Boy labour is exclusively employed in these fish-traps, and women are supposed to bring bad luck. Whenever I read official publications about native activities in Singapore, or newspaper articles about anything, including politics, and find the words 'labourers', 'workers', 'supporters', 'manpower', 'personnel' and so on I close my eyes and think of the chirruping little boys to whom these words refer. In Singapore, where half the population is under the age of twenty, there are boys everywhere. They all look exactly the same, with slanting, dancing eyes under long, dank locks of hair, tough little brown or yellow bodies clad only in a pair of dirty blue-and-white striped shorts, and noses that spread all over their pug faces. In the fish-traps they hopped about all over the wooden framework of the structure like birds. Their feet were broad and seemed almost prehensile like those of monkeys. They wound up the net for us to see the catch and sorted it out with exclamations of surprise, though they must have seen the same thing happen a dozen times a night. When we sat down on the mats they had arranged and ate our fried chicken they stood around watching with passionate interest. Only the old headman stirred his cauldron and took no notice.

These fish-traps become slightly different as you go north up the Straits of Malacca. Around Penang the long, guiding palisade of poles is absent and all you can see is a palm-thatched chalet standing on a platform on stilts above an enclosure with a lift net and a light.

Malacca itself, with Penang, is one of the original Strait Settlements and, until the Independence of the Federation of Malaya in 1957, was British territory, as opposed to a British-protected Sultanate like the Malay States themselves. Before that it was Dutch and before that Portuguese. It has handsome Dutch houses, Portuguese ruins and lovely elaborate Chinese temples. It is the oldest Straits Chinese community in Malaya. It is old and historical and smelly, and lies sweltering in the heat, dreaming of the past. It is surrounded by an enchanting countryside of rice fields and coconut groves, in which stand Malay houses with steep, pointed gables of palm thatch, quite unlike the rest of the west coast. Covered ox-carts sway slowly along the roads, and there is an unhurried, leisurely air about the place which is refreshing to tired spirits after the noise and rattle of Singapore. From marshy creeks and inlets along the coast of Malacca fleets of flat-bottomed, open boats go out and set long lines of drift nets in the shallow, turbid straits.

Drift nets are walls or curtains of netting set so as to hang across the tide so that the fish swim into them and become ensnared in the meshes. They may be either 'gill' nets or 'tangle' nets. Gill nets consist of a single wall or curtain of meshes made of fine thread. The meshes are of such a size that the fish they are designed to catch will just be able to get their heads through them, but no more. They cannot withdraw, because the fine threads of which the meshes are made hold them behind the gill covers. Thus it follows that gill nets catch only fish of one particular size. In the herring drift-net fishery round the coast of Britain this is convenient enough because the shoaling herring are all of the same size. In the frenzy and excitement of their 'runs' or 'swims' inshore the great shoals of them charge into the hanging miles of netting and become stuck fast in the meshes in countless thousands. Tangle nets, on the other hand, consist usually of three curtains of netting, a small meshed curtain hanging between two curtains of much wider mesh made of fine strands. The fish run up against the triple curtain and strike the small meshes, but in turning to avoid the obstruction they become caught in the web of fine, wide-meshed netting. The more they struggle the more entangled they become. Tangle nets, therefore, can catch fish of almost any size, since meshes of three different widths may be used. But one of the disadvantages is the labour of disentangling the fish from them, and another the constant repairing and replacement which are needed, since the fish in their struggles always damage the nets severely.

In the Straits of Malacca the shallow wooden barges, each with an eye painted on either side of the bows, without which no boat can see where it is going, are towed out to sea in long strings by a single powered boat. They set fine nylon tangle nets to catch, among many other sorts of fish, the diamond-shaped black or white 'pomfret', which is considered to be a very high-class fish and a great delicacy at Chinese feasts.

Farther up the west coast, between Port Swettenham and Penang, lie the lovely Pangkor Islands, where there is quite a different sort of fishing. In the season of the south-west monsoon shoals of green and silver mackerel, called *kembong*, appear around the islands and are caught by Chinese fishermen with ring nets. These mackerel shoals appear in the south-west monsoon season along all the coasts and islands of the Indian Ocean from East Africa to Malaya. They disappear in the months of the north-east monsoon and no one knows where they go to. Their natural history is almost unknown. In the Seychelles the creole fishermen catch them close inshore with hand lines armed with many small hooks. In India and Ceylon they are caught in shallow waters with nets towed between two boats. But around Pangkor the water is too deep for this, and when the mackerel shoals see or hear a net approaching they disperse and dive, reforming behind the net. The Chinese fishermen of Pangkor, therefore, use a ring net or 'purse' seine. The shoal is swiftly encircled with a ring of netting, which is then drawn together at the bottom to form a bag or purse beneath the shoal. Great skill, precision and speed are required for this as well as absolute quiet, for the fish are very timid and disperse and dive at the slightest sound. The shoals can only be seen on calm, moonless nights when they make milky patches of phosphorescence as they move about at the surface of the water. The boats watch for these patches and approach them with great caution and stealth. No engines can be used, because the beat of a screw can be heard by the fish a long way off. The boats paddle forward making as little sound as possible No talking is allowed, no lights may be shown and there is no smoking. The boats work in pairs, one of the pair carrying the net and paying it out while the other takes the end of it quickly out in a wide circle round the shoal. Skilful and successful as the Chinese are at this, their catches would be much greater if there were some way of locating the shoals other than by watching for the patches of phosphorescence they make on dark nights. The radar 'fishlupe' may be the obvious answer, but it seems impossible to approach the shoals with any boat driven by any sort of engine. The fish can hear the beat of the screw and of the engine from a long way off and are just not there when the ship gets to the spot.

Some years ago the Malayan Fisheries Department acquired a small Scottish 'purse' seine boat and a team of expert 'purse' seine fishermen, who came out from Scotland to try their hand at catching the *kembong*. In order to work up to the necessary speed and precision they practised for weeks with masses of bits of torn-up paper scattered upon the water. But the bits of paper could not dive and disperse when the boat approached. When the Scotsmen came to try their skill upon the fish themselves they failed to catch any at all and eventually had to admit defeat—another example of the difficulty of improving on old fishing methods with modern apparatus.

On the east coast of Malaya the fishermen, who are Malays, live and work by the weather to an even greater extent than on the west coast. From October to April the north-east monsoon blows upon this open coastline from across the hundreds of miles of the South China Sea, bringing high winds and heavy rains, so that in these months there is not much fishing except in sheltered river-mouths. Most of the fishing is done in the hot, calm months of the south-west monsoon. Then the days are hot, but the land cools during the clear, still nights. In the morning a land breeze blows from the cooled coast on to the warmer sea. As the land warms up during the day the breeze is reversed, and in the afternoon a sea breeze blows in the opposite direction, from the cooler

ea on to the warmer land. Along the coasts of Kelantan and
Trengganu, therefore, the fishermen take advantage of this
daily change of wind which has always been part of their
lives. Their slim canoes, with high prows and stern posts
and lateen sails, put out in their hundreds with the dawn land
wind and return on the evening sea breeze. From this it has
become the tradition among Malay fishermen to stay out at
sea for one day only. They may spend a night or so at some
other village along the coast, but on the whole, like many
other sensible people, they prefer to spend the night in their
own beds and under their own roofs.

Most of the fishing on the east coast is for the small fishes
which move about in shoals, great or small, in shallow waters,
such as various sorts of herring, mackerel, sardines and
anchovies. These resemble but are not the same as our northern
ones. The shoals appear in the months of the south-west
monsoon and can be seen by day as a stippling on the surface
of the shallow sea like a cloud shadow on a meadow or the
pattern of the wind upon a field of corn. On calm, moonless
nights, again, pale patches of phosphorescence show where
the shoals are moving at the surface. The fishermen make
artificial shelters to attract the fish, making use of the fishes'
habit of collecting wherever there is shade. Ropes are moored
in the sea all along the coast with a stone sinker at one end and
a bamboo float on the surface at the other. Fronds of coconut
palm about ten feet long are fixed along the length of this
rope about six feet apart. These artificial trees are left in
position throughout the fishing season and renewed when
necessary. Small fishes collect together in the shade of the
palm fronds, though why they do so is a mystery. It is possible
that they congregate there because other small creatures on
which they feed collect there too, or perhaps it is simply that
they enjoy the shade. The second explanation seems the more
likely of the two. Most of these small fishes feed on the tiny
drifting life of the sea, the plankton, which they sift out of
the water by means of sieve-like processes which project
across their throats from their gills. But the plankton is not
necessarily more abundant in the shade than elsewhere, and
anyone who has observed fishes at all knows how they love
to seek shady places. The trout lurks under rocks in his

mountain stream and the salmon lies in shadowy pools. In the sea the young of many fishes congregate in the shade between moored boats, under jetties or beneath the overhang of roofs. Off Zanzibar there was a half-sunken wreck of a steel ship the hollow shell of which made a calm, shady tank where young mullet used to collect in dense masses, constantly circling and inter-weaving in the gloom. In Dar-es-Salaam, in Tanganyika, there was, and probably still is, a diving raft under which, unknown to all but a very few, large barracuda used to lurk, and probably still do, quietly asleep in the shade while the bathers dived and shouted around them.

Before the fishing operations start each day the Malay fishermen visit their artificial shelters in turn to see if there are any fish there. If there are they swiftly draw an encircling net round them, which may be a gill net or simply a large bag like a seine. Or they may cunningly draw the fish away over a big lift net slung between four boats.

An even more cunning way of fishing which the Malay fishermen use on the east coast of Malaya involves listening to the voices of fish under water. It is known that many sorts of fish do, in fact, make noises under the water, and records have actually been taken of their strange gulping, croaking sounds. Even prawns are said to make a clicking sound as they swim. It is not known exactly what the significance of these sounds may be. It is doubtful if the fish are really communicating with each other in any way, and the noises they make are probably mechanical and fortuitous, perhaps caused by their fins or tails in swimming, or by the bones and teeth in their throats in the act of breathing or eating. One of the noisiest and most talkative of fishes is the Jewfish, or Croaker, which forms dense shoals close inshore along the coasts of Malaya and Borneo. It is a good fish to eat and gets its name from its rounded semitic profile.

Some of the east-coast fishermen are experts at detecting shoals of Jewfish and locating them by listening under water to the sounds they make. Some fishermen are more skilled at this than others, either because of long practice or because this is just one of God's strange gifts which He bestows capriciously upon mortals. Thus, just as some people can sing while others have not a note, and some can paint pictures while others cannot, so apparently some people have the rather more outlandish gift of being clever at listening to fish under water. Malay fishermen who are especially gifted in this way are regarded with awe by their fellows and become leaders among them, headmen of the companies of fishermen who own and man the big drag nets which are used for catching Jewfish and other shoaling fishes. The headman, who dives and listens to the fishes, is known as the *juru selam*, and the better he is at detecting and locating the shoals the more easily he can win recruits from among the young men of his village to man the net.

The companies of fishermen sail on the dawn wind in their long, graceful, canoe-like boats with high, tapering ends and spar-rests painted and carved in ancient traditional designs. The spar-rests are passed down from old boats to new from year to year, for they carry the spirit of the boat with them and pass the good will and luck of one boat on to her successors. Each boat has a crew of fifteen or twenty men with the *juru selam* as their leader. In the big boat a large encircling seine net is carried folded down amidships, while forward athwartships a small row boat is carried. When the big boat reaches the fishing ground, which may be twenty miles offshore, the small boat is put over the side and the *juru selam* is paddled about in it by one of the crew. A pair of goggles is the only concession he makes to modern science, and these have only come into fashion in the trade quite recently. From time to time he goes over the side of the small boat to listen under the water, sometimes holding on to the gunwale with one hand with his head under, at other times swimming and diving. If fish are about he can hear them talking. I once heard a *juru selam* give an imitation of the sounds he said he heard, but his imitation was more like that of a flock of ducks than a shoal of fish. If he is a clever *juru* he can tell whether the shoal is near or far off and in which direction it is, and whether it is a large shoal or a small one, whether it is compact or scattered. Even the sharks, the fishermen say, have a respect for the *juru* and will not attack so gifted a man, but swim away in shame. When a suitable shoal has been located by the *juru* he gets back into his small boat and from it directs the operations of the big encircling net which is laid round the shoal, one wing fixed to a float while the big boat pays out the rest of the net, moving in a circle.

These are only a few of the cunning and ancient methods of fishing which have been used on the east and west coasts of Malaya by humble fishermen for many centuries. They operate only in the shallow coastal waters within ten or fifteen miles of the coast. They served well enough in their day to provide fish for the scattered villages of the coastal strip. But they cannot nowadays possibly bring in enough fish to feed the steadily increasing populations of great industrial centres such as Singapore, where alone the population has doubled itself in the last ten years, and will have reached the two-million mark by 1970. A large fraction of this population, too, is made up of Muslims who cannot eat pork, so that fish from the sea, always an important staple food in all countries, is even more important in Malaya than elsewhere.

To the east of the Malay Peninsula, and to the north of Borneo, a gently undulating submarine plain slopes away for about four hundred miles. It is dotted with numerous islands and has an average depth of between thirty and forty fathoms. The mud has been laid down by the torrential rains of countless ages washing away the soft soil of the neighbouring coasts. Turbid rivers, swollen by monsoon rains, carry the fine silt out to sea and drop it on the shelf which joins Indo-China and Borneo. Along a line running roughly north and south about four hundred miles east of the coast of Malaya the shelf descends steeply into the abyss. The great expanse of the South China Sea over this shelf, nearly as large as half the Mediterranean, has remained since the beginning of human history unfished, largely unexplored and unexploited. Across it for half the year the north-east monsoon wind blows strongly, piling up heavy seas with enormous swells that roll into the Borneo river mouths. But among the fishermen of the neighbouring lands no seafaring tradition exists, nor is there any capital for building or equipping ships to undertake the necessary voyages in search of fishing grounds.

This shelf of oozy mud, its southern boundary the coast of Borneo and its western boundary the coast of Malaya, merges to the northward into the great mud plain of the Gulf of Thailand, laid down by the outflow of the Mekong River.

To the east extends the South China Sea far northward to Formosa and Japan. But this was only part of the area which we, my two young scientists and I, had to explore. To the west of the Malay Peninsula there lay the funnel-shaped passage of the Malacca Strait between Malaya and Sumatra, floored by another muddy shelf, widening out and deepening to the Indian Ocean where the Nicobar and Andaman Islands ride, crowning steep-sided ridges which go down to great depths. Singapore stands at the centre of all this, commanding the junction of these two great expanses of shallow sea.

No one had ever really defined the limits of our area, and our terms of reference were extremely wide. They were 'to explore and investigate the offshore waters of Malaya and Borneo'. We felt justified in assuming that this meant all the waters outside the ten-fathom line within a reasonable cruising distance from the Malayan and Borneo coasts. Obviously there would be no point in covering an area greater than could be economically worked by commercial fishing boats operating from the only available base, Singapore. Nor was there any point in going beyond the limits of the muddy continental shelf to the east and west of the Malay Peninsula where the fishing grounds, if there were any, might be expected to lie.

Very little fishing had ever been done in these offshore waters. When I arrived in Singapore in 1952 there were two or three couples of Japanese-built 'pair' trawlers working in the South China Sea. 'Pair' trawling is a method which is used by Hong Kong sailing trawler junks and is much favoured by the Japanese. A trawl is in essence merely a bag of netting which is pulled over the sea bottom by wires, called 'bridles', attached to its two lateral wings. In the British-style single trawling the ship lies beam-on to the wind and pays away the trawl over her side. When the trawl is out she turns and tows it behind her. But in 'pair' trawling two ships work together, hauling the trawl between them. One of the pair shoots the net over her stern and then passes the bridle attached to one wing of the net to her sister ship. The two ships then steam or sail ahead a mile or so apart with the great net sweeping along the bottom between them. This method makes possible the use of much larger nets with a bigger gape, but

E*

is of course just twice as expensive as single trawling, since two boats cost twice as much as one. In Europe this method is used by Spanish fishermen in the Bay of Biscay fishing for hake. During the war these *pareja* trawlers called in at Milford Haven, having been taking advantage of the absence of British trawlers from the southern grounds. For a while after the war the idea of 'pair' trawling caught on with Milford Haven fishermen, but now the Milford Haven trawlers have fallen on hard times and 'pair' trawling has ceased.

In Singapore the 'pair' trawlers were old and cranky little ships. They had a curious chunky, junk-like appearance, with square stern and narrow beam, and cumbersome simple Jap diesel engines which could tonk along happily for month after month without any attention. Manned by Chinese crews recruited in Hong Kong, they seemed to operate chiefly on liberal doses of hope, and it was always rather alarming to see them setting out with black smoke belching from their exhausts and a forty degrees' list, they looked so low and small and near the water. They fished mostly near the beautiful palm-covered islands, Tioman, Aur and Pemanggil, off the east coast of Malaya, on a soft, oozy bottom, heavy and diffi-cult for trawling. But so slender was the financial shoe-string on which they worked that one or two unsuccessful trips, due to bad weather or poor fishing, were enough to bankrupt the owners. They certainly could not afford to try new grounds or risk going where they would not be certain of their catch. And so one by one, or rather two by two, the little ships went out of business during my first year or so at Singapore and ended their days sadly rotting on the mud in Kallang River.

Besides the trawlers there were several long-lining boats from Hong Kong, and they did rather better. Long-lining is a method of fishing which, in northern waters, is used on the grand banks of Newfoundland for cod and ling, and off Iceland on the continental edge where the great halibut are taken on the slope down to the abyss. On the Grand Banks the long-liners lay miles of line with hundreds of hooks, each hook at the end of a short branch called a 'snood'. The lines are carried in round baskets each containing some hundreds of hooks, and are laid from flat-bottomed open boats called 'dories'. There are many days of still weather on the banks, otherwise such a method would not be possible. The 'dories' are carried on the deck of a mother-ship and put over the side when the ship reaches the fishing ground. Each dory carries three or four men, who pay out the lines from the baskets with a marker buoy and an anchor at each end. The lines lie on the bottom all night and are picked up in the morning. This is, however, by no means as simple as it sounds, and long-lining is a highly specialized form of fishing. There is probably no trade in the world in which specialization is as great and varied as in sea fishing. A trawlerman is not necessarily a good long-liner or a long-liner a good trawlerman. Many fishermen specialize all their lives at long-lining, and others at trawling, or seine-netting, or ring-netting, or drifting, and cannot leave their chosen calling for any other kind of fishing. Part of the long-line fisherman's art is to get his long line of baited hooks swiftly away and down past the 'guard' fish without losing the bait on its way down to the bottom, where the true fish are. The 'guard' fish are the small second-grade fish which swim to and fro above the bottom and take the bait on its way down. Fishermen say they are guarding the fishing ground, and look upon them as enemies to be thwarted. In the tropics another problem is to get the hooked fish up safely without having them devoured on the way by sharks, barracuda and other predatory, hunting fish so that all that comes aboard is a head and a bloody stump. Once on the bottom the bait may be sucked off the hook by fishes with mouths too small to take the hook, or nibbled off by crabs and other creatures which live on the bottom. In long-lining, therefore, the character of the bottom and the kinds of animals that live on it have to be taken into consideration as well as the kinds of fish that live on the bottom and above it.

The long-liners in Singapore came down from Hong Kong, where, off the coast of Kwangtung, long-lining is an important fishery. They used very fine, light lines, with nylon snoods, carrying thousands of small hooks. They weighted them with round blobs of concrete, which they made themselves. They made all their gear by hand, and we used to watch the tough, square little men, in white singlets and black cotton trousers, with plate-like straw hats on their heads, sitting on the jetty with their hands rapidly busy among the fine lines and clouds of nylon, white as spiders' webs, coiling them down with exquisite precision in bamboo wicker-work trays. Their ships, too, were small and old and cranky. They lived herded on board them with all their families, their women and their children, their pigs and their chickens. The women cooked and smacked the children. Their oiled hair was always done up tightly with gilt pins through the coils. They glared resentfully if you stepped on board, even if only to cross to another ship. White devils were unlucky, and their influence had to be exorcised with joss sticks. On the fishing grounds, near the islands of Tioman, Aur and Pemanggil, they put bamboo rafts over the side, each with two men on it. From these the lines, carrying several thousand hooks baited with salted herring, which were bought by the barrel before the ship left port, were paid out and hauled in. The rafts, with two or three men on them, were left to drift all night while the ship went far out of sight to put down more lines from more rafts. In the morning she went round collecting the rafts and the men on them with their catch. Presumably she picked up as many rafts in the morning as she had put down the evening before, but it is doubtful if a season could pass without some casualties. The fishermen had no fear on that account. We used to come upon their bamboo rafts adrift in the South China Sea, the nearest land a mere faint loom in the far distance, and no sign of any ship. The little men, sitting or standing on the rafts, the warm waves lapping round their feet and legs, were not in the least perturbed. They had been sitting there all night.

'Ask them where their ship is,' our Skipper said on the first occasion. 'Ask them if they want any help.'

Our Chinese cook leant over the rail and shouted something in Cantonese. They replied.

'No good,' said the cook. 'A few snappers. Bad fishing.'

'I said "Ask them where their ship is," you bloody fool.'

The cook spoke again in Cantonese.

'Hong Kong—six months,' said the cook.

'Good God! Isn't she coming back?'

'Yes, yes. Come velly soon. Ship coming.'

And presently she did come, far off and low down on the horizon, a plume of black diesel smoke. She had been away putting down other rafts and had now picked them up and was returning to gather up her chickens. How she knew where they all were was a mystery, for she had no radio, radar, echo-sounder or any other modern devices. She had her skipper's sense of direction and sea craft, and she had bought luck from the gods before she sailed by scattering the necessary amount of imitation paper money on the water. Perhaps it was because she never failed in this that all the little men on her rafts came safely back to port.

These long-liners did quite well in the months of the south-west monsoon. In the north-east monsoon the weather was too rough. They caught the big red snappers which are the staple fish all over the Indian Ocean. But it was a specialized form of fishing which only these few Hong Kong boats could use, and what they brought in was a trifling contribution to the great mass appetite of the population. And the trawlers all failed and lay on the mud in the river.

The Government itself had made several attempts to explore the shelf area of the South China Sea with trawlers of its own in the hope of finding likely fishing grounds. In 1926 the Malayan Government of that day bought an old British steam trawler which fished up and down the east coast among the islands. But she failed to get good catches and lost so many trawls that the attempt was given up as hopeless, and nothing further was done for nearly thirty years. Then the Government had another try with a small motor fishing vessel which had a longer range and was able to go farther afield. But she was not powerful enough and could not trawl successfully on the heavy, muddy bottom of the South China Sea. Her trawls bogged down in the mud while her screw thrashed the water under her stern.

David was the Master Fisherman who had charge of these unprofitable operations. He was the Milford Haven trawling skipper with whom I had sailed around the Seychelles and Mauritius and whom I felt I knew by now as a brother. The title 'Master Fisherman' is a kind of honorary rank bestowed on an expert professional fisherman whose job it is to catch fish, take charge of fishing gear, or direct fishing operations. In David's particular case his position was a somewhat invidious one since, as Master Fisherman, he was in charge of the fishing operations, but not of the ship which was carrying them out. The ship was commanded by a Malay skipper or *nakhoda*. Not surprisingly this dual control was not a great success.

Much water had passed under many bridges since David and I had last sailed together. When the work at the Seychelles was completed David joined the commercial venture, sponsored by the Colonial Development Corporation, which attempted to exploit the grounds we had surveyed. He took command of one of the fishing vessels which the venture sent to fish on the banks. During a voyage between the Seychelles and Mombasa the ship developed engine trouble and was adrift helplessly in a heavy monsoon gale for over a week. David saved the ship by his coolness and sagacity and received the M.B.E., of which he was exceedingly proud. He said it stood for 'My Own Bloody Efforts'. But the Seychelles venture flopped, and David found himself with an M.B.E. but no job. In 1952 he came to Singapore as Master Fisherman with the intention of joining my outfit as Skipper as soon as I had a ship for him to command. I rejoiced when I heard that he was coming and felt safe. He had lost none of his Welsh fire and his eye could glitter as coldly as ever.

But at that time my outfit, to which I referred officially as 'my organization', and which was called 'The Singapore Regional Fisheries Research Station', consisted of my Tamil stenographer and me, and a rapidly growing mass of files in which I kept copies of the minutes I wrote to the Government.

'. . . I would request the favour of an early reply.'

'. . . Grateful for a reply.'

'. . . Request some degree of priority.'

'. . . No reply has yet been received.'

'. . . Glad to know your views.'

8

My Ship

In the seas of the world everywhere, whether in the North Sea around the coasts of Britain and Europe, or in the warm and muddy waters of the South China Sea and Malacca Strait, there are two main classes of fishes. There are, firstly, those which spend their adult lives on or near the sea bottom, and secondly, those which spend their adult lives at or near the surface.

All fishes start life as small fry which, as they develop from the egg, float passively at the surface at the mercy of tides and currents. These young fry are, in fact, members of that community of drifting life which is known as the 'plankton', from the Greek word πλαγκτός, meaning wandering. The newly hatched fry at first feeds on the remains of its egg yolk, which hangs down like a sac beneath it. When that has all been used up the fry is clearly recognizable as a little fish, and it begins to feed on microscopic living things which it takes in at its mouth. These are largely the unicellular plants and protozoa which make up the finest and smallest creatures of the plankton. As the fry grows it becomes able to make more and more independent movements of its own and to feed on the larger members of the plankton. At about this stage the two classes of fishes diverge from one another. Those of one class sink down and spend the rest of their lives swimming about at or near the bottom. At the same time they change their feeding habits and take to a diet of crabs, shellfish, worms, sea-urchins and other creatures which crawl over, or cling to, or burrow into the muddy, sandy, stony or rocky bed of the ocean. These are called 'ground' fishes or 'demersal' fishes. In British waters over three-quarters of the fish that reach the markets are ground fishes, such as the cod, the haddock, the whiting, the plaice, the sole and many others. They are caught with trawls or seine nets or lines. In the South China Sea and Malacca Strait the great staple ground fish is the red snapper, or *ikan merah*, which is the Malay for 'red fish'. It is a large, dark red, voracious beast with formidable teeth which feeds on almost anything it can find on the bottom, including the young of its own species. It has a cousin in the Seychelles where the staple fish is a very similar red snapper.

The second great class of fishes comprises all those which do not sink down to the bottom of the sea in their youth but remain all their lives swimming at or near the surface. These are known as the 'pelagic' fishes, and they mostly swim about in shoals, which may often be of immense size, containing thousands of fish united in a common purpose and direction by some mysterious bond which is not yet understood. It is not known what influence or instinct it is which makes shoals of fish move and act as though the whole host was in fact one organism with a single will.

The most important pelagic fish in European waters is the herring, which appears off the east coast of the British Isles every summer in enormous shoals. It is caught by means of drift nets, curtains of netting hanging in the water so that the fish, charging against them, get stuck in the meshes by the gills. About a quarter of a million tons of herring are caught by British drifters alone every year, and far more than that by the drifters of other nations. There are also many other pelagic, shoaling fishes in our waters, such as the mackerel, the sprat, the pilchard or sardine and the anchovy.

All the pelagic shoaling fishes feed on plankton. Most of them sieve the plankton out of the water by means of filaments on their gill arches. These are called 'gill-rakers', and they form a sort of grid across the gill apertures. As the fish takes in water by its mouth in order to breathe, and passes it out through the gill apertures, the grid formed by the gill-rakers strains the plankton out of the water. The pilchard and the American 'menhaden' feed on the very finest microscopic plant and animal life of the plankton and have very long gill-rakers, but most other pelagic fishes feed on larger members of the plankton and so have rather shorter gill-rakers, which sieve less efficiently and let through all but the larger animals which the fish needs. On the other hand it is believed that the herring, which has quite short rakers, actually goes

n pursuit of small animals and actively captures much of its
ood rather than passively sieving it out of the water.

In the Far East there are many kinds of pelagic shoaling
ishes, such as mackerel, sardine and anchovy. They are
mostly caught with seine nets, or with lift nets with lights
:o attract the fish, like the *kelongs* around the coast of Singa-
ore. They are all taken close inshore by individual fishermen or groups of fishermen operating with their own private
oats and gear. The waters farther from the shore, beyond
he ten-fathom line, were unexplored, but in planning our
operations we had to go by analogy with the waters of other
parts of the world where it was known that as you go farther
out from the coast into deeper water the pelagic shoaling
fishes become less abundant and at varying distances from the
coast peter out altogether. There are, however, other types
of pelagic fishes which might perhaps be taken some distance
from the coast, such as the giant mackerels like the Tuna,
the Bonito and the Yellowfin, or the fierce swift hunters of
the sea, the sporting fishes, such as the Wahoo, the Sailfish
and the Barracuda. Some of these are migratory, particularly the Yellowfin, and their migration routes often take them
far from land, but on the whole, since they feed on smaller
shoaling fishes, they too tend to follow the coastlines and the
edges of banks and reefs.

The fisheries of Malaya, Borneo and Singapore, like those
of all tropical countries in Asia and Africa, are based on
mainly inshore fishes and are operated by men working
singly or in small groups. In Malaya and Singapore these
inshore fisheries were saturated—that is to say, they were
taking out of the inshore seas as much fish as they would
ever be able to get. Any future increase would have to be
obtained by a movement of the fisheries away from the inshore waters into the hitherto unexplored waters farther out
beyond the ten-fathom line. It therefore seemed to us that
it was the demersal or ground fishes which we must chiefly
look for. There were not likely to be pelagic fisheries in
deeper waters awaiting exploitation. We must therefore survey
a wide area of open sea to start with and, if ground fish were
found in likely quantities anywhere, we must return to those
places at a later date, after we had surveyed the whole area

as closely as possible, and give the new grounds, if we found any, a more detailed study, find out how the population on them varied from season to season and what the population was composed of.

A ship engaged in this kind of exploration has to do a great deal more than catch fish. All marine life is ultimately dependent on the plankton. Pelagic fishes feed directly on it, while the ground fishes are dependent on it at first remove. They feed on the fixed, burrowing or creeping things of the sea bottom and these in their turn are directly dependent on the plankton. They are indeed part of it when they are young, since many bottom-living animals start life as tiny larval youth forms which drift about as part of the plankton. At a certain stage they sink down and change into their adult form and spend the rest of their lives fixed to a rock, like an anemone, or burrowing in sand like a lug-worm or creeping cautiously about like a sea-urchin. Many bottom-living animals feed on the decayed remains of plant and animal life which rain constantly down from above as the plankton animals themselves die, or on the rain of excrement from the plankton in the upper layers. Other bottom-living animals feed on their companions on the bottom. The sea is a jungle, not red but blue or green or opalescent, in tooth and claw, and it is fairly true to say that almost everything eats almost everything else. Biologists amuse themselves by building on paper great structures like genealogical trees showing, not who begat whom, but who eats whom in the submarine underworld. These are called 'food chains', and they show that all creatures in the sea from the largest whale, or indeed man himself, down to the smallest speck of microscopic jelly are closely interdependent and interrelated. At the bottom of the tree or chain, however, always stands the green plant life of the sea, the diatoms. These unicellular plants, with complicated skeletons of silica—glass, in fact—floating at the surface of the sea in uncountable millions are the grass of the ocean. They occupy much the same basic position in the economy of the sea as does the grass in the economy of the land. In temperate waters, such as those around the coasts of Europe and North America, there takes place a great outburst of this plant life in the spring. It proliferates in the summer and

lies away again in the autumn. The spring outburst is followed
a few weeks later every year by a similar outburst of minute
animal life with a similar proliferation in the summer months.
This small animal life feeds upon the microscopic plant life,
and during the course of the summer steadily grazes it down.
In tropical waters, such as those around Malaya and Borneo,
there are also proliferations of plant and animal life in the
sea, but they are linked, not with a spring and summer season,
since these do not properly exist in that part of the world,
but with the alternating and opposite monsoon winds. It is
these which dominate the cycle of life in tropic seas.

The plankton, both plant and animal, and its variations
both in time and place, therefore obviously occupy a key
position in any study of a fish population. And there is more
to it than that.

If the plants of the plankton, the diatoms, can be compared
with grass on land, so can the sea-water in which they live be
compared with the soil. Just as plants on land build up carbohydrates from carbon dioxide in the air, using the green
chlorophyll in their leaves as a catalyst, so do the plants of
the marine plankton build up carbohydrates within their
tiny cells. Their cells contain chlorophyll, exactly the same as
that in the leaves of land plants, which fixes the carbon dioxide
of the sea-water with the aid of sunlight. And as plants on land
suck up nourishment from the soil by their roots, so does the
drifting plant life of the sea absorb the same nourishment
from the water through the cell walls. Sea-water, therefore,
really acts for marine plants both as soil and atmosphere,
and those plants, such as the seaweeds, which are fixed to
the bottom use their roots for holding purposes only. They
have no absorptive function whatever. This then leads us to
the chemical constitution of the sea-water itself, the chemical
build-up of the soil. Obviously the plant plankton will be
directly dependent on what kind of water it can thrive in best
and on the circulation of the ocean which keeps the soil in
constant motion. The animal plankton will be dependent at
second-hand on these conditions. The avenues of research
that open up before us when we consider this aspect of the
matter are endless. The currents, the tides, the outflow of
rivers, the whole circulation of great sea-basins, bear upon

the drift and blooming of the plankton, and thus upon the movements and distribution of fish.

We might well have quailed at the prospect before us when we arrived upon our virgin field of endeavour. We knew that only now, after more than half a century of inquiry by most of the governments of northern Europe, with teams of devoted scientists of international fame, are we beginning to understand something of what goes on in the North Sea, the most investigated area of sea in the world. It was not a tithe of the area of our province, where no work had been done at all—or almost none.

We did not quail. Two of us were young and eager, the third was sceptical. But the governments who had to find the money did the quailing for us. They quailed in loud voices at painful interviews, banging on desks and making trays full of paper-fasteners quiver. 'It's no use coming to us and saying you want money for research,' they said. 'What we want is something we can ring on the counter. Show us what we are going to get for our money. How long will it be before the results start coming in?'

'Who knows?' I said, doodling on my scribbling-pad. 'It might be a lifetime.'

It has always seemed to me that research has been wrongly sold to the governments of colonies and less well-developed territories, whether dependent or independent. There seemed to be an altogether mistaken idea of what scientific research is and does. It had come to be looked on as a magic cure for well-defined and specific maladies. There were no fish in such and such a colony's waters. So you sent out two chaps to do some research and then, after a stated number of years, they should have made some fish in those waters. If they hadn't done so they were pretty useless at research. In our case money had been provided for a five years' project the terms of reference of which were very vague. The general idea seemed to be that I would arrive on, say, Friday, June 28th, 1952, and that on Monday, July 1st, at 0900 hours I would start doing research. At 1700 hours on June 30th, 1957, I would lay aside my pen or my scalpel, put away my microscope, and, with a deep sigh of fulfilment, rise from my seat, my research completed, the problems solved. I would then depart, after uitable farewell handshakes, leaving behind rows of contented faces. The markets would be crammed with fish summoned from the vasty deep as a result of my efforts, their market price would be so low that it would be scarcely worth-while to take the money, and all the fishermen would be driving about in solid gold Cadillacs. Some such idea, surely, was in the mind of the Government official who, at one of the painful interviews after I had been in Singapore about three years, said with icy politeness:

'I hope it's no reflexion on anyone when I say that it seems to us that we've been pouring money out for three years and getting absolutely nothing for it.'

'Well, I don't know about that,' I said. 'You have a well-planned and equipped laboratory, a well-found ocean-going ship and a qualified staff. None of these existed even on paper three years ago.'

That these tools for the job had to be acquired and that labour and time would be used in acquiring them did not seem to be understood, and was not accepted when it was explained.

In my mind's eye there cruised majestically, breasting the murky waves of my enormous parish, the ship I thought I ought to have for the job as I saw it. I knew that she would remain a dream-ship, a figment of my imagination, because such a ship could not really exist. In the first place she was a steam-ship with a good old-fashioned triple-expansion steam-engine, like those whose gleaming, ponderously revolving cranks I had loved to watch on my first cross-Channel voyage. However, this was not just a nostalgic vision, for it is a fact that steam is the most satisfactory form of propulsion for a ship which has constantly to start and stop and make frequent variations of speed. Great flexibility and ease of handling are the advantages which steam gives, and it is a universal provider of power. It can be carried about the deck and all over the ship in pipes to winches large and small for hauling and lifting, and to pumps and machines of all kinds. They, too, all have the flexibility and elasticity which steam gives.

Against these advantages, however, must be weighed the most important consideration of all. Steam-engines are nowadays very expensive to run. No modern ships are fired by coal

nowadays, owing to its high cost, bulk and general inconve
nience, but oil fuel is also very costly. Further, steam-engine:
are very large and take up a great deal of space amidship:
which is needed for other purposes.

So I knew that in reality my ship would be a diesel job
though in my dreams she went by steam. She would be able
to cruise for great distances, and would carry enough fuel and
fresh water in her bunkers to stay at sea for at least a month
without replenishing. Accordingly she would have to be a
civilized sort of vessel with reasonable eating and sleeping
accommodation not only for her skipper, officers and crew, but
also for two or three scientists whom she would have to
carry. She would have laboratory accommodation for the
scientists to work in under the wheelhouse, and probably
aft as well. Here living creatures could be dealt with, examined, pickled, labelled and stowed away in thousands of
screw-topped jars. These thousands of jars of every size are
a vital cargo, part of the equipment of any ship doing this sort
of work, and there would have to be storage room for them
down below. There would have to be workshops where
instruments could be kept and repaired. In thinking of this
I had, incidentally, forgotten the tropical climate, which makes
the below-decks compartments of any ship like a series of
small ovens. If I had thought of that I would have included in
my dream the air-conditioning of all cabins and compartments below decks. To hell, I would have said in my imagination,
with the expense! But that, of course, is just the thing one
never dares to say.

My ship had plenty of deck space both fore and aft and so
we could all move about and examine in reasonable ease
what the nets brought in, instead of jostling and floundering
over one another's bodies and clutching wildly at one another
each time the ship rolled. There was running sea-water piped
to the deck so that animals could be kept alive on board.
There was a wide poop-deck with lifting tackle above it
for handling heavy gear over the stern and, though this was
a strange fantasy, for few ships are built with such a thing
these days, an old-fashioned cut-away counter-stern. This was
necessary so that nets and other gear with heavy metal frames
could be lifted aboard clear without crashing against the

hull plating or catching on projections, which happens with
the bulging cruiser-sterns which most ships have nowadays.
Forward my ship had a raised fo'c'sle, which would protect
the forward fish-deck from the weather, and a flared bow to
throw the waves out and away instead of scooping them up
like a spoon.

The ship I eventually found did not have all the points
of my dream-ship, but when I first saw her in 1953 she had
few of them. She had still more when, after a long sojourn
in a shipbuilder's yard, she arrived in Singapore nearly two
years later. I hardly recognized her for the pleasure-yacht I
had seen lying at Lymington, in Hampshire, nearly two
years before.

I had been staying with friends at Lymington, and my
host had made me, at my age, row nearly half a mile in a
whaler to see a boat which he had designed. As we pulled
towards the jetty on the way back my host pointed to a fair-
sized diesel yacht lying at the jetty. She had a black hull
with white upperworks and a yellow funnel. She had a low,
upswept bow with no raised fo'c'sle and long, clean lines leading
to a counter-stern.

'What about that? There's a ship for you.'

'Somebody's yacht?'

'Yes, but the owner wants to sell. Expensive things, yachts,
these days.'

I rang up the owner that evening. He had a large house
not far away.

'I hear you want to sell your yacht. Could I go on board
and have a look at her?'

'D'you want to buy a yacht?'

'I might. How much?'

He named a figure. I felt very grand. I had never bought
a yacht before and I don't suppose I ever will again.

The *Manihine* (a New Zealand name, I think) and I were
twins. She had been built fifty years ago as a steam-trawler.
Her hull was therefore elderly, but sound, like mine. In 1937
she had been converted to what the documents called 'a
pleasure-yacht', though they never specified what sort of
pleasure went on in her. But whatever it was it necessitated
removing the steam-engine and replacing it by two 200-h.p.

diesels. By 1953 these had become rather old-fashioned and
cumbersome, but they were slow-revving engines and good
enough. This meant, however, that the *Manihine* was a twin
screw ship, which was rather a black mark against her, for
twin screws, although they give great ease of manœuvre
are not very good in fishing-vessels because the propeller
are laterally placed and endanger the nets. But to offset thi
black mark was the fact that the engine-room was right aft
leaving room amidships for a fine range of cabins, all lined
with mahogany veneer and fitted with running-water basins
I seem to remember there were no fewer than three tiled
bathrooms, though one of them was removed to make way for
a workshop. On the main-deck aft of the bridge was a dining-
room with a fine galley adjoining. The fore-part of the deck-
house at main-deck level was occupied by a big lounge. I
was all chintz and shining brass when I saw it in Lymington
Harbour. It had four roll-up windows looking out forward
over the well-deck, and as I sat on the luxurious stuffed sofa
and drank the tea the Skipper brought us, I gazed around
mentally converting it into a fine ship-board laboratory. It
was just the place, I thought.

In the end the Colonial Office bought the *Manihine* and she
was converted to a research ship by a famous firm of yacht-
builders in Southampton to the designs drawn up by an equally
famous firm of naval architects. The conversion proved to be
surprisingly difficult. One of the items which gave the greatest
trouble was the fitting of the powerful trawling-winch which
would be necessary for trawling on the heavy muddy bottoms
of the South China Sea. When the ship was taken over she
had no winch of any kind, so we had to buy one and install it
In modern trawlers the main winch is either driven by a vertical
belt from the front of the main engine crankshaft or else by
electricity. This is where the first snag was met with in the
Manihine. Her engines were so far aft that the drive for the
winch could not be taken from them by a belt or gearing or
any other kind of drive. Electricity could not be used because
her generators did not develop enough juice to drive the
powerful motor which would be needed. There was no room
to install a bigger generator or motor and, more important,
no funds. The only way round the difficulty, therefore, was to

drive the winch by means of a separate independent diesel engine on the deck. But this could only be done by housing it in the main lounge at the expense of my beautiful laboratory. Accordingly a huge hole had to be cut in the curved front of the lounge, removing two of its windows. A big bay was built in the lounge so that the fine, spacious room became a cramped, rectangular U-shaped compartment. This quite spoilt the laboratory as it finally appeared, and broke my heart. But it had an even more unfortunate effect. The weight of the heavy diesel engine on the main-deck, and the heavy steel strengthening which had to be built to carry it, made the ship top-heavy. She was in some danger of rolling over in the dock at Southampton. She rolled ominously if you walked from one side of the main-deck to the other. Accordingly several tons (I forget just how many) of iron bars were distributed about below deck in order to bring down the ship's centre of gravity. This was successful enough, but it made her ride so low in the water that her portholes were only just above the water-line when she was in harbour and below it when she was at sea. At sea I had a submarine view through my cabin scuttle, as in an aquarium, and could see the surface of the ocean from below. This meant that the scuttles could never be opened even in the calmest weather, so that in the tropics the accommodation below decks was sweltering hot. I could never sleep in my beautiful mahogany-panelled cabin but always rigged up a canvas camp-bed and slept in the laboratory. I could just fit my camp-bed into one of the legs of the U. The atmosphere was pungent with formalin, but it was cool.

The ship was bought at the end of 1953, but it was not until early in 1955 that the work of converting her was far enough advanced for David to fly home and take over as Captain. Some months before she was ready to sail from England I was to get a crew together and send them home by P. & O. to man the ship and bring her to Singapore.

In about April I heard from David and set about this novel and unaccustomed task. I went to the Office of the Master Attendant and said I was looking for a crew for my ship.

The Master Attendant is the Port Captain and Queen's Harbour Master. The Shipping Office, to which come all sailors looking for jobs, was part of his organization and occupied the top floor of a big building on the waterfront. Here, too, came all those who wished to employ sailors in ships. A counter divided the would-be employers from the would-be employed. Every morning, in this office full of registers and of clerks writing things in them, there gathered Malay seamen, Chinese drivers and firemen and stokers, old men and young and mere boys, the tough and the lazy, the honest and the rogues, the hopeful and the disillusioned. They brought their tickets and certificates with them, those almost disintegrating evidences of their occupation from which old photographs taken years ago looked out with the shocked surprise or scowling ferocity characteristic of all photographs in all passports, licences, certificates or documents whatsoever. They waited all the forenoon until twelve o'clock, when the labour market closed for the day, and then went away. If nothing that suited them turned up they came back again the following morning and every day until they were suited, or gave up hope.

When I appeared behind the counter the room was full of young men and boys standing about or sitting on benches along the wall. There were others outside on the balcony that overhung the Singapore River. There was a movement of interest, a turning of faces in my direction, and the buzz of conversation died down. The wings of hope were fluttering on the grimy ceiling above the electric fans. Was I a job? Was I a meal at last, perhaps the first for weeks, for some family in Pulau Brani or Geylang Serai? Was I dollars in the pocket, a packet of cigarettes, a new pair of shoes or a haircut?

The presiding genius in this bazaar, where some men sold what skill they had for a fixed sum and others bought it, was Mr. Ezekiel, the Shipping Master, a large, friendly Tamil. He had worked in this office for years and knew many of these men well, the older ones anyway. He had seen some of them coming in and out for years on and off with their tickets and their increasingly improbable photographs. He could recommend this one and point out that as a reliable man or a hard worker. Frequently you had to interpret between the lines of his conversation, for he would never actually

ay that such and such a man was a scallywag or a sea-lawyer
or a trouble-maker or a lazy son of a bitch. You had to infer
information of that sort from his pregnant silences, a pursing
of the lips perhaps, or a slight shrug of massive shoulders.

'If I were in your position, Doctor,' he said, as if my position
were a most unenviable one and he devoutly hoped he never
would be, 'I should choose my *serang* first and let him pick
his own crew. After all he has to look after them. If he chooses
them there can be no complaints that any of them is no good,
and all that, if you understand me, isn't it?'

In a ship with a Malay crew the *serang* is the bosun. But
he is rather more than a bosun would be in a ship with a
European crew, for in many ways he is the father of his men
and their leader. He is the liaison, and the only one they have,
between the men and their European officers. He is often their
interpreter and has to transmit the officers' orders and speak
for his men to their officers in all matters. He holds the ship
in his hand, next to the Captain, for the lives and souls of
the native crew are known to him and are his. He is, therefore,
a man of great importance and great dignity. A good *serang*
means an efficient ship and a contented crew. When a *serang*
was seeking employment, therefore, he did not hang around
with the crowd in the Shipping Master's office. He left his
address and papers there, and if a possible employer showed
up a note was sent to his house saying there was a possibility
of a job and would he please present himself for interview
next morning?

Taking Mr. Ezekiel's advice I set about the task of finding
a *serang* first, extremely conscious of my total lack of experience in this sort of thing, and wondering whether I should
know a good *serang* from a bad one. Unfortunately there were
very few *serangs* free at that time, but I was presented with
a small bundle of well-thumbed documents to sift through,
each with an unprepossessing photograph, scowling or goggling among the faded writing, and a non-committal record.

At length I chose, from about six competitors, an elderly
man whose photograph I thought looked fatherly and benign.
He had served in a well-known local steamship company,
but there seemed little to choose between any of them in the
matter of past record. Each one carried the letters V.G.

('Very good') all the way down opposite the name and dates
of each ship the man had served in. Sailors seldom bear any
other testimonial. If a captain feels he cannot, even by turning
a deaf ear to his conscience, truthfully write V.G. on a man's
ticket when he is discharged, he writes D.R. ('Decline to
report'). But that is very damning and if your ticket bears
those letters it is better to pretend to have lost it and start
afresh. Anyhow, no one whose ticket had these letters on it
would be likely to get as far as *serang*. The best evidence
about a man is the length of time spent in each ship. Too
long in too few ships may be as bad a sign as too many ships
and too short a time in each. Those whose job it is constantly
to be choosing crews get to know just how long and how many
ships. But I had never chosen a crew before and I am afraid
my first essay in this direction was not an unqualified success.
However, a messenger was sent with a note, written in Jawi
(Malay in Arabic script) telling the man of my choice that
a job was about to offer itself, and that if he wanted it he was
to present himself to me the following morning in the go-down.

At the appointed time a very dignified, but very elderly,
Malay in a sarong and *songkok* appeared before my desk
after being kept waiting for the required ceremonial five
minutes by Jim. He was much older than had seemed probable
from the photograph in his certificate, but that was no doubt
because I had forgotten, as I often do, the lapse of years.
He bowed. I agreed to take him on and explained, through
Jim, that he was to sign on the *Manihine's* articles here in
Singapore and then 'proceed', in the parlance used in the
agreement, 'by tourist passage to U.K.' to join the ship.
There were to be four Malay seamen and a cook and a Chinese
fireman going with him. The fireman had been chosen already.
Would he please select the four seamen and the cook as he
thought best and bring them to the go-down for approval
tomorrow? He bowed, and so did I.

The next day he duly returned at the head of his troops.
They were an unlikely-looking lot, but I supposed if they
were good enough for him they would suit me. I rather wondered what David would say when he met them at Southampton.
I told them that tomorrow they must bring to the go-down
their passports or seamen's registration-books for inspection.

by the immigration authorities. They must then take their bodies to the hospital, which was, of course, at the other end of the town, to be X-rayed and inspected by the medical authorities. When these formalities were completed we would all go to the Shipping Office and sign the articles. Then they could draw their first pay-packet and everyone would be happy. Unfortunately they did not seem to think so. They withdrew into a huddle outside the door of the go-down, where I heard long consultations in Malay taking place. These went on for a long time, until Jim at last went out to see what was the matter. He came back laughing what I have learnt now, after years in the East, is the laughter of embarrassment. The Chinese especially, but also Indians and Malays on occasion, have a way of smiling when they have to say or do anything unpleasant, to convey bad news, to refuse a request or make any sort of disagreeable pronouncement. They laugh or smile too if they themselves are in any sort of unpleasant predicament or embarrassment. I once saw a very pretty and well-dressed Chinese girl being sick in public. She was roaring with laughter. Jim came back giggling.

'They say,' he said, 'tee-hee, they say they want their fares paid from their homes to this office every day, tee-hee-hee.'

'Well,' I said, 'I'm sure I've no objection, but I'd better find out what the rule is about that.'

I rang up Ezekiel. He was not available. The old Malay and his troops squatted down in a row outside the door of the go-down. Meanwhile it was lunch-time. When I came back in an hour's time they were still there.

'No,' said Ezekiel over the phone. 'They're not employed by you until they've signed the articles, and not entitled to any payment until then.'

'But,' I said, 'I've got to get them here in order to have their passports and registration-books inspected and to get them medically examined.'

'Well, that's up to you, Doctor. But I can't authorize any payment.'

By this time the troops' blood was up. The light of battle was in their eyes. They told Jim, at enormous length, that they intended to be paid for any journeys they might make

in the future and also for coming here that day. And they were
not going away until they got the money. The *serang* said
he must be paid for coming from his house to the Shipping
Office in the first place. I hesitated. It seemed fair enough to
me, but I wondered what sort of minutes I should be writing
for the next month or so to justify the expenditure. Should
I save time and all that bother by paying this, after all very
small, sum out of my own pocket? This solution is always a
weak one and I know that hardened and capable administrators
never do it. But I am not a hardened administrator and doubt
whether I am a capable one, and I wanted to get this boring
business over and finished with. Then the *serang* saw me
hesitating and came to the conclusion that the enemy was
on the run. He began talking again volubly to Jim.

'What does he say?' I asked.

'He says they demand full pay from this morning when you
agreed to take them on. Tee-hee!'

'Tell the old b—— to go to hell!' I said.

They arose, picked up their sarongs around their knees
and with great dignity filed across the go-down to the other
door, in full and delighted view of all the clerks in the office.
Across the dockyard basin I saw them still walking in single
file, the picture of offended dignity. I was without a crew, but
I did not think they were much loss. They had begun sea-
lawyering really a little too early in the voyage.

I went back to the Shipping Office. 'I'm looking for a crew
for my ship,' I said.

The crew I eventually got together were not a very likely-
looking lot either, but they were young. They made no
difficult demands and I avoided the transport problem by
compromising and driving them around in my own car.
They went with docility through the incredibly involved
formalities of getting travel documents and being passed
medically fit. They bore gently with a lot of quite unnecessary
rudeness and off-handedness from clerks and understrappers
in offices, were kept waiting for hours hanging about in waiting-
rooms or leaning hopefully against counters. I wonder what
happens to the myriads of forms that even the humblest of
us has to fill in as we go through life. I had to do a good deal
of this for them as none of them could read English, and one

or two of them could not write. They signed with thumb-
prints. But eventually I got them all passed diplomatically
and medically fit to travel. Then I had to get them warm
clothes, for it was February and they would arrive in England
in March. I found it surprisingly difficult to get warm clothes
in Singapore, for nobody has any use for such things. However, the seamen's hostel came to my rescue with a miscel-
laneous collection of garments, for which I was very grateful,
and the men ought to have been but were not. The garments
were not exactly becoming, but they would keep out the
bitter winds of an English spring. Then the day came when
I led my crew, gentle and obedient as ever and holding one
another by the hand like little boys, down to the tourist deck
of a big P. & O. liner and saw them installed in their hot
little cabins. I took the *serang* to see the Chief Tourist Class
Steward and made sure that as good Muslims they would
not have to eat anything unsuitable. Then I shook them all
warmly by the hand, saying '*Selamat jalan*—peace to your
journey.' '*Selamat tinggal*,' they replied. 'Peace to your staying.'
Then I went down the gangway with a sigh of relief, feeling
that something at any rate had been achieved.

The *Manihine* sailed from England in August 1955 and made
a good voyage to Singapore. In the Indian Ocean she met
with violent gales, for the south-west monsoon was at its
height and mountainous seas caught her abeam. But she
behaved splendidly, and there was no sign of any instability.
But the poor crew whom I had sent to take her over were
prostrated with sea-sickness.

One day in September I received a radio message announ-
cing the time of her arrival at Penang. The Director of Fisheries, Derek Le Mare, and I put to sea in the Malayan Fisheries Department's small wooden fishing vessel to go and meet
the *Manihine* and escort her in. A young man from Radio
Malaya with a broadcasting apparatus was on board also.
For me this was the crowning moment of three years' working
and planning. Now the apparently endless essays in com-
position, the boring memos all saying the same thing, the
correspondence and the arithmetic were all about to be justified. As we chugged out of George Town the shores of the
Perak were dark blue and dim on our right and the peaks of

Penang Island rose on our left. The sea was glassy and heave‹
gently as though breathing. The radio message had said th‹
Manihine would be off a certain point north of Penang Islan‹
at a stated time. We approached the rendezvous. The sea wa‹
vacant and empty, but we were a little early. We cruised roun‹
in a circle, and when the appointed time arrived and th‹
horizon all around was still blank I felt sure that the *Manihin‹*
had missed her way and gone aground, or rolled over in
heavy sea, or struck an old Japanese mine. We anxiousl‹
scanned the empty sky and sea. Then far away a small speck
It was a bird on the water. It was a floating log. It was a ma‹
in a canoe. It was a fishing-junk. It was a ship. But not th‹
Manihine, surely? Impossible. Yet as she drew near sur‹
enough there was her name on the bows. She was unrecog‹
nizable and not in the least like the yacht I had seen at Lyming‹
ton two years ago. This, of course, was due mainly to he‹
having sunk down so much in the water owing to the weigh‹
of the winch-engine on deck and the ballast in her belly. I‹
was also due to the whaleback fo'c'sle which had been adde‹
to her and to the new cabin for the Skipper which had bee‹
built abaft the bridge. But she was a proud sight with he‹
flags fluttering, a cock's-comb of white foam at her bow an‹
the little blue plume at her funnel which told how sweetl‹
the two engines were running. She was my ship. I had create‹
her out of paper. Dave stood on her bridge-deck and wave‹
I had received many caustic letters from him since he ha‹
flown to England to take her over, all in his round, fisherman'‹
writing, ending up 'Well Dick. 'Bye for now. Be seeing yo‹
soon.' He was proud of the ship too and that in itself was a‹
achievement, for he was hard to please. We turned and escorte‹
the *Manihine* to her anchorage. Then we went alongside an‹
for the first time I stepped aboard my ship. We shook hand‹
and met the new Scottish Mate and the Welsh Chief Enginee‹
Someone said, 'Excuse me, Doctor. . . .' It was the youn‹
man with the broadcasting apparatus. I had forgotten him.

'I feel that with this ship we shall really be able to do some‹
thing of value for the people of Malaya.' And the extraor‹
dinary thing is that at that moment I think I really believed i‹

9

At Sea

From their high thrones among the clouds old gods looked down upon the *Manihine* as she moved slowly, like an insect, upon the disc of the South China Sea.

This sea is dotted with many islands. Some, like the Anambas and Natunas two or three hundred miles to the east of the Malay Peninsula, are quite large, and most of them are Indonesian territory. But close to the coast of Malaya there are many small islets and rocks which are Malay territory, and we often anchored under their shadow for the night. Four of them, named Tioman, Aur, Pemanggil and Tingi, are majestic peaks on each of which a tall chimney of granite among the clouds surmounts palm-clad skirts that sweep down to the water's edge, where the huts of Malay fishermen huddle together. These are lonely and remote little villages full of gay and charming people who ran out laughing to meet us when we went ashore. The children tumbled in the sand, and the young men ran and shouted and kicked a football from one to another and showed off their suppleness and grace. Each castellated knob of rock far above the upper limit of the palm trees, sparsely clothed with grass, is venerated as a deity by the people of the island it crowns. They pray to it for good fishing and fair weather and tremble when the clouds gather upon it and the lightning flashes. And who can blame them? For these peaks are grand and awe-inspiring enough, especially when half hidden by the clouds of the north-east monsoon, rattling their mantles of coconut palms and spouting cataracts. Sometimes we climbed the steep slopes where the palm trees got smaller and smaller and the grass shorter and shorter to the high uplands of short grass like the grass on the hills of home. Here the white-bellied sea-eagles sailed around us, and we could look across the sea to the other peaks. The wide, vague sea was dotted with the canoes of Malay fishermen, their crescent sails filled with the light monsoon. Sometimes

F

a Chinese long-liner or a small trolling boat from Singapor
crawled across the face of the world trailing the plume of i
exhaust, the tonk of its diesel loud and clear across sever
miles of water.

The *Manihine* made nine trips up and down the South Chin
Sea and three in the Malacca Strait during her short stay i
Malayan waters. In the South China Sea she trawled up an
down along parallel courses from north to south and bac
again and followed the coast of Borneo as far as Brunei an
Jesselton. On the west side of the Malay Peninsula she wer
as far north as Southern Burma to Mergui and Junkseylc
Island. On these voyages we three scientists went by turn
My turns took me out across the South China Sea, to Tioma
and Aur, across to the Anambas, which we saw only as a fain
loom, and then down to Sarawak and Brunei.

Every day we began trawling at dawn. From my camp-be
in the laboratory, among the chink and rattle of bottles an
the stinging aroma of formalin, I would rise painfully, thinkin
that I was no longer young and this was no life for a *tua*
besar in the fabulous East. But the sun was already coming u
over the wine-dark sea and I did not envy the other *tuan*
besar so much after all. The world was filled with the pearl
light of a new day. Let them sleep with their legs over thei
'Dutch wives' and sarongs draped over their hairy paunche
Dave was already on the bridge-deck with his mug of te
He had taught the Creoles of the Seychelles the mysteriou
virtues of that brew of strong, sickly sweet liquid in a thic
china mug, and now he had taught it to the Malays. Ever
hour or so a Malay sailor came up on the bridge with a ne
brew and smiled enigmatically at the strange habits of Euro
peans.

The crew were already getting the otter-boards ready an
free on the gallows for paying away.

'Now wait a minute,' I said. 'Not such a hurry. Let's tak
a water sample and temperature first.'

'Oh, hell!'

David was a trawlerman. Like all trawlermen he wa
happiest when trawling. When the wires were out and th
bag was on the bottom, that was the life for him. Life had
unity and purpose then. His pride and joy was to see the cod

d, the tapering end of the bag, break surface upside down
ulging with fish, to watch from the bridge when the cod-end
ing over the fish pounds, slung up on the gilson wire, and,
the knot was tugged loose, spewed its flapping, gasping,
oaking harvest on to the deck. For David there was no
shing really but trawling, and like most fishermen he pri-
tely thought little of science. So, when I stopped him in the
t and said I wanted to take a water sample and a temperature,
made a small exclamation of irritation at such waste of time.
e stopped the ship and the way slowly came off her. It was
fine morning with only a light, soft breeze, so there was no
ed to bring her into the wind. She could lie broadside and
ot drift too much.

I called down the fo'c'sle companion ladder and, after the
sual significant pause, a sleepy young Chinese boy came up
ad only in a pair of blue-striped pyjama trousers. The water-
ampling instrument, the reversible cylinder with thermo-
eters attached, was to be lowered into the water on a wire
hich ran from a drum over a special davit on the port side.
he drum was operated by a small petrol motor for hauling
e wire up after it had run out. The motor had to be started.
or this the Chief Engineer had to be called. I hate starting
ngines by hand, and am always afraid they will backfire
nd break my wrist, or explode in my face and singe my
yebrows. I am not at all mechanically minded and regard
ll machines with suspicion, especially those that work by
lectricity. They seem to have evil intentions and if they can
ossibly let me down they always do so. The Chief Engineer
ame from aft. He was always smiling and always wiping his
ands on a piece of waste. He was a burly and marvellously
enial Welshman.

'Good morning, Doctor.'

'Good morning, Mr. Tamlyn.'

In conformity with the curious tradition of the Merchant
ervice, or at any rate the fishermen's branch of it, one never
ddressed the Chief Engineer nor the Scottish Mate by their
urnames without the prefix 'Mister'. After a few weeks in
ingapore the Mate and the Chief Engineer became firm,
lmost inseparable, buddies and frequently went out on
arties together, did the town together and, when necessary,

saw each other off and saw each other home. But never und
any circumstances did either of them forget to address tl
other as 'Mister'.

Mr. Tamlyn bent himself to the starting-handle of tl
winch-engine. It would not respond. He swore gently ar
persuasively. That sometimes had a magic effect, but not th
time. He tickled it in an intimate place and it gave a fe
reluctant spurts. My assistant composed himself for slee
again, draped against the rail. David leaned over the rail
the bridge-deck looking very impatient and frustrated. Tl
crew, halted at the start of their job, were now squatting c
the deck chattering unconcernedly in Malay. None of the cre
I had selected to go to England and bring the ship out ha
survived the first fishing trip. They all found the work to
hard, and that is hardly surprising for they got no extr
money for the hard sweat of trawling—or, rather, what the
regarded as a hard sweat. This was one of the difficulties
running this sort of ship in these lands where there is n
class of fishermen to draw upon for recruits for the crev
It means that the ship's crew is constantly changing. At tl
end of every voyage usually one, but sometimes more, me
signed off, having found the life harder than he was accustome
to. Yet we only made about three or four hauls a day and hardl
ever trawled at night. In commercial trawlers in Europea
waters the ship trawls day and night for a fortnight or thre
weeks at a stretch, using two trawls alternately, one on eac
side. When one is on the bottom the catch from the othe
is being sorted, gutted, washed and put below in the fish roon
The crew therefore work on deck continuously throughout th
twenty-four hours, taking four-hour watches in turns. The
turn in on their bunks fully dressed in their watch below. A
the end of a three-weeks trip the men sometimes fall forwar
face downwards among the fish in the pound, overcome wit
fatigue. But in the *Manihine* we used only one trawl. Th
catches were small and soon dealt with. As is usual in tropic:
waters the fish were washed but never gutted. This used t
astonish me when I first came to the tropics, for in a ho
humid climate decomposition begins first in the gills of
fish the instant it comes out of the water and soon spread
to the guts and head. One would have thought that thoroug

ad instant cleaning would be regarded as highly important
i tropical countries. Yet no fish is ever gutted in any tropical
ountry so far as I know, and very often the catch is left lying
bout in the sun before it is collected for the market. It may
pend more hours lying about in a heap on the market slab
efore anyone buys it. Yet if a fish has been opened or tampered
ith in any way it is unsaleable in the tropics. The public
ill not buy it and believe that it has been spoilt. In the
Manihine, therefore, unless the fish were required for examina-
on in the laboratory, they all went straight below into the
sh-room after sorting and weighing according to sizes. The
ctual work of the crew consisted only in paying away the trawl
nd bringing it in, flinging the fish into tubs of running sea-
rater and then stowing them away in the fish-room in baskets.
'aying away the trawl was easy work and took about ten
iinutes. Bringing the trawl in took about half an hour from
ie time the trawl came up to the time the last fish was below.
.hese simple operations were carried out about once every
ur hours. Yet we found it hard to keep a crew. Men were
ontinually leaving on one pretext or another and without any
eal reason stated. They seldom said they thought the work
oo hard, but some of the reasons given for signing off were
o unconvincing that we could only guess what the real reason
vas. In every ship, however, a combing-out process has to take
lace at first. It lasts for a longer or shorter time, but in the
nd the chaff is winnowed away and the good grain remains.
'his happened in the *Manihine* after we had made some six
oyages. By then we had a tried and reliable crew under a
;ood *serang*, but then the *Manihine's* time in these waters
vas coming to an end.

Mr. Tamlyn loved machines and was loved by them. He
ised to explain them to me, but his explanations went in at
>ne ear and out at the other. The little engine, tickled lovingly
n the right place, burst into life, and I roused my assistant
rom his sleepy brown study over the rail. He screwed the
netal cylinder to the wire, and Mr. Tamlyn took the brake
»ff the drum so that the cylinder descended into the water
nd sank out of sight. The depth of wire lowered into the water
vas shown on a recording pulley over which the wire ran.
Ve let enough wire run out to bring the cylinder to a halt

about five metres (about fifteen feet) above the bottom of th
sea. The echo-sounder on the bridge told us what the dept
of the sea actually was at the spot where the ship was stoppe
Then my assistant clipped a brass weight on to the wire an
sent it sliding down, trailing a comet-tail of bubbles. Onc
or twice he sleepily fumbled it and dropped the weight int
the sea. When he did that he looked at me guiltily like
puppy who has done something naughty and expects to b
slapped. But having done the same thing myself all over th
world's oceans many times, years before my assistant wa
born, I only laughed and made a clucking noise.

When the weight struck the cylinder near the sea botton
the wire gave a little shudder which you could feel with you
hand. Mr. Tamlyn engaged the clutch of his engine, and th
wire began to run in, trailing a shower of glittering drops
Presently the cylinder glimmered upwards from the depth
and came to a stop at the rail. Sometimes, through inadver
tence on the part of whoever may be operating the engine
these instruments fail to come to a stop and go shooting u
to strike the measuring pulley on the davit with quite spec
tacular results. This has much the same thrill as throwing
wooden balls at a china-stall at a fair, but is very much mor
expensive.

The cylinder, having been closed when the weight struc
it, now contained a couple of pints of water from near th
sea bottom. By turning a tap at the base of the cylinder w
ran off some of it into a glass bottle with a spring-clip top
Curiously enough it looked exactly like sea-water from th
surface or any other level, but it would in fact, on chemica
analysis, be found to differ slightly in salt and oxygen conten
from the water at other levels, or at the same level in a dif
ferent part of the ocean. It is these small differences fron
one level to another, from place to place and from montl
to month, which make it possible to trace the movements o
bodies of water and map the flow of currents.

We read the temperature on the thermometer attached t
the cylinder. These thermometers are constructed to recorc
permanently the temperature at the moment when the cylinde
was reversed. When we had done this, and emptied the cylinde
and taken it off the wire, we signed to David. He had beer

vaiting on the bridge with some impatience, looking out of
he wheelhouse window over his mug of tea.

'Away we go!'

He turned the ship so that she lay with the wind on her
tarboard side. The trawl lay ready along the starboard rail.
The head-rope, the upper lip of the bag, carried a line of metal
nd glass floats. The foot-rope, the lower lip of the bag, which
vas a good deal longer than the head-rope and would sweep
ike a big U over the sea bottom, was bound round with more
ope so that it would not stick in the mud which was universal
ll over the area, or almost all over it. The two rectangular
otter-boards, shod with iron along their lower edges, were
riced up to the gallows. After the bag had been put over the
ide and was fairly away, Dave went ahead. The trawl is
lways shot broadside to the wind so that the ship drifts away
rom the net. Now it floated out away from the ship's side and
ank like a gaping mouth into the darkness. The engine telegraph rang, and the *Manihine* came gracefully and beautifully
ound into the wind, drawing a lovely, frothing, dimpled
curve upon the water. At the same time, with a shout, a rattle
nd a splash, away went first the forward and then the after
otter-boards, or 'doors' as they are sometimes called. The
wo steel trawling wires ran out from the winch, and we saw
he bag fall astern and sink from sight.

There is a style and dash about paying out a trawl, a moment
of beauty that never fails. The ship leaps forward with throb-
oing engines, drawing arcs among the clouds with her fore-
ruck. The wires run sweetly out, and the great maw sinks
lown gaping hungrily into the dark. There is the same poetry
ind magic in this moment as there is in the sight of a train
eaving a station, an aeroplane taking off, a ship in full sail
or a destroyer steaming ahead with pennants flying. Everyone
on board feels it and stops whatever he is doing to look for
in instant. It is as though the moment is marked in the mind
ind stamped on the memory with an asterisk. The men shout
ind laugh though they have seen it a thousand times before,
a figure with a handful of oily waste appears in the engine-
room fiddley and Dave leans on the starboard-bridge rail
with his mug of tea in his hand and a look of satisfaction and
ulfilment on his face. It is the confident look of a man who

knows his skill and has used it once again in the job which is
his life. Aboard northern trawlers on the grounds life is thus
and this is one of life's moments. Another is the momen
when the cod-end breaks surface as the trawl comes up an
there is the catch gleaming in it, a silver harvest. But out her
in the South China Sea our crew had no particular interes
in the trawl or in what it caught, for it meant nothing to ther
and no money in their pockets. Yet at this instant of payin
away the Malays caught the feeling and laughed, showin
their gold teeth.

'One twenty!' sang out Dave, meaning a hundred and twent
fathoms of warp paid out, three times the depth of the sea
which at this spot, we will suppose, was forty fathoms.

The trawling warps are marked in twenty-fathom length
by tufts of rope yarns threaded through the steel strand
one tuft at twenty fathoms, two at forty, three at sixty, fou
at eighty and five at a hundred. They begin again with one tuf
at a hundred and twenty. So, when the second single tuf
arrived amidships, the winch was stopped and the two trawlin
wires were clamped together by a heavy steel clamp jus
astern of the after gallows. Like this, with the warps clampe
together at deck level, but widely spread below the surfac
of the sea where the otter-boards carried them apart, th
Manihine dragged her trawl slowly across the bottom of th
South China Sea.

At the end of each haul Dave came out on to the bridge
deck with an expectant look and said, 'Right! Knock out!'

This was the order for one of the sailors to knock free th
clamp, which held the warps together, with a heavy hammer
They sprang apart trembling and making a shower of drops
Then the winch-engine, started by Mr. Tamlyn with a lou
wheezing explosion inside its housing under the bridge, bega
to rumble and the wires began to run in. The single tuft
marking the one hundred and twenty fathoms, slid fron
amidships forward, flicked round the bollard and back on t
the winch-drum. Presently came the group of five, up out o
the water, over the gallows sheave, round the bollard and bac
to the winch. Then the four, the three, the two and the one
following each other as though they possessed a life of thei
own. Meanwhile Dave had brought the ship round with th

wind once more on her starboard side, and soon the head-rope of the trawl appeared with its floats like a string of beads on the water.

This is the moment for which, in a northern trawler, every-one waits. If the haul has been a good one, and the bag is full of fish, the cod-end—that is, the narrow, tapered end of the trawl—breaks surface now some yards from the ship's side and floats there, a great balloon, stuffed with silver treasure. But in the South China Sea this scarcely ever happened, and, more often than not, the cod-end was a poor flaccid thing, a deflated finger. If there were one or two decent-sized fish in it we thought it a fairly good catch. Usually it spewed a little heap of spiny trash into the pound with indignant crabs, furious at such an affront, scuttling sideways into the scuppers, octopuses, writhing and contorting and clinging with their many suckers, sea-urchins, starfish and quantities of shells and under-sea growths like ferns. Only near Great Natuna Island, which is Indonesian territory, and south-westwards towards Tioman and Aur, did we find catches big enough to float the bag up to the surface with the great scarlet and speckled beauties in it. And Dave would say, 'Well, now, that's a little better! That's more like it!' and he would come down from the bridge and stand gazing at them, his trophies of war, wrested from the cold, dark fastnesses.

The first haul of the day, which we shot before breakfast and hauled afterwards, was of about two hours' duration. When the trawl came in at the end of it the crew carried the fish to the after-deck in baskets after they had roughly sorted them according to sizes. There stood the scientist, myself when I was on board or, if not, one of the other two, like an executioner with gutting-knife in hand, a measuring board like a rack beside him and spring balances like instruments of torture. On the after-deck the fish were sorted according to species, as nearly as possible, weighed and measured. Some were slit open to find out what sex they were, whether mature or not, whether ripe or not. Our young assistant helped at this without seeing much point in it all. Another of the strange habits of Europeans.

In order to sort the fish out into their many and various species (there are over two hundred different species of fishes

F*

in Malayan waters) we arranged them in little inconvenient heaps all around the after-deck—inconvenient because anybody walking by with bare feet was liable to get his toes unpleasantly spiked by sharp spines, and because the deck soon became horribly slimy, so that if the ship was rolling it was difficult to stand up. There were more different species than we could find room for on the cramped deck, and, if the ship rolled, the heaps got muddled up together. Sting-rays made slimy heaps, crevallies made heaps that gleamed like piles of silver coins. Boxfish, cowfish and porcupine-fish, the trash and rubbish of the haul, made prickly, spiny heaps that wounded toes and fingers. Hair-tails made heaps like piles of mermaids' tresses. Puffers lay blown out with their silly pouting little mouths pursed into prim shapes. Tongues of sea came licking along the scuppers and played a kittenish game with our piles of corpses, scattering them about the deck and even whisking them off back to their native element through the freeing ports. On one occasion the wind blew all my notes over the side, and I raved and swore. The young assistant looked at me in mild astonishment, obviously thinking I had gone out of my mind. In the north-east monsoon we sometimes worked in torrential downpours of tropical rain, warm but very wet, streaming through the awnings and cascading down from the ship's structures. We wore swim-suits, and my notes turned to pulp. In the south-west monsoon the sweat streamed off one's forehead and body and anointed the fishes on the deck. We weighed and measured and slit open the best and biggest fish first, the biggest snappers, bream and scavengers, and threw them into wooden tubs full of running sea-water. All this lasted most of the morning, but since we were new to the South China Sea there were many fish we did not know and could not immediately identify. These we put on one side and took along to the laboratory later. Very often I was still poring over them far into the night when Dave came in to get a last orangeade out of the fridge before turning in.

We found that a haul of two hours' duration gave us enough work to keep us busy for several hours, often into the afternoon. After the first short haul at daybreak, therefore, we continued on course, making hauls one after the other of three or four hours' duration. From these the catches were much bigger and more satisfactory from David's point of view, but too large for me and the boy to get through in detail. The catches from these long hauls were therefore sorted roughly into sizes, weighed in baskets and put down below in the fish-room, after being washed in wooden tubs of running sea-water. I had caused these beautiful tubs to be made in Singapore especially for this purpose. It was one of my minor crosses that they were often used for storing coal for the galley stove.

As a result of trawling laboriously to and fro across this sea we found that the best fishing-grounds lay near the islands or along a shallow trough to the east of Tioman, the highest and the noblest of the four Malayan sisters. It was from these grounds that we took the big snappers and sea-bream. This was perhaps to be expected. The monsoon rains, streaming off the islands, pour into the sea immediately around them a flood of water full of salts dissolved out of the soil, and of decaying animal and vegetable matter. This promotes the growth of plankton in the seas close to the islands. The plankton dies and constantly rains down upon the bottom to make a rich pasture for all the bottom-living creatures on which the fishes feed. All down the east coast of Malaya, and down the west coast as well for that matter, great murky rivers, like the Pahang River on the east and the Muar River on the west, carry down a mass of mud and decaying organic rubbish and drop it on the sea-bottom. Out to a certain distance from the coast the ever-settling silt tends to choke and suffocate the life on the bottom, but farther out, after most of the mud has rained down and settled, the bottom population gets a chance to grow. Close inshore nothing but myriads of crabs inhabit the muddy bottom, but farther out we found the filter feeders, the shellfish, the brittle stars, the starfish and the urchins, on which the bottom fishes feed.

But by far the greater part of the South China Sea for hundreds of square miles was virtually barren of fish. Everywhere we found the bottom consisted of an oozy, sticky grey mud, the deposit of countless ages washed out of Malaya and Borneo. Sometimes the trawl would get stuck fast in it. Over it grew a great forest of lace-like sea-fans and other wiry submarine trees with branches which seemed to be made of metal. The fans spread out their huge, flat, reticulated surfaces at right-angles to the current so as to offer to the countless polyps, growing on the lacy branches, the maximum exposure to the stream of plankton on which they live.

Farther south, however, towards the Karimata Strait, which separates Borneo from the Malay Peninsula and the Indonesian Islands to the south of it, we came into a region of enormous cup-sponges. They were shaped like bowls, chalices and vases four or five feet high and two or three feet across with fluted sides. So still and quiet was the dark world where these amphorae stood in their thousands that they had nothing to anchor them in the mud. They stood upright on round, hard bases in the ooze, and nothing came to upset them until our trawl swept them up. They were a terrible nuisance. One or two of them in the bag and there was no room for anything else whatever. They were very heavy and made the trawl difficult to bring aboard. When, after a great deal of heaving and straining, we got the bag in there were almost no fish in it. And yet these trophies from the sea-bed were often of such lovely shapes, like gigantic drinking-vessels from a lost submerged civilization, that I was unwilling to throw them back into the hidden world they came from. I wanted to keep them. But we had nothing large enough to put them in, and if left lying about the deck they soon began to rot and stank horribly.

There were other nuisances besides these. Inside the twenty-fathom line along the coast of Malaya and Borneo enormous sting-rays came up in the trawl. Some of these were flattened mounds of inert flesh ten feet across from wing-tip to wing-tip with long, whip-like tails. The eyes were knobs close together on top of the mound. We gave them a wide berth at first, for the sting, which is a little jagged pointed dagger at the base of the tail, or sometimes two or even three, can give an agonizing and occasionally fatal wound. But they were far too overcome by their own weight to move at all and just lay there, brown speckled heaps exuding slime. When we lifted them up to weigh them with a hook through the gill slits they gave a feeble flap or two with their giant wings, and we could see their lugubrious mouths on their white undersides. Yet in their own element they can rise from the bottom on which they lie and flap through the depths with ponderous grace and lithe, rippling movements of their wing-like fins. Like collapsing tents they settle down again amid a smoky cloud of mud or sand. The sting is an enlargement and modification of the small denticles that lie embedded in the skin of all sharks and rays. When one sting wears out a new one appears beneath and behind it, and often another behind that, so that there may be three in a row. Along each side of the sting runs a fine groove fitted with glandular tissue. When the dagger pierces the flesh of a victim this tissue is ruptured and secretes the poison which killed Ulysses. The first thing, therefore, which the Malays did when they found even a baby sting-ray among the heap on the deck was to break the sting out with a knife or with a thick leather glove.

Sometimes we brought up other strange giants. There were the large 'guitar fishes' with triangular heads. They cruise about over the bottom feeding on shellfish and crabs, are half-way between the sharks and the rays, and are harmless and quite useless. But to us, again, they were a nuisance because they weighed a great deal and filled up the bag with their useless bulk. Sometimes, too, we took 'cat sharks' with round, pussy-cat faces and long tails for all the world like gigantic, speckled, sand-coloured tadpoles. But most of the true sharks we caught were very small, and we only once caught a really big one near the Borneo coast.

We were often ourselves a considerable nuisance to other people, for whenever our large ship—large for those waters—went blundering into shallow coastal waters our trawls and wires were liable to become entangled with the lures, made of coconut-palm fronds, which the Malay fishermen anchor in shallow water to attract small fishes. In the Malacca Strait there was also a danger of our trawls fouling the drift-nets which the fishermen set for 'pomfret' and 'threadfin'. We learnt to keep out of shallow water. At night we usually anchored or just lay wallowing in the monsoon while I rolled like a log from side to side on my canvas bed, to rise stiffly with the first light. And my assistant slept down below in the fuggy fo'c'sle the solid, dreamless, uninterrupted sleep of the very young in his blue-and-white striped pyjama trousers.

The *Manihine* operated in Malayan and Borneo waters for

eleven months, from August 1955 to July 1956. During that time she made twelve cruises, lasting each from two to three weeks, and was at sea altogether for 182 days. She travelled altogether more than 15,000 miles, as far north as Mergui on the western side of the Malay Peninsula and as far east as Jesselton along the coast of Borneo. On every trip one of my two young colleagues went as scientific officer or I went myself. It was our job to sort and measure the catch. I found my turns fairly gruelling and usually went to bed for twelve hours when I had got back to my house after each one. I awoke stiffly next day and decided that I must be getting old.

We shot the trawl altogether 207 times and caught about twenty-eight tons of fish and seven tons of shark or ray. Since our cruises were exploratory, of course, we often fished on barren ground, since it was just as important to find out where the fish was not as to find out where it was.

But in the summer of 1956 two very sad events brought all my plans to an end and left me hanging in the air without any aim or purpose—and even, as seemed probable at the time, without a job.

The first of these was that the Government of Malaya, which paid about thirty-five per cent of the running costs of the outfit, decided that after it had achieved independence in 1957 it would withdraw its contribution. It was not so much that Malaya had decided that *Manihine* and research did not go together as that in Kuala Lumpur they had never really understood what we were doing far away in the South China Sea. They did not really like financing something which was based in Singapore and therefore, since Singapore was separate from Malaya, not really under their control. It was 'felt very strongly', as the saying was, that if Malaya were to finance any fisheries research it must be done by their own people. In view of the prevailing mood and the tendencies of the times this was only to be expected, but it meant that without Malaya's contribution there would not be enough money for us to run the ship. All the other Governments concerned, when approached on the subject, thought it was all most regrettable, but began with one accord to make excuse. They decided with regret that they could not pay any more. In the end Singapore also decided to withdraw the eleven per cent which was her own contribution, and so we were left worse off than ever. Indeed, it had been a sad disappointment for me to discover as the months went by that in Empress Place they very much disliked the *Manihine*, and disliked her more and more as time went on. 'Many people think she's a white elephant,' I was told. I have often thought that this must have been my fault and that I ought to have explained more often and more clearly and more loudly what exactly we were doing. But God knows I wrote enough reports.

But the second event that happened in 1956 was far more sad and touched me much more closely. In July, on what proved to be the *Manihine*'s last voyage in the Far East, David, our indomitable little Welsh skipper and my friend of years of bouncing around on tropical oceans, had a heart-attack while at sea off Penang. The ship put in to George Town and David was carried off to hospital. He never recovered and was pronounced medically unfit for sea. After some months in and out of hospital in Singapore it was decided to send him back to England.

I was late getting down to the quayside on the day he sailed and had only just time to shake him by the hand and wish him luck before the big P. & O. liner pulled away from the jetty. He looked terribly frail and ill, a shadow of the man he used to be, and he could scarcely walk up a short flight of stairs. But his eyes above his hollow cheeks still shone bright and humorous.

'Good-bye, lad. Be seeing you!' he said.

He died a few days after the ship reached London. So Dave joined the great company of the dead who increase and multiply around us as we grow older.

The loss of our skipper meant that a new officer would have to be appointed to the ship, for by law she could not go to sea without a certificated skipper and mate. But it was by then September, and Malaya had already given notice that she would withdraw at the end of March 1957. It would not have been worth while, or even possible, to bring another man out from England for so short a time. So finally it was decided to lay the ship up and she went to a buoy in the Johore Strait to begin that slow decline into death which overtakes ships that swing for a long time at buoys.

In April 1957 she was rescued from this dismal fate. After some agitated correspondence and negotiation the Colonial Office, whose property she was, decided to move her to East Africa. When I went to Empress Place to report this development the Treasury official smiled up at me from behind his battlement of files and picked up the telephone.

'I've good news about the *Manihine*,' he said into it. 'We're getting rid of the beastly thing.'

I celebrated my birthday in a melancholy way that year and was conscious, not for the first time, of the strange circularity of life. I stood on the jetty outside the go-down, among the little men in black trousers and white singlets making up their long-lines, and watched the *Manihine*, which had once been my especial pride, draw away with a new skipper in charge, especially flown from England. She turned south-westwards towards the islands and diminished into the sunset. I have never seen her since that day, though I have heard of her and read about her often. She went to Zanzibar and is still there, thus merely completing another circle. My fine laboratory on the sand-spit on the easternmost point of the island, after being inhabited for only five months, was closed down at the end of March 1957 and has stood empty and forlorn ever since. But the oleanders and casuarina trees I myself planted are doing well. Jim, my Tamil steno, loaded his numerous family and furniture on to a lorry. He was the last of my staff to leave. I watched the family depart, sitting on top of their furniture, with a fluttering of handkerchiefs and small dark hands, and a flashing of brilliant smiles. When they had gone I closed the wire gates behind them, and sat down on the contemporary-style concrete entrance-steps all alone and wept.

Part Three

LANDSCAPE:
TOKYO
HONG KONG

10

Tokyo

About every two years a conference of fisheries experts from all the nations of South-east Asia meets under the auspices of the United Nations. They discuss their fishy problems and meet each other. It is always a salutary experience, if sometimes a chastening one, to meet the man in another country to whom you have been writing polite letters. 'So that's what you look like, is it?' The delegates to the conference assemble by invitation of one of the interested Governments, a different one each time, and in 1955 Japan had the pleasure. She was at home to a variegated assembly of about a hundred or more experts, more or less, of whom I made one. I was present as chief delegate for the United Kingdom and headed a delegation from all the territories in South-east Asia then under British rule. They sat behind me in formidable and distinguished array.

We met in a magnificent panelled room in a new building in Tokyo. At one end of the room was a dais with banks of flowers topped by a row of flags of all the nations represented. Below that was a long baize-covered table for the Chairman, Secretary and dignitaries, if any. Facing them was a large baize-covered horseshoe with places around its outside for all the delegates. There was a gallery for spectators and committee-rooms leading off. It was a room especially designed for conferences in an age of conferences, and directly we had finished our deliberations and dispersed after a fortnight another conference rushed in to take our places.

Every delegate around the horseshoe had the name of his country on a board in front of him, and a microphone. On his left, just under the table, there was a battery of buttons and switches to which a head-set was connected. When a delegate wished to address the meeting he must first press the button on the microphone itself before beginning to speak, having also raised his hand to attract the Chairman's attention. If he forgot to press the button, as he often did at first, nothing came through the microphone, and all the other delegates around the horseshoe were aware only of silent mouthings like a ciné-film when the sound-track fails. The two official languages were English and French. The French delegates always used the latter so that when one of them spoke the other delegates, except those from Viet-nam, hurriedly pressed a button under the table on their left. What the French delegate was saying into his microphone in French then came through everyone else's headphones in English in a feminine voice with a French accent, being simultaneously translated by a clever lady in an eyrie high above the conference-room under the ceiling. If, as also often happened when the conference was young and we were inexperienced, one forgot to push the button again after the Frenchman had ended, the next delegate, say the representative of India, who always addressed the meeting in most fluent and mellifluous English, continued disconcertingly to come through the headphones in a feminine voice, but in French.

We sat around the horseshoe in alphabetical order, so that I had the quiet, shy delegate from Thailand on my left and the delegate from the United States on my right. Britain and the United States, I regret to say, carried on quite a lot of sly negotiation by means of winks, nudges, digs in the ribs and pencilled notes. Behind me sat the delegates from the British territories and behind the United States delegates various supporters from Honolulu and points west, such as Guam and Okinawa. Two charming characters represented one American-held island which had once been Japanese. One was a musical-comedy American who only needed a Stetson hat and a six-shooter to complete the picture. He greeted everyone with 'Hi-ya, fella!' without, so far as I remember, making any other contribution to the deliberations. The other was his buddy, who was an enormously broad and squat islander. He was, I suppose, in fact a Japanese, but he indignantly repudiated any such suggestion. The only occasion when I heard him say anything was when this apparently outrageous imputation was cautiously made. 'Doggone!' he said. Apart from that he was completely silent and left all the talking to his American friend.

'Oh, no, brother! Don't you get no ideas like that! John
here's a United States citizen same as me. Yes, sir, he's
gonna tag on right along with Uncle Sam. Now that's one thing
makes John kinda wild, being called a Jap. Why, one time in
a bar in Palao some guy called John a Jap, and, boy, d'you
know what John did to that guy? . . .' Looking at John one
hated to think.

Across the horseshoe from me sat the Indian delegate,
a suave and polished Bengali. He made more contributions
to the debate than anybody else. In deliberations of this sort
Indians are always particularly at home. How fortunate for
India that she attained her independence in the era of conferences. For Indians shine in debate, and the subject of the
debate is of far less significance for them than the fact of
debate itself. The wording of minutes and the phraseology
of resolutions are of transcending importance. The fact that
business may be held up for hours by discussions of the use
of 'shall' and 'will' in a resolution means nothing to them.
They enjoy the dialectical exercise. 'What a tower of strength
he is!' people said, with an admiring sigh, of the Indian delegate outside the debating-hall. But I must confess that there
were moments when my heart sank as the Indian delegate
raised his hand, reached forward to press the button on his
microphone and began to address the meeting in his smooth,
slightly Welsh intonation. 'Mr. Chairman, if I might, perhaps,
be permitted to make an observation or two . . .'

Farther down the horseshoe, near the U, sat the large
and distinguished Japanese delegation. Japan spends enormous
sums of money annually on research into various aspects of
fisheries, which are, indeed, her life-blood. Many of her
research-workers are among the most distinguished in the
world and produce work of the very first class, although the
fact that a good deal of it is published in Japanese script
leads to a certain amount of duplication of Japanese work
by the West and vice versa. So there, across the hall from me,
sat some of the world's most distinguished research-workers.
They were little wizened men with pebble-glasses in plain
blue suits with batteries of pens and propelling-pencils in
their breast-pockets. Something happens to the Japanese of
both sexes round about the age of thirty. They do not decline

slowly and—dare we add?—gracefully into middle age, late middle age and old age as we do, or as we flatter ourselves we do. But at thirty, over the young Japanese man or woman, it would seem, a mysterious wand is waved, and suddenly youth and beauty vanish. There is left a little homunculus in a blue suit and pebble-glasses, or an elderly matron in a kimono which has somehow suddenly become a dressing-gown. And sometimes, as I sat with my head in my hands, while the Indian delegate's mellifluous voice ran on and on, the blue suits and propelling-pencils of the Japanese delegation faded away and were replaced by baggy khaki drill and peaked caps. There were sentries with fixed bayonets behind them.

The Japanese always addressed the meeting in English. As a race they are not good linguists, and of all languages English seems to present them with especial difficulty. Their struggles with this barbarous occidental tongue were often painful to behold, and they would preface every sentence with inarticulate groaning noises as though they were indeed in labour with words.

Next to the Japanese delegation sat the Indonesians, handsome, self-conscious, aloof and prickly. They all wore the Malay *songkok* and were aglitter with rings and wrist-watches and chains and bracelets. They spoke very little English and made only small contributions to the debates, but livened the proceedings at the end, just when my head was beginning to sink on to my hands again, by formally objecting to the words 'Netherlands New Guinea' being included in any part of the reports of proceedings. It should be 'West Irian', their leading delegate said. The Chairman ruled that the point was out of order, but I was grateful for the interlude and so, I think, judging from the way everybody round the sleepy horseshoe seemed to perk up and take notice, were all the other delegates.

The Korean delegate also occasionally enlivened the somewhat soporific proceedings by injecting a welcome political note. He directed his artillery mainly against the Japanese, upon whom he seemed to have a heavy piece more or less permanently trained. It seemed to be triggered ready to explode into a torrent of oratory on the least stimulation.

The sufferings of the Korean people, the wrongs they had endured first at the hands of the Japanese and lately at the hands of the Communist aggressors, who, as all the world knew, by an unparalleled act of unprovoked aggression, and in violation of the most sacred human rights . . .' All this arising out of a proposal that member states should investigate the total production of plankton per unit-volume of the waters of their areas. I was most grateful for the diversion.

After a few preliminary sessions around the horseshoe we split up into committees, to each of which was assigned some aspect of fisheries problems. I found myself chairman of a committee which light-heartedly took over the vast realm of sea fisheries as its province. I had not then much experience of being chairman of a committee, although I have much more now. I had, however, sat on innumerable committees and listened with irritation to them maundering on and on, spending two hours and fifty minutes on the first item on the agenda and ten minutes on the other five because it was suddenly lunch-time or train-time or some other time. But now, I think, after some experience, I can say that I am rather a good chairman. I will not let them wander off the point and I seldom make the mistake, which is common to so many chairmen of so many committees, of leading the debate myself and turning the proceedings into a monologue by the chairman. At any rate a meeting when I am in the chair usually comes to an end at the appointed time with all the items on the agenda adequately discussed. All the members of the committee go off in plenty of time to their lunches or their clubs or their trains feeling that they've put in a pretty useful morning's or afternoon's work and given the spokes of the wheel of destiny a push.

In Tokyo I decided before long that the wheel of destiny must be given an occasional push. There were times when it seemed to get terribly bogged down in the mud of verbosity. One of these occasions was when, after several preliminary sessions, the assembly round the horseshoe came to break up into its constituent committees. The horseshoe broke up all right, but the assembled delegates, like quicksilver spilt when a thermometer is broken, dispersed into fragments and went hither and thither and could not be joined together again.

The committees just seemed unable to get themselves formed
The Korean delegate had something of special urgency t
say to the Burmese delegate, who wore with an air of impassiv
amiability his charming national dress. The Indian and Sin
halese delegates were engaged in earnest conference. Th
Sinhalese was a good-looking and self-assured young ma
who lost no opportunity of intervening in debates on behal
of his lovely, quarrelsome island. 'I would like if I may,' h
would begin in his cultivated labial accents, 'to draw the assem
bly's attention, Mr. Chairman, to the very excellent wor
which is being done in Ceylon on this particular subject.
There was, it appeared, no branch of fisheries research o
development in which excellent work was not being pushe
ahead with unflagging zeal and vigour in that fortunat
island. And now my own delegation, confound them, had go
in among the little men with pebble-glasses, and across th
room I could hear the ominous sounds of the English languag
in parturition. It was too much! A whip must be cracked,
could see!

'Will all members of Committe One kindly assemble forth
with in Room A,' I said in very loud and British accents
after clearing my throat ominously several times. Our voice
sounded extremely regional and none, I am afraid, more s
than mine. I was back in the Navy again, telling my watc
in a voice of brass, to 'get fell in'.

'Now, listen!' said the United States delegate, amid gale
of laughter, 'you jest can't be that way around here.'

But it worked, and quite soon I had a room full of littl
men from many nations, with paper and propelling-pencil
poised, and stacks of files and resolutions and agenda in from
of them on the baize-covered table, all ready with bows an
polite, diffident smiles to tackle the vast ocean and its many
mysteries.

Meanwhile around us roared and pulsated, like a giganti
heart, the huge and horrifying city of Tokyo, metropolis o
the new Japan.

It is, I think, the ugliest capital city in the world. There i
not a single distinguished building in it, except, perhaps
the Imperial Palace, and that is invisible across a moat an
hidden by trees. The streets are dirty and full of pot-holes

Wires are strung crazily about from raw poles, giving the whole place a Wild West look. There is mud everywhere, and every building has a stand in the entrance with water for cleaning the gum-boots which the citizens all wear for wading through the all-pervading slush. The traffic roars and shrieks up and down the wide, shabby streets. When the lights turn red at the intersections the crowd pours across the roadway like an avalanche. When they turn green the traffic charges forward like an advancing mechanized army going into battle. By day Tokyo seems like a huge wen of wooden shacks and mean concrete commercial blocks, of roads leading God knows where, and rattling trams and many-tracked electric railways reaching out like tentacles into the distance. Along them the trains shuttle to and fro, like bobbins weaving together ten million lives compounded of hard work and worry. How to exist, how to feed, how to educate, how to marry and how to die. Like any other enormous frightening city, I suppose. But by night it flowers into great rivers of light, of which the main street, the Ginza, is the largest and the noisiest, ablaze and aglitter after sunset with many colours from end to end. From it, and from the other main wide rivers, run tributary streams of light.

The Japanese are an artistic people and, as is often said, their taste is faultless. Yet where architecture is concerned they have developed in recent years a blind spot. But they are not alone in that. Yet once inside the hideous exteriors of their buildings, one may find oneself in that exquisite, stylized, feminine world of paper and flowers, very old and artificial, where everything is faultlessly formal and arranged. One's mere presence is liable to seem grotesque and outrageous. One is much too big. One's hands are too red, and there is a hole in one's sock.

My apparently gigantic size, which had never really occurred to me before, struck me forcibly and disconcertingly from the moment of my arrival in Japan. In my hotel, which was extremely western in intention, my bedroom had a bathroom and lavatory, tastefully tiled and, as everywhere in Japan, spotlessly clean. But the shaving mirror was so low down that, while I could shave my navel, I could not shave my chin without the most painful contortions. On the pedestal, of the latest pattern, I was all pudding and no plate, a midget's pedestal, and the bath was a 'sitz' bath, with the knees up to the chin. In the Kabuki Theatre I found that the seat was much too small for my behind—a shoe-horn was almost necessary—and after the first two and a half hours of a performance which seemed absolutely interminable I felt I could endure no more cramp and came out.

But it was when I came to essay the Japanese style of life that I became most conscious of my sheer outsize. The mattresses that were spread on the floor for me to sleep on were invariably too short, and so were the coverings, so that my feet and ankles stuck out nakedly and icily over the end. The tables from which one ate were only about a foot high, and one had to kneel at them to eat with the legs somehow tucked away beneath the buttocks. Cramp set in long before the meal was over, and I usually finished it propped up on one elbow, Roman style, with my legs splayed out away from the table. And next to the Japanese style I suggest that the Roman style must have taken the biscuit for sheer discomfort when eating. The Japanese, indeed, in their own houses must spend most of their time in some posture which to us would seem hideously unnatural and uncomfortable. They must be perpetually on their knees, for all domestic furniture is only about two feet high, with any drawers, shelves or cupboards where one could keep anything low down near the floor. In fact, in Japanese-style hotels one is evidently not supposed to keep things at all, and all that is provided are a few hooks from which to hang one's, it must be assumed, exiguous garments. Mirrors, if any, are similarly placed so low down that one has to kneel to look into them. Sanitary arrangements, which are always spotlessly clean and neat, are apt to be on a similarly minuscule scale, often with not much privacy and paper-thin partitions. My visit to Tokyo was in October, before the weather had really become cold enough for any heating to be necessary. Yet I could not quite see how these papery, elegant but comfortless rooms could get really warm in the rigorous Japanese winter. All this kneeling and squatting about and living generally off the floor, surrounded by screens and partitions made of bamboo and paper, seemed to me to have a Polynesian flavour, as though many centuries ago people from the tropical islands of the Pacific had arrived in their canoes at these wintry islands and planted their flowery, papery, bamboo-and-mango civilization there. But, throughout the centuries, during which they had been subjected to the suave and sophisticated influences from the Chinese mainland, they had never really adapted their tropical ocean-island way of life to the rigours of the climate of the temperate islands of Nippon. I decided, anyhow, that I really preferred the way of life in that other temperate island, with an equally rigorous climate, half a world away across the globe, and that the Japanese way was not for me.

Luckily, perhaps, our hosts seemed anxious that we should experience and admire the new westernized Japan. None of this out-of-date oriental stuff. So we stayed in a hotel which had been the palace of a wealthy prince. It was a hotch-potch of various styles imported from Europe—Tudor, Louis Quinze, Italian Renaissance, Dutch and Regency. My bedroom was Italianate with heavy curtains, cords and bobbles. It was quite creditably like Bexhill-on-Sea except for the incurable malady of littleness which affected some of the most important aspects of life. Over the Japanese formal garden, with its rockeries, bridges and dwarf trees, straddled a huge television tower.

At nine o'clock every morning, after a European-style breakfast served by maids in aprons and caps *à la* Bexhill, a motor-coach drove us to our deliberations and brought us back again at five. After that the whole great roaring city, with its beckoning lights and their myriad implications, lay waiting for us.

The Ginza is a great canal of light after sunset. Up and down it drifts the crowd of those who want to buy and those who wish to sell. They buy and sell pleasure, of sorts. Those who want to buy it are not quite sure what it is they are looking for, nor how much they are willing to pay for it when they get it. They have a kind of secret feeling that somewhere among all these glittering lights and momentarily glimpsed faces it must be possible to find pleasure for nothing. There must be eyes that are kind and not hard, responsive limbs and hands whose touch is gentle. But those who want to sell know exactly what they have to offer and worry only about how much they will get for it. They have a kind of secret feeling that somewhere among all these glittering lights and faces and voices (mostly American) there must be a mug who will pay their price and even more.

The Ginza, in fact, is the centre of Tokyo's famous night-life. You do not have to go very far along it. Someone has fallen in step with you already. 'You like a nice bar, sir? I show you some beautiful girls.' A young man in the ubi-quitous uniform of a university student, dark blue-buttoned jacket and peaked cap, approaches. 'I can offer you a very re-markable entertainment, sir, if you will be so good as to step this way,' he says, in much too faultless English.

'You like a very nice Besbian show?' whispers somebody else at my elbow.

Somebody presses a card into my hand. 'Wellcome', it says, 'to the famous Blue Lagoon Bar. Come and have a Good Time. Excellent foods and drinks, smooth services, lovely girls, nudes.'

Well, that later, but first we must eat.

The Sukiyaki Restaurant is a low-ceilinged, dimly lit but elegant room. The fireworks of Tokyo's sky-signs twinkle and glitter through the windows. Dozens of low tables are scattered about the room at which American G.I.s in civilian clothes and in every attitude of discomfort are sprawled about eating *sukiyaki* out of little bowls and pretending to enjoy it.

Sukiyaki is the only really edible dish, so far as I could make out, in the whole Japanese cuisine, which has nothing like the range and variety nor the epicurean quality of the Chinese. *Sukiyaki* is a kind of beef and vegetable *fondue* cooked at the table over a charcoal stove. Most Japanese food I found rather uninteresting, with a good deal more attention paid to its visual appeal than to its other qualities. There is a fish dish done in batter, called *tempura*, and another of raw fish cut in slices and tastefully garnished. The latter is considered to be a great delicacy. Only small mouthfuls should be taken and savoured with deliberation, in the manner of one savouring the nectar of the gods. I found it rather tasteless.

As always, when entering any Japanese house, we removed our shoes and put on sandals. We were, as is the custom, welcomed at the door by several charming little Japanese ladies in kimonos, who bowed and laughed as though we were the very first guests to arrive at a very special dinner-party given in our honour, instead of the two millionth foreign customers arriving at a public restaurant.

In parenthesis let me add here an entirely unnecessary and superfluous (because it has so often been done so much better before) note on the beauty and charm and grace of Japanese women. They so often combine the rose and cream of the West (idealized) with the upslanting eye and exquisite drawing of the oriental face. They do not have the coarse, parchment sallowness that spoils so many of the Chinese. If Japan has so quickly charmed her way, as she has, back into the comity of nations it must surely be at least partly due to her lovely, utterly feminine women with their air of dignified humility, their graceful, poetic movements, their knowledge of how to please and flatter, cajole and tease the western male.

Conscious of the hole in my heel I picked my way across the great thews of the western males sprawled about at the little tables. They wore blue jeans, open-necked shirts and often some kind of lumber-jacket with zips. Their universal presence everywhere in Tokyo gave it the air of being the least dressy capital city of any in the world. They wore crew-cuts. When I tripped over their enormous legs they drew them in politely, but with difficulty, saying, 'Oh, pardon me.' Every G.I. had a girl with him. Some had Japanese girls, but most had Americans, very formidable and Max-Factorized. They looked as though they unscrewed their heads and went to bed without them in order to preserve their make-up and their hair-do. The noise in the room was deafening and seemed to be all made by the women.

We sat down uneasily at one of the little tables. I folded my legs underneath me at first, but soon gave it up and half lay with my legs asprawl like the others. When anyone tripped over them I drew them in politely, but with difficulty, and said, 'Oh, I beg your pardon!'

Presently a little girl in a kimono set bowls of tea before us and then a charcoal brazier on which bubbled, exhaling a lovable fragrance, a sort of stew of beef and vegetables. We ate from little porcelain bowls with small, light chopsticks, easier to handle than the long, heavy Chinese ones of ivory or bone. We were helped continually by the little lady in the kimono, who sat at one end of our table and kept plying us with morsels and filling up little cups with saki (rice-wine) from an attractive little jug. When the attractive little jug was finished another one appeared, and the little jugs became more and more attractive as the *sukiyaki* bubbled and sizzled over its charcoal flames. The little girl tended the flames and the room got hotter and hotter and there was a general removal of lumber-jackets. The little girl giggled and made bird-like noises and kept bringing more and more little jugs.

At one end of the room was a low dais making a sort of stage on which four girls sat wearing kimonos and elaborate hair-dresses with things that glittered and sparkled and looked very delightful. They played sad little tunes on guitars and, occasionally, sang in high soprano voices sad little songs that seemed to have no melody. Then two of them did a dance with fans, that most enslaving of all feminine toys that the Japanese have retained to hide their laughter and their tears.

Unfortunately, at a moment possibly determined by the number of attractive little jugs, the sad-gay feminine performance of the girls on the dais suddenly became too much for the American audience. Or, perhaps, I should say it suddenly became not enough for them. An enormous blonde woman like a horse unfolded herself from one of the tables, dragging a very unwilling but obedient crew-cut male with her.

'Oh, c'mon!' she said, mounting the dais. 'Gimme that cute little banjo!' She seized the guitar, a triangular affair, from one of the girls, tried it without success and handed it to the boy friend, who plucked at it sheepishly without making any sense.

'Gwon! Swing it!' shouted the audience.

'Well, now, isn't that jest the cutest thing?' said the woman, seizing the fan from one of the dancers and making ogling passes with it. The little girls, their act thus rudely interrupted, stood about giggling the oriental giggle of embarrassment. But the American lady was not in the least embarrassed. She was having herself a time. She did a dance on the stage that was very sad in a way that was not intended, while the audience clapped in rhythm. The Japanese atmosphere was torn to tatters, and I felt nothing but unspeakable embarrassment for the whole of those warm-hearted, brash, unfeeling, unperceiving United States.

Naturally, in a few weeks, and not meeting many Japanese to talk to, I could not gather much of what the real feelings of the Japanese were towards their late conquerors and occupiers. Their feelings about the war were explained to me by an American who had lived in Japan for years. 'Our propaganda about the war is all wrong,' he said. 'It is predicated towards making the Japanese feel sorry and ashamed about it. They are not in the least sorry or ashamed, except that they lost it. They thoroughly agree that their war leaders should have been executed, but only because they led Japan into defeat instead of into the victory they promised.'

The Japanese have certainly embraced the less attractive aspects of the American way of life with an almost hysterical fervour. The love of the East for the gadgets and toys of the West seems to reach its apogee in Japan. Things like baseball and rock-'n'-roll, which the Americans take more or less in their stride, have become a kind of nightmarish religion to the Japanese. Baseball is everywhere, like a fever. On every playing-field and vacant site you will find boys of every size playing it, dressed in the appropriate costume. Huge baseball-parks are packed with humanity, shouting and screaming, every week-end. They have cheer-teams and cheer-leaders who go through all the frenzied antics just as in America, but with a kind of grim, humourless intensity, as though it all mattered dreadfully. There is none of the mad, crazy abandon which the Americans bring to it and which saves many of their activities from being merely pathological. 'The Americans are all mad,' an English naval officer said to me once during the war after his ship had returned from a refit in the States. 'But all in the nicest way.' The Japanese seem to have been bitten with the madness, but, being a people totally devoid of humour, there is something not quite nice about it. When I was in Japan hill-billy and rock-'n'-roll were the teen-age crazes, and no doubt they are so still. For this western cowboy dress appears to be necessary, and nothing looks sillier than little Japanese boys, with their doll faces and slanting eyes, dressed in the ten-gallon hat, tight trousers, boots and belt of a cowboy from Texas. But then the same might be said of the many cowboys of Leytonstone and the Gorbals. In the main streets of every town of any size there are huge and glittering pin-table saloons. They are always crammed with highly respectable, and often elderly, citizens pulling knobs and watching revolving numbers or gyrating balls for hours with serious, intense, humourless concentration as though, again, it all mattered very much and was something that simply must be done in this competitive westernized world. You see them entering with their umbrellas and leather brief-cases for half an hour's necessary devotion after the office closes, as though it were good for the soul. The housewife with her shopping-bag drops in on her way to the station and the electric train. They adjust their spectacles before they put their nickel in the slot.

There is television everywhere. The great steel Wellsian colossi straddle the roof-tops and tree-tops of Tokyo and spill down their trivia on to a million flickering screens in public squares, in railway-station concourses, in hotel lounges, in restaurants and in bars. Half the mouths of Tokyo are open in a fish-like gape, half the eyes agoggle.

And yet what are their feelings towards the bringers and originators of all these blessings? One cannot tell. The Japanese face is closed in an inscrutable smile. You see only the top of his head as he bows. Yet one with whom I went out one evening turned back at the door of a restaurant crowded with crew-cuts, lumber-jackets, blue jeans, blue hair-rinses and costume jewellery. 'I am sorry,' he said, bowing me to the door. 'It is just that I cannot bear these people.'

After the *sukiyaki* we launched ourselves again on to the canal of light, the Ginza, that flows through the sad heart of Tokyo.

'Harro, dahring,' said a voice. The Japanese cannot pronounce their *l*s, any more than the Chinese can pronounce their *r*s, and have, like the Chinese, thereby given rise to many a side-splitting, hearty joke.

'A really quite remarkable entertainment, if I may say so, sir.' It was the University student again.

'Very nice Besbian show,' said the other patient voice.

But at that moment a sign across the road caught my eye.

Blue neon wrote across a concrete façade—'Blue Lagoon Restaurant and Bar—Drinks, Music, Floorshow, Wellcome'.

remembered about the smooth services, lovely girls, and nudes.

'What about this?' I said, and we dived into the Night-Life of Tokyo.

It was very dark, as it always seems to be in any night-life, but when presently our eyes became accustomed to the gloom we saw that there were tables all round the room. On each was a dim red light, and at each, reclining so far back against the dark cushions that you could hardly see them, and some half under the table, were apparently the same young men that we had seen in the restaurant we had just left. They were not the same, of course, but so similar as to make prac-ically no difference. Each one had himself wrapped round a bundle of feminine deliciousness, and some were exploring with their hands and some with their lips and some with both. There was nothing particularly Japanese about the bundles of deliciousness except their upturned eyes. For the rest they were passably American and wore short, flared skirts and pony-tails and their mouths worked incessantly on gum. They were not noticeably different from a million other b.s of d. in a million similar joints all over the Far East.

As we entered and groped our way to a table a band composed of Japanese, dressed in what presumably represented Cuban costume, began to make an ear-splitting noise from a dais at one end of the room and couples emerged from the dark recesses and began to gyrate on the dimly lit floor.

At that moment I discovered that I too had a b. of d. with me, and all the rest of the party had one each also.

'Harro, dahring,' said mine. 'Gimme drink,' and she leant backwards against me, rather like one getting into a hot bath, so that she could receive embraces but did not have to give them. The waiter, without being asked, brought a tiny thimble of coloured fluid for my girl friend and a glass of beer for me. My beer, I afterwards discovered, cost about 75 yen or 1s. 6d., but the thimble of coloured fluid cost about 400 yen or about 8s. 6d. She had several before the evening was over. She placed herself so that my mouth was full of her hair, and I thought it tasted not bad, though hardly worth all that.

The dance came to an end and there was a roll of drums. A brilliant beam of light shone a circle on the floor in front of the dais and the band-leader made a triumphant, but totally unintelligible, announcement. Suddenly the beam and the circle were occupied by a smiling plump girl in blue sequins and wispy veils. The music started up again, something Spanish, and she began to quiver. She was quite silent, smiling and shaking like a jelly. I felt a rather unorthodox feeling of excited anticipation. I ought to be ashamed of myself, I expect, and am, but was not at the time. At the end of every few bars she took off one of the wispy veils, which seemed to be very cunningly and loosely attached, and let it float gently into the lighted circle of floor like a dying wraith. Soon she was almost completely naked, but still wobbling. She still kept a small triangular *cache-sexe* of sequins and a thin band round her hips. Then she stepped from the lighted circle of fallen wisps on the floor and, followed by her private moon of light, went jellying and wobbling round the room. Sometimes she stopped at a table, especially if it happened to be occupied by an elderly and particularly unattractive man, and wobbled her breasts near it, or at him. Perhaps it was a compliment that she did not wobble them near me. But I was pleased to see her. She had small, rounded, carmine-tipped breasts and a well-shaped bottom and I was sorry when her private moon went out and left me with my bundle and another eight-and-sixpence worth. There were some other much duller turns and, at about two, the place closed. On the stroke of the hour my bundle, who had become a bit muzzed by then, sat up, grasped her handbag, looked at herself in her compact with the intense concentration which women bring to that operation, tidied herself around the ears a bit and rose from the table, pulling her skirt straight, like a typist rising from her typewriter. She walked away without a backward glance, leaving me metaphorically under my oil-cloth cover. We paid and departed, feeling that this particular bit of the famous Tokyo night-life had nothing more to offer. My bundle, I found, had chalked up a round half-dozen eight-and-sixpences. As we left I saw her walking out of the door to catch her late bus in earnest conversation with a companion. It was the lady of the sequins, becomingly dressed in a smart coat and skirt.

So that was the famous night-life of Tokyo, and so much for the celebrated nudes. Further acquaintance with the great metropolis proved to me that this really was so, for all the night-spots I visited, in a kind of frenzy to find something gay or different or original, were variants of this first one into which we dived at random on our first night. Some were larger, of course, and noisier with several bands and rows of undressed girls and more numerous and more resplendent bundles of deliciousness. Others, at the other end of the scale, were dark, dim little bars with a radiogram and a few couples in the middle of a tiny floor and people lolling and fumbling in dark recesses. In all of them there were the same young Americans apparently dressed for walking or climbing or fishing or cutting down trees, but not really for a night in town. In all the larger ones there seemed to be a certain desperate earnestness, an anxiety lest it should not come up to standard and fail to be night-life as she is lived. How frightful if our famous Japanese night-life were not quite right in the eyes of these barbarians who have come among us! Supposing our vice was not really vicious enough! What a lowering of honourable prestige, what loss of face! In all a sad, indefinable boredom seemed to linger, for night-life is really terribly boring and how one longs to go to bed!

One night I went to one of over a hundred bars in Tokyo which cater for the minority. It was much the same as the others, only more respectable. In the middle of the room several couples of young men, dressed in a vaguely outdoors get-up, were dancing together to a radiogram. And, tell it not in Gath, Pa., publish it not in the streets of Askalon, N.J., there were G.I.s there too.

Life is what you make it, and every evening did not end quite like the first one.

'You come to friend's house, Poppa-san?'

Friend's house was miles away down those interminable Wild-West roads, all trams and poles askew, which lead from the lighted centre to other lesser centres, and then out, one supposes, to some undiscovered country whose bourne

endlessly recedes. The taxi rocked and bounced along and
the rain fell pitilessly, red- and blue- and yellow-streaked in
the neon. It had been raining for four days and nights without
stopping.

The house, when at last we reached it, was small and
low and made of wood behind high hedges. An electric railway ran not very far away at one end of the little side-road
and a tramway at the other.

Friend opened the door with many smiles and knelt to
remove Poppa-san's shoes. The house was sparsely furnished
but in simple, lovely taste with low tables and single flowers
in vases and mats spread on the floor.

The bath is the central feature of every Japanese house.
It occupies a dominant place in Japanese life and is the pivot
around which turns the routine of day and night. It cleans
the body and heals the soul. It is the place for conversation,
for meditation and for love.

In Friend's house the bathroom was the largest room. On
one side of the kidney-shaped sunken pool was a floor of sea-
pebbles, covered with mats. On the other was an overhanging
rockery of ferns and dwarf trees, with little dripping grottoes
that talked among the greenery. Paper lanterns shone like
moons among the leaves.

You must never soap yourself in the bath. You do that,
or have it done, first and wash the soap off with a shower.
You then step into the bath and let a great peace sink into you.
We lay in the warm water and the South China Sea seemed
very far away. The ocean could keep its ancient mysteries for
all I cared.

'Poppa-san!' she said.

We put on kimonos and went into a flowery dimly lit room,
where we sat on cushions while Friend brought in a little
low table. Kneeling and laughing she served us little bowls
of tea and of raw fish. All three of us knelt (I very awkwardly)
and laughed and toasted each other in tea. Then Friend brought
in mattresses which she laid on the floor and took the table
away. She bowed, touching the floor with her forehead between
her hands, and dowsed one of the paper lanterns.

The electric trains rattled past towards the undiscovered
country. When the darkness outside the opaque windows

began to pale they began rattling past again in the other direction, bearing towards the great city once more those who must face another day of worry about how to live and how to die.

At the week-ends, exhausted by the ocean and its mysteries, we left our baize-covered tables and memo-pads behind and went on conducted tours to see the sights. These entailed even more exhausting journeys by motor-coach or train.

These journeys were exhausting because of another of those neuroses which the Japanese seem to have caught from the Americans. They simply cannot leave you alone. They must entertain you constantly and divert your mind from the least stirrings of thought. Mental processes must at all costs be avoided. Every motor-coach, therefore, which was always a magnificent, aluminium stream-lined affair like a juke-box on wheels, was provided with a hostess whose job it was to interpose herself between her charges and their thoughts. At the least symptom of mental activity on their part she took energetic action. She was always dressed in the impersonal, sexless, sheath-like coat and skirt and little peaked cap which air hostesses affect, and she belonged to that same impersonal, international, slightly dehumanized race of young women which also includes receptionists (hotels, doctors, dentists), air-line booking-clerks and senior nursing-sisters (inside the hospital only).

I am one of those who, in buses or trains or aeroplanes, like to fall into a pleasant state of mental abstraction. Or even, I must guiltily admit, I sometimes read a book. I avoid getting into conversation with my neighbours, and if they insist on getting into conversation with me they find it rather hard going and are not encouraged. But in motor-coaches in Japan all this was quite out of the question. No sooner had we started and were lumbering through the traffic of Tokyo and threading its busy intersections, than the little hostess began to address us through a portable microphone, first in Japanese and then in English. She was very pleased, she said, to welcome us aboard her coach and hoped we would have an enjoyable trip. If there was anything we wanted please to ask her. She was there to help us. Today we were going to visit Kamakura, which was about twenty-five miles distant from Tokyo, where we would see the famous Kanon Buddha. Now this Buddha . . .

When she had finished she smiled charmingly and said, '*Dom arigoto*—thank you velly much'—and instantly turned on a record of an American crooner through the loud-speaker. Thus, to the sound of canned music, the dope of the East, we trundled and jolted our way over Japan's rough roads, through her swarming townships, and at last into her pine-clad, hillocky, bamboo countryside, where the little houses with ridge-and-furrow roofs and upturned cornices huddled together amid rice-fields and valleys full of streams.

Sometimes the microphone was handed round among the company in the coach and we were each in turn invited to sing or tell stories into it. When the microphone, on its dread, remorseless journey from hand to hand, inevitably came to me I suddenly found that my brain had stopped working altogether. I was a vegetable without any mental processes at all. My memory had completely forsaken me, and if I had known any songs or stories once upon a time I could not recall a single one now. If the microphone had been red-hot I could not have been more anxious to get rid of it. In fact almost everyone in the coach found the thing too hot to handle except one of the Indonesian delegates and the handsome, self-assured young man from Ceylon. The Indonesian, holding the microphone in an elegant, beringed hand, intoned into it a long, monotonous chant in a minor key. I was able during it to drift off into a pleasant state of self-communion, watching crowded, industrious Japan wheeling past the windows. 'That is a song the Javanese fishermen sing in their canoes,' the singer explained. I could well believe it. The delegate from Ceylon, on the other hand, was well prepared and equipped for this situation, which, it would seem, had occurred before in his life. He grasped the microphone, cleared his throat and began—

'The sun was declining behind the green mountains—'
We were safe for the next half hour.

Japan is simply bursting at the seams with people. This could scarcely be otherwise with a population of ninety millions in a country about the size of the British Isles. It bursts especially with the young. Everywhere you go there are troops and hordes of young men and boys in uniform, blue tunic with a high neck, trousers and round peaked cap, or girls and young women in a female equivalent costume. They are school and university students, and it is perhaps a symptom of the education they receive that they all look, and appear to move and think, exactly alike. Usually they are being herded and marshalled by superiors into companies and columns and marched off somewhere to see something educational or instructive. They are alarming by reason of their sheer numbers and of the earnestness with which they do everything.

When travelling by train one is especially struck by the vastness of the population, by the incredible numbers of Japanese in Japan. The railways are mostly electric, near Tokyo anyway, and very efficient. Everyone uses them, because the roads on the whole are narrow and motoring is expensive. On the National Railways the coaches are built on the American pattern with seats like pews on either side of a long aisle. But there are many privately owned lines, covering the country with a close network, on which the coaches have the same plan as those on the London Underground, with longitudinal seats facing each other, side-doors and straps to hang from. Both kinds of train are always crowded, and in general travelling by rail in Japan is like a very long, rather slow and very crowded journey on the London District railway. Since all the station names are written up in Japanese characters and nobody speaks any English the chances of your getting out at the wrong station, or of not getting out at all and being carried on heaven knows where, add a spice of excitement to the journey.

When we visited Hakone, which is up in the mountains and from which there is a wonderful view of Fujiyama, I travelled in one of the trains of the District variety, standing up tightly wedged for about three hours. We got out at the right station, after several false descents, because, I think, the train did not go any farther. We then bundled into a waiting motor-coach and roared and zigzagged, to the accompaniment of canned music, for several hours up a tortuous mountain road. But we did not have to sing, and indeed long before we reached

Hakone we were too tired even to talk and most of us were nodding in our seats. We were a very distinguished company, and among the tired forms slumped in the upholstered seats were scientists of international repute and directors of world-famous scientific institutions. Some of us were snoring distinguished snores by the time we stopped at the lighted doors of the hotel, and had to be awakened.

Hakone is a lovely spot. You climb up and up through wooded gorges and past waterfalls. Holiday resorts fill the steep valleys with wooden houses perched over precipices and over cataracts. It was Saturday evening, and the week-end crowds thronged the narrow, brilliantly lit streets all wearing the kimono into which the Japanese love to change when the day's work is done. They feel relaxed in it. Like all national costumes whatsoever it has an enhancing effect on the wearer's appearance, but only, strangely enough, if worn by the race for whom and by whom it is designed. European women often make a great mistake in the East by wearing the *cheong-sam* or the sari. It almost without exception looks wrong on them.

Hakone itself stands beside a big crater-lake with steep wooded shores, and the hotel was surrounded by a charming garden which sloped to the water's edge. But it was dark when we arrived, so that all we could see were Japanese lanterns shining between pine trunks and, as usual, little girls in kimonos waiting on the steps to welcome us with bows and laughter and bird-like twitterings.

The world-famous scientists and directors of institutions climbed stiffly and wearily out of the coach. The thought of a bath, shave and change, and then perhaps a drink, was at that moment a very enticing one. But this was a Japanese-style hotel and the mention of a bath set moving an inexorable train of consequences. With many bows and chirrupings and smiles the guests were led along a passage to their rooms. Protesting, but impotent, the world's most distinguished scientists and directors of institutions began to have their clothes forcibly removed piecemeal. Some rebelled at this point, overcome by the indignity, and decided after all, with regret, to forgo a bath. Others got as far as being led along the passage, draped in a kimono, to the bathroom. But here they in their turn shied and fled back to their rooms. For it was obvious that they were all expected to bath together in the same pool and be sponged and towelled by the little, gently amused ladies. To the puzzled regret of the girls the distinguished company decided almost to a man not to have a bath after all, tired as they were.

The least distinguished and humblest of the scientists, however, had had all this treatment before and knew what to expect. Myself I do not particularly mind about being seen naked and feel only a slight loss of dignity when I lose my clothes. I cannot be a very engaging spectacle with nothing on, but no worse than others, and no one need look who does not wish to. So I allowed myself to be undressed and soaked myself in the bath and then put on a kimono over my underclothes, which is the Japanese way. When I rejoined the company they were all sitting round a roaring log fire, on low rush stools or on cushions on the floor, for it was a very chilly night and we were several thousand feet up. But I found that in a kimono, as in the kilt, one has to be practised to sit on a low stool or on a cushion on the floor. It was also very chilly, so I decided that there was such a thing as being really too Japanese, and went and put my trousers on like my colleagues.

The distinguished scientists need not really have worried, for their unclothed forms would have meant as little to the girls as would their learned scientific papers. The Japanese are quite without emotion about nudity. It means nothing to them whatever. In their public baths men and women all bathe together naked without a thought. In the fields you often see, as the train flashes past, peasants of both sexes working almost naked. In some parts of the coast the fishermen have worked naked on the beaches by tradition for centuries, until the Americans came along, like the serpent, and told them it was rude. For the Japanese do not consider that the human body is rude and have a totally different approach to the question from ours, and a far more wholesome one. Goggling at nudity is incomprehensible to them, and nude shows in Tokyo are only for foreigners. Perhaps all this results from their never having read the story of the Fall, where all this nonsense about the human body began.

We all slept Japanese-style on mattresses on the floor.

My feet, projecting over the end, grew colder and colder towards morning. Loud scientific snores shook the paper-thin partitions between the rooms. When we awoke it was a lovely autumnal morning with dew on the grass that sloped down to the glittering lake. Far away at the end of the wooded valley arose the white-tipped cone of Fuji-san, the sacred mountain, symbol of Japan.

11

Hong Kong

I had, of course, foreseen all the sad events leading up to the collapse of my plans in Singapore and to the loss of the *Manihine*. In Tokyo I had met David Barker, who was the young and energetic Professor of Biology in the University of Hong Kong. In the years since the war the University had enormously expanded and was still growing. David had built up a department of biology which was shortly to split into two separate departments, one for zoology and one for botany. Affiliated to the zoology side was a Fisheries Research Unit, which at present lacked a director. At the end of 1956 I had applied for this post. In due course I was successful and arrived in Hong Kong by air in September 1957.

What the world knows as Hong Kong is an irregularly shaped peninsula of the mainland of China and a constellation of mountainous islands, of which the most important is the island of Hong Kong itself. Immediately to the west of them the great Pearl River estuary, formed by the confluence of three great streams draining from the heart of China, empties itself into the South China Sea.

This geographical entity has acquired since the war an importance and significance far greater than its size would indicate. Sometimes it is spoken of as 'a pimple on the backside of China', as though it had no permanent future and would soon be engulfed by its monstrous neighbour, at others as a 'menace to our standard of living and way of life'—that is, to our five-day week and three-weeks holidays with pay. Its Colonial Government is either depicted as 'the last outpost of an outdated colonialism', or as a 'model of paternalistic government'. The British are of no importance and could be thrown out tomorrow, or they are sitting oppressively on the heads of several million Chinese. It all depends on the point of view. The fact is that no one quite knows what to think of this curious enigma, for it does not really obey any of the rules. With its striving, thrusting, industrialized population and its liberal Colonial Government, its lack of any movement towards political independence, yet with its defiant attitude towards fate and life and towards the outside world, it is quite unlike any other community on the face of the globe.

The island of Hong Kong—the name means 'Fragrant Lagoon'—is about ten miles long and two or three miles wide. It is a steep irregular ridge of scrub-covered mountains. On the northern slopes of these, facing the mainland across a narrow strait, huddles the city of Victoria—a name which is very seldom used—with its maze of canyon-like streets, commercial skyscrapers, blocks of flats, old terraces and steep alleys and its swarming, shouting, nineteenth-century stews. On the other side of the strait is the peninsula of the New Territories, really a tiny projection of the Kwangtung province of China. The city of Kowloon, a dusty commercial wen without charm or grace, sprawls along the northern shore of the strait up to the feet of the mountain of Tai-mo-shan, which stands like a bulwark to the north. From Kowloon-side, as the Chinese say, the island looks like battlement upon battlement of geometrical blocks climbing up the steep mountainsides. By night it is a glittering palisade of coloured lights. From Hong Kong you can only see Kowloon properly if you climb up the Peak by car or by cable-tram and watch it unfold itself like a dingy patchwork carpet. By night both cities are like twin galaxies spilling their stars up to the skirts of the mountains and into the farthest corners of landlocked bays. Between them anchored ships glow upon the dark water, and the lighted ferries weave to and fro like meteors darting from one galaxy to the other.

The peninsula known as the New Territories is about the size of a small English county, very irregularly shaped, with mountains and fjords and lovely valleys on the east, and low-lying farm-lands, rice-fields and swamps on the west. The peasant people, many of whom still live in walled villages four hundred years old, belong to the Hakka tribe, who fled from the mainland and took refuge here in the seventeenth century. They wear sombre black clothes and huge, plate-like straw hats with no crown and a wide hanging fringe around the brim. When I was in Hong Kong in 1945 the peace of the Hakka villages with their upturned eaves and large shady trees had not been disturbed. The paddy-fields made lakes of brilliant green in the steep-sided valleys, and the bamboos were huge fountains of trembling green. Today these valleys are being invaded by industrial development, and modern earth-moving machinery is changing geography and making history. Yet everywhere you look, even today, the landscape is ancient and traditional and utterly Chinese, and you feel, driving through it along the macadam roads and dodging the military lorries, that you have seen it and known it all in some other life and that it is for ever.

The peninsula is a strange territorial muddle. A large part of the city of Kowloon, together with its waterfront, is British territory by right and was ceded with the island of Hong Kong in 1841. But the mountainous hinterland up to the Chinese border about forty miles away, and most of the surrounding islands, were leased by the British from China in 1898 for ninety-nine years. Thus in 1997 they are due to return to China if the lease is not renewed. Nobody knows what will happen then and nobody seems to worry very much. The threat is a remote one at present. The British, as usual, think that some compromise will be arrived at, but meanwhile the only effect that this, as yet, distant cloud has on life in Hong Kong is perhaps that it creates a demand for quick returns for capital outlay. For instance, the rents of flats in the vast blocks that are springing up everywhere are very high because no one quite knows what lies in the future and landlords want their money back quickly.

In the middle of Kowloon is a curious little enclave which, for some reason, was not included in the lease. This is the old walled city. The walls have disappeared, but the small area they once enclosed is still Chinese territory, where, theoretically at any rate, the Queen's writ does not run. English is not the official language, and nothing but Chinese script is seen there. It is said to be a haven of refuge for criminals on the run from the Hong Kong police, but it can only be a very temporary one for the police have the place well under observation and control. Nevertheless, when the air-field, which is near by, was being enlarged the old city was encroached upon and there were protests from the Chinese Government against this trespass on its territory.

In 1945 the population of the whole colony was about half a million, about a million having fled over the border from the Japanese. It seemed to be swarming with people even then. When, in 1949, the Communist armies surged up to the border and stopped, thousands of refugees streamed the other way, into British territory. Many came by road and others by sea at the rate of thousands a week. Today the population numbers about two and a half million and they are still coming, though not in the former enormous numbers.

The result of this is that for its Chinese inhabitants Hong Kong has become a kind of human jungle where competition is fierce and desperate. Wages are low and hours long. There is no security and little future in that other world in which the Chinese live in Hong Kong. It is a world which we Europeans have long forgotten about. We look back at it from the comfort of our welfare state and hope that we shall never return to it. Yet it must have once existed in England, in the middle years of the industrial expansion during the last century. In Hong Kong now, as in England then, the faces of the poor are ground. In the new textile factories, until the introduction of new legislation at the beginning of 1959, the workers did fourteen hours a day with half an hour's break for lunch, Sundays included and no holidays. I once met the European manager of one such establishment, who prided himself on the enlightened conditions of employment in his particular factory. His people only worked twelve hours a day with half an hour's break and they lived in, in long, bleak dormitories. They were perfectly happy, he said, and thankful to have their jobs. And that I could well believe. In most Chinese shops, though not in the European ones, the assistants work eight or nine hours a day, Saturdays and sometimes Sundays included.

Such conditions astonish us with our welfare-state outlook, but the fact is that the Chinese have an attitude towards work itself which is totally different from ours and incomprehensible to us. Labour for them, no matter what it may be, is an integral part of their lives, part of their natural daily bodily activity, like the heart-beat or the motion of breathing. It is a complement to eating and sleeping. They do not cultivate leisure, which seems to be something strange and foreign to them. The idea of 'relaxing' and consciously unloosening their stays, which seems to have come to us from America, is unknown among the Chinese. There is no quiet abstraction over a 'cuppa', and even their method of eating is designed to take up the minimum time and space. You eat where you work. Comfort, too, is not really understood by the Chinese. They sleep on boards and squat rather than sit. Perhaps they have never had time for ease or leisure. Perhaps in the mid-nineteenth century the English working-people, too, had never cultivated leisure because they had no time to do so. So now for the Chinese work is a habit. In occupations like Government service or the University, in which holidays and annual leave are regularly given to the lower-grade staff, it is often difficult to make them take advantage of these facilities. They go on leave and may come and say good-bye to the boss at great length. But after a day or two it is quite likely that they will come back again saying they are bored and do not really want a holiday. In many cases no doubt this is the result of the overcrowded conditions in which they live. It is better to be in the office or workshop than in an overcrowded tene-ment surrounded by squawking children and other people's radios and noises generally.

More stringent regulations to control working hours are now being introduced, but whether they will stop the people from working is very doubtful. In the hours not taken up by their jobs they will probably find other work. They will cer-tainly not use them for leisure, a word which scarcely exists in the Cantonese vocabulary.

In my own case I could not help noticing the contrast be-tween Hong Kong and Singapore, which was very striking. In Singapore I had to go round the building every day in order to see if the boys, junior assistants, had done their jobs—such small chores as washing glassware, cleaning floors, even keeping lavatories clean. For a large part of their time the boys sat, lolled or squatted in a state of gentle, bemused abstraction with nothing much going on between the ears. They only uncoiled into any sort of activity if they heard official-sounding footsteps approaching.

'Now, have you done so-and-so today?'

'Oh, no, Doctor. I was just going to.'

'Well, why haven't you?'

'You never tell me, Doctor.'

'I did, you know. I told you to do it every day.'

'Very good. By-and-by two minutes I do.'

But the next day it would probably be just the same, and eventually one gave up the unequal struggle. But in Hong Kong it is seldom necessary to give an order more than once. And I notice that the boys are seldom idle. They are constantly repairing things, making things, cleaning things, or reading little books in Chinese script on how to repair or make things or gain more knowledge or more skill.

The fierce competition, which is life, has produced, as it did in England a hundred years ago, an extraordinary inventiveness, ingenuity and drive. New industries and ways of earning a living spring up with vegetable profusion. The textile industry is an example, entirely new to Hong Kong since the war. There are many others, and most of them have the United States as their main export target. The export of large, edible (but rather tasteless) prawns, the cultivation of oysters for oyster sauce, the manufacture of genuine old Chinese furniture, ceramics and carpets and the building of boats are all examples of the determination of the Chinese not to be beaten and to keep their ends up. The result is that Hong Kong is now no longer merely an *entrepôt*, importing and re-exporting. It is now a manufacturing centre in its own right —a menace, in fact, to our standard of living. And its own standard of living, although there is poverty and want, is on the average an extraordinarily high one for so small and overcrowded a 'pimple on the backside of China'.

Toughness and self-reliance are the key-notes in Hong Kong. If you do not help yourself it is very certain no one else will. Every corner and alley of the crowded streets is occupied by someone making a living somehow. Fate cannot daunt these people. It is as though for many centuries they have borne her blows and know the worst that she can do. Now the enemy has no more shots in the locker. The Cantonese face life and all its tricks defiantly, with heads erect, a deadpan expression and a fathomless fatalism and scepticism.

If competition for a living is fierce, that for a place in which to live it is fiercer still. The tremendous influx of refugees in the last ten years has created a nightmarish housing problem. On the steep, scrub-covered mountains of Hong Kong Island and on the barren, dusty hills behind Kowloon wretched shacks of corrugated iron, scraps of planking and beaverboard and canvas, cover the hillsides like a pox. They serve to house the driven poor, who are thankful for even that much shelter. They look down upon the ever-rising geometrical blocks of flats with their lifts and built-in garages, the 'hi-fi', the re-diffusion, the 'telly' and other horrors. Many of these are empty because their rents are so high and the landlords can get their money back if only a few in each block are let. Along the waterfront and in the purlieus of the two cities are the tenement stews and steep alleys lined by old houses, many of them very elegant if you could see them unencumbered by sign-boards and festoons of washing. They frequently collapse from age and the workings of termites and dry rot, burying their many inmates. In these slums people live in rooms many times divided into cubicles by wooden partitions. Four or five people live in each cubicle, and there may be five or six cubicles to a room. Recently in heavy rain two old houses collapsed, burying over seventy people who were living in them. One old man, when dragged out of the rubble, complained only that he had lost his pipe. It was just another blow of fate.

In order to house the invading hordes which streamed over the border from China the Government, refusing to lose its head and being unhindered by party politics, built row upon row of blocks of low-cost tenements, in which they have succeeded in housing a very large number of refugees. These buildings are not things of beauty. They are of a strictly utilitarian design, but so stark and bare of all inessentials that they do in fact achieve a kind of forbidding symmetry. They stand in long, gaunt perspectives on the foothills of Kowloon, as bare and unornamented as the rocks around them. They look like prisons, but they are gay with washing hung out to dry, the challenging symbols that decorate every Chinatown. They swarm with busy, vital humanity and must be, for those who brought them into existence, their own reward.

The surprising fact is that the great army of the jobless and destitute which flooded into Hong Kong since 1949 has somehow or other found work to do. Most of these people are making a living of some sort. You see many signs of poverty around you in the streets, but little of disease and almost none of starvation.

Because of the overwhelming majority of the have-nots, all furiously competing for a living, Hong Kong is probably one of the easiest places in the world today for the haves. Everywhere there are dozens of people only too glad to be of service in any way you like. Servants are comparatively cheap and easy to find. There are firms who will contract to keep your flat clean for you and do all the polishing and chores. Restaurants will send meals up to your flat, deliciously cooked and hot, saving you the trouble of putting your nose outside the door. Tradesmen take orders at your front door (not your back door, for flats in Hong Kong are curiously constructed and seldom have more than one entrance). If your car needs servicing the garage will collect it for you and drive it back without extra charge. Rents are high, but food is cheap and clothes very cheap, about a third of their price in London. Young married couples, used to the rigours of the kitchen sink and the forenoon's journey to the Home & Colonial and Sainsbury's in England, grow lyrical about the joys of life in Hong Kong. But there are too many and too frequent reminders that one is living well because many are living poorly to allow one to feel too comfortable—if one pauses to think about it. But very few Europeans in Hong Kong, I think, indulge in that unpleasant exercise.

The contrast in wages, for instance, between Europeans and Chinese is startling. A Chinese friend of mine is a qualified schoolmaster with several years' experience. He teaches mathematics and Chinese literature. His salary is about HK$750 (about £47) a month, which is considered quite high. An English friend of mine, starting up a branch office for a famous London firm, engaged a Chinese office-manager of many years' experience at a salary of HK$1,000 (£55) a month, which was considered very high—'for a Chinese', as Europeans always add. On the other hand I knew a young Englishman who arrived from Malaya, where he had thrown up his job, hoping vaguely to find something in Hong Kong. Within a fortnight he had landed a business job at HK$2,000 a month with no experience at all. Young Europeans in banks and offices draw salaries at this level with paid leave and quarters, so it is perhaps not very surprising that they studiously avoid thought.

There are beggars everywhere, who make the avoidance of thought difficult at my age. They are not only in the streets, where mothers use their children to charm your cents from you, and the deformed and sick use their afflictions as their stock-in-trade. They come to your office and to your house with long, elaborately prepared hard-luck stories. Soon you begin to feel that everyone in Hong Kong is after you. You develop a callous crust and a harsh manner to keep at bay the armies of the needy, the poor, and the down-and-out. You feel, if you feel at all, that you are surrounded by a great, dark ocean of human misery and unhappiness.

But one of the more hopeful signs in this day and age is the general feeling of responsibility, which has got itself spread around, for what is happening to one's fellow human beings. Because of it a very large number of charitable organizations and kind-hearted individuals swim bravely against the tide of want and misery, which seems to be steadily rising. One of these is devoted to the care and upbringing of castaway babies who have been dumped in other people's rubbish-bins by their despairing parents. Girl babies, who are no insurance for the future, are especially liable to this fate. From America, as always, comes a continual river of charity and good works. Hospitals, schools and homes are run by American institutions and religious bodies, and if souls are not saved at the same time as the bodies it is certainly not the fault of the droves of earnest ladies and gentlemen who pour into Hong Kong in an endless stream, all looking curiously alike and all ready with their views on what to do and how to do it.

On first arriving in Hong Kong it seems a very foreign city and gets no less so as the years go by. You always seem to be on the outside looking inward, never absorbed and always a stranger. It is far more foreign and less European than Singapore. The more Singapore cocks a snook at Europeans the less foreign it really seems to be. It is the indifference and deadpan politeness and exclusiveness of the Chinese which makes one feel that one really has no place in this most Chinese of cities. Away from its commercial centre, with its temples of mammon and slightly London atmosphere, you soon find yourself in streets where no English is spoken or understood and where life is ferociously Chinese. Everything goes on in the street, buying and selling, eating and drinking and sleeping, and even dying. Things for sale are draped and hung in festoons inside crowded shops and outside, from roofs and beams and stalls. You push and jostle your way along. Babies and women are under your feet and everyone is furiously at work, intently minding his own business. They are not in the least hostile, only totally indifferent and uninterested, unless they think you wish to buy something. As a rule they do not even bother to look up from their rice-bowls as you pass. If you address a word to anyone he replies with a vacant look and 'Ha?' The clip-clop of sandals strikes through the shrill of voices and even through the blare of radios from open doors and upper windows.

The people who push and shove and elbow around you are so foreign as to seem to be almost another species. Their voices are harsh and strident, and the language they speak has a curious sing-song intonation with an upward lift at the end of sentences. Many of them have well-shaped bodies and fine legs. In the Chinese face the mouth is often good, with regular white teeth, but the eyes, under upslanting brows, are dead.

They love bright colours, and looking uphill along the crowded narrow alleys you see a constantly shifting pattern of many hues. The women wear pyjamas of bright flowered patterns or of plain black. Those of the servant class wear the white tunic and black trousers, their hair tightly coiled, or, if they are unmarried virgins, hanging down their backs in a long plait. Mothers carry their babies in a sling on their backs, poor heads nodding in sound sleep so that they look as though their necks would break. But, judging by the swarms of children everywhere, impish and beguiling and perpetually laughing, one must assume that their necks very seldom do break in infancy. Many of the men still wear the Chinese dress, a loose suit of blue or white or black material, buttoning to a high neck with wide, floppy trousers. In winter they wear a dressing-gown affair with wide sleeves. Elderly gentlemen carry fans, and labourers smoke long bamboo pipes that rest on the ground between their knees.

Rickshaw-pullers run between the shafts of their two-wheeled carriages wearing shorts and wide straw hats. I seldom use them because I dislike undignified arguments in the street about money and because they always assume that I want to go either to a brothel or a bar. There are moments in my life when I do not particularly want to go to either.

You may live for years in Hong Kong, I think, without ever going into a Chinese home. This is partly because as a European you are an alien and an outsider, and partly because the conditions under which most Chinese families live, so overcrowded in their tiny apartments, make entertainment impossible. It is certainly not because the Chinese are inhospitable, but circumstances force them to live in public and in the street, like the French. Entertainment usually takes place in restaurants, and you often see large parties with all the women and children present and the amahs coaxing and smacking while the grown-ups chatter and pick their teeth.

A party in a Chinese restaurant is an experience in its own right. I had been to many in Singapore, of course, but in Hong Kong it is different. It is the difference between dining in a French restaurant in London and dining in Paris. With your food and wine you absorb an atmosphere and drink in a culture, a very old and self-assured one like that of the eighteenth century in Europe.

I had not been in Hong Kong many days before a Chinese Singapore acquaintance, whom I met in the street by chance, invited me casually to dinner. 'Just a little party, you know. Nothing much—a few friends. You like Chinese food, Doctor?'

'Of course,' I said.

There are innumerable restaurants in Hong Kong where you may dine in any one of many styles, in that of Canton or Peking, Shanghai or Szechuan or several others. Or you can eat 'steamboat' style in little restaurants run by northern Chinese Moslems. A charcoal brazier in the middle of the table heats a circular trough of water in which you seethe rolls of raw mutton or liver or vegetables. The water in the trough transforms itself into a soup which you drink at the end of the meal. The only thing you cannot do is eat quietly. There are large noisy restaurants with dance bands where acres of floor space are divided up and partitioned off by movable screens. You shout across the crash of the band and the rattle of mah-jong chips which goes on behind the screens, and across the plaintive mooing of a glittering little figure in a shining *cheong-sam*. She is mouthing American 'pop' tunes into a microphone. This is 'Miss Carmençita Romero, the atomic sex bomb of 1957 [or any other year]' and her rather listless, unemphatic rendering is due to the fact that she has learnt the words off parrot-fashion without having the least idea what they mean. Or you may dine in small, unpretentious noisy restaurants with spittoons on the floor and dishes of melon seeds on the tables. Or, less pretentious still, in the crowded and even noisier cafés open to the pavement where the juke-boxes throb and the coolies look up from their bowls of rice with only faint interest and amusement as you enter.

I am always something of a joke to the Chinese, and they often laugh unashamedly and outright when I appear. My entrance into a restaurant is often greeted by amused stares and even giggles. I was puzzled by this when I first arrived in Hong Kong, so I asked a European woman who had lived for years in Peking what the reason could be for the stir my appearance seemed to cause.

'It is because you are a good omen,' she said. 'You resemble General Kung, a figure in Chinese traditional opera. He is a big, red-faced, benevolent General who confers benefactions whenever he makes an appearance.'

So now I take Chinese stares and giggles as a compliment and hope the omen, which is me, brings them the good luck so many of them so much need.

On a warm evening in September, then, a few days after my arrival, I climbed up through the steep, narrow alleyways to the first of many Chinese dinner-parties that I have attended in Hong Kong. The declining sun made searchlights in the dusty air between the dilapidated houses festooned with washing and aglow with Chinese characters in neon.

We assembled in a little restaurant with a low ceiling,

brilliantly lit by white mercury-strip lights. It was not air-conditioned, and there were only a few wall-fans humming and rotating on brackets. They stirred a vitiated air. There was a fungus-ridden mirror on one wall with Chinese characters in gilt and some improbable Chinese ladies with operatic complexions advertising soft drinks. It was a somewhat crumby little place, but I have since learnt that the externals are the last things by which you should judge a Chinese restaurant, as a French one. The longer you have to wait for your food the better it will be. Part of the small room was screened off around a circular table set for about twelve people. The places were so close together that it was difficult to imagine how twelve people were going to sit at them.

A flock of little waiters in white coats and black trousers pulled out chairs for us. The stout, paunchy boss bowed us into the screened-off recess. We sat down and waited.

A table set for a Chinese meal is a most inviting sight. Merely to look at it seems to stimulate the anticipatory juices that are so important. At each place is a plate, two porcelain bowls—one larger than the other, two porcelain spoons with short handles like medicine-spoons, a pair of ivory chopsticks and two small round dishes. One of these contains mustard sauce and oyster sauce and the other usually soya-bean sauce. There is a paper napkin beside each place and beside every other chair an enamelware spittoon for the gentlemen. All this inviting array looks very sad when the feast is at last over, because it is not considered to be particularly bad manners to make a mess on the tablecloth. That is what tablecloths are for. The result is that when the guests rise from their places in two and a half hours' time the table looks indeed as though an orgy had taken place. As a matter of fact the Chinese spill their food about very little, but Europeans, who are less skilled, do. When I have finished, the floor around my chair is usually covered with spilt rice as though snow had been falling.

The other guests on this occasion were one European, a Government servant, some Chinese business-men, a lawyer, and their wives. They came round the screen and we bowed as we were introduced. Then we sat down as directed by our host cheek by jowl, or rather hip to hip and thigh pressed against thigh, on little metal chairs around the enticingly laid-out table. As usual the meal began with little bowls of jasmine tea, delicious and fragrant, and damp hot cloths were handed round on a tray from which they were proffered to us with tongs. On these we wiped our hands and the men their faces, but not the ladies for fear of spoiling their make-up. In the good old days, whenever those were, these cloths were soaked in rose-water, but in these degenerate times it seems to be nearly always disinfectant. Then the meal began. A sort of *hors d'œuvre* came first, tiny cockles from northern China in their shells, minute fragile birds, which could have been larks, eaten whole, and slivers of 'abalone', which is the *Haliotis* shell. After that I cannot recall the sequence of dishes, but I remember that at first I looked up in eager anticipation as each one arrived. As a rule there are as many courses as there are diners, so that presently my eagerness turned to misgiving, and then to dread, and finally to despair. Sweat burst out on my forehead. I felt I was beginning to swell visibly and began furtively undoing buttons. I have learnt better now and know that you must hold your horses and attack the first few dishes lightly. Even if you take only a few mouthfuls from each dish you are sure to have eaten more than enough before the end comes. The succession is in the opposite order to that of a European meal, beginning with chicken, duck or meat, or all three and sometimes more than one dish of each, followed by fish (several perhaps) and then soup. Lichees or sliced oranges or baked apples dipped in syrup usually bring the meal to a merciful end. Everything, needless to say, is of celestial deliciousness. The Chinese are perhaps the most skilled cooks in the world, and all their various cuisines are the products of centuries of trial and error and perhaps also the products of centuries of famine and shortage when all sorts of things had to be eaten and made palatable. The Chinese, indeed, eat practically anything, birds' nests, sharks' fins, toads, frogs, lizards, all cunningly disguised to please fastidious tastes. Behind the scenes in any Chinese restaurant, no matter how smart its external appearance, is a spectacle of inferno-like squalor, where celestial foods are nonchalantly prepared, amid clamour and steam and shouting and clatter, angry sizzlings and licking tongues of flame.

Out of these infernal regions there were borne in to us, and set down steaming before us, sucking-pigs of which one ate only the crackling, ducks which seemed to have fallen asleep with their bills beneath their wings while being cooked, but which fell apart at a touch and were stuffed with lotus seeds. There were fledgling pigeons which were eaten whole, skull, beak, skeleton soft as jelly, entrails and all. There was chicken with walnuts and carp cooked in ginger, rice and bamboo shoots and sharks'-fin soup, which has the same indefinable satisfying quality that oysters have. Finally there were apple slices cooked in syrup. You dipped them in cold water so that the syrup turned to toffee. It is impolite to pass over any of these delicacies even if one's eyes are not, as mine are, larger than one's interior. So that it was really with unspeakable relief (I could scarcely speak by now in any case) that we at last greeted the arrival of a dish of sliced oranges, which really meant the end.

We drank Chinese rice-wine, or *shau shing*, which is served warm and is rather like a volatile sherry, rich and giggle-inducing. After the meal we drank a fiery liqueur also made from rice. It traced its course in neon lights down to the midriff, where it stayed and glowed like a small coal.

We talked little during the meal. While we were sipping our jasmine tea at the start we made a certain amount of conversation. No, this was not quite my first visit to Hong Kong. I had been here just after the war. You would hardly recognize the place now, of course. I had lived for five years in Singapore. On the whole I thought that Hong Kong was hotter than Singapore in the summer but cooler in the winter. Yes, I had used chopsticks before. Oh, you flatter me. But immediately the first dish arrived conversation ceased. In my case, as a matter of fact, it had begun to languish before the first dish arrived since I was seated between two Chinese ladies neither of whom spoke very much English. They seldom do and prefer to leave all that to their husbands.

Though there was little talk during the meal there were many murmured politenesses. My two neighbours sat very upright and prim in their *cheong-sams* with high collars, one yellow and one blue, and showed no signs of the heat at all, nor of that overstuffed feeling which overcame me. They made little delicate pecking movements at their food with their chopsticks, which looked like birds' beaks. It is polite to help the lady (or gentleman) on your right or left before you help yourself. You are supposed to choose morsels of especial delicacy for your neighbour. You pretend to be doing this even if, like me, you are merely making random dives. Having done it you may then plunge into the dish on your own behalf as often as you wish. If there are several dishes on the table together, as there usually are, you may flutter from one to the other like a butterfly. The chopsticks are held between the thumb and the first and second finger of the right hand and made into a pair of pincers of which the stationary arm is the stick that lies along the thumb, and the one that lies between the two fingers is the mobile one. It is bad manners to carry the food straight from the dish to your mouth. It should be transferred first to one of the small bowls, which should then be raised half-way to the mouth with the left hand, holding the fingers under the dish and the thumb on the rim. When eating rice the bowl should be held right up to the mouth with the rim touching the lower lip. The rice is then shovelled into the mouth with a skilful rotary motion of the chopsticks, rather difficult to acquire. This was usually where I made the snowstorm on the floor all round my chair. Meat and poultry often seem to have been cooked after having been first bashed into unrecognizable fragments with a hammer. One is therefore always having to deal with and discard splinters of bone. These are rejected with delicacy and a far-away look in the eye on to the chopsticks and placed in one of the small bowls and will presently be removed by the waiter. From time to time you toast your host and your neighbours, and your host does the same to you, in *shau shing* which is drunk from little porcelain cups. When the sharks'-fin soup comes on to the table it is *de rigueur* for the host to salute this climax of the meal by toasting each of his guests in turn. When toasting, or responding, you raise the cup to your lips with your right hand, keeping two fingers of your left hand supporting the bottom of the cup. With your eye on your victim you drain the cup to the dregs, saying, '*Yan seng*,' or 'Drink to the end' or, less literally, 'Bottoms up'. Then you point the empty cup like a pistol at your victim

) show that you have indeed emptied it to the last drop.
After the orange slices had made their appearance more
owels soaked in disinfectant came round, and we picked our
eeth, keeping the palm of the left hand over the mouth as
ve did so. All the gentlemen belched, except the only other
.uropean beside myself, and he was too well-mannered. But
vhen in Rome I always do as the Romans do, so I belched
vith the best of them. I belched, they belched, we all belched.
loosened a few more buttons and wondered if it was per-
nissible to set out on one of those voyages through the shades
vhich in any Chinese restaurant eventually lead to a dingy,
dorous, cockroachy corner which serves a simple and necessary
urpose. There is certainly no temptation to linger there and,
' you must relieve nature in a Chinese restaurant, try to do
o after the meal rather than before it since, if you are at all
queamish, it may put you off your food. I am not in the
east squeamish.

Just as I was beginning to think that I must make myself
onspicuous and rise from my place our host pushed his chair
ack and rose from his. He bowed to his guests. 'Thank you,
adies and gentlemen,' he said. 'Good night!' We shook hands,
aid, 'Thank you' in return, and the party was over. That
s the order of a Chinese repast, the greetings, the conversation
as brief and non-committal as possible), the food and drink,
he repletion and the abrupt farewell. This always seemed to
ne so much more civilized and sensible than the European
ustom by which you sit, drowsy and overstuffed with roast
uck, baked Alaska and sour wine, until midnight. At that
vitching hour the senior lady present at last says brightly,
Good gracious! Just look at the time. I'd no idea it was so
ate. We really must tear ourselves away!' And so, as at the
vave of a wand, must everybody else who has been waiting
or this signal and has known perfectly well what the time
vas really all along.

So, after our party in Hong Kong, the little waiters with
he soiled white coats and black trousers and tiny slippered
eet bowed and smiled. And the manager with the big tummy
nd the bald head smiled too and hoped we would come again.
.he little girl in the black *cheong-sam* and ear-rings, behind
he desk, too, looked up from her abacus and smiled and said

'Good night'. So did the pert little boy at the door in the pill-box cap, and we were out in the lovely neon-lit coolness of the street. But their eyes did not smile and you could not tell what they were thinking, or know whether they were for you or against you, friend or enemy, right or left. Or merely waiting to see, as the Chinese have waited for thousands of years.

The Chinese in Hong Kong are deeply divided into two opposite camps, the Communists and the Nationalists, while the British hold the balance, so that an uneasy truce prevails. Big Brother sits just over the border. But strings of Communist barges come into Hong Kong every day from Canton bringing vegetables, pigs, eggs and other kindly fruits, and the water-front is aflutter with red and gold Communist flags. If they did not come Hong Kong would starve. A busy traffic shuttles to and fro along the single-line railway to Canton, but, in spite of long negotiations, the two sides have not yet been able to agree to run through carriages. At the border you get out of your British diesel train and get into a steam Chinese one. You may, and do, spit in the British train, but if you do so in the Chinese one an official may give you a long lecture about hygiene, or you may even go to gaol, and quite right too. At the border, which the public are not allowed to approach, British police and Chinese guards exchange cigarettes and say 'Good morning'.

From the windows of my flat, which, like all flats in Hong Kong, commands a lovely view of mountains and harbour, I look down every morning upon little Communist boys and girls doing eurhythmics or playing basket-ball on the roof of their school. Sometimes they are encouraged by an ampli-fied loud-speaker, for the Chinese love noise. At night a flood-light sheds its glare on their activities, which certainly look innocent enough from where I observe them. Farther up the hill, above the University, is another Communist school, which occupies an old Victorian mansion with a garden where I see the boys and girls at their physical training, or sitting in rows listening intently while someone lectures them. Some time ago this school was told it would have to close, because the old house was said to be unsafe. It was umoured that the Government had long had its eye on this chool and was only using the condition of the building as n excuse to close it down. There was an outcry in Canton, vhich always seems to have a telescope directed upon Hong Kong. This was an example of colonialist oppression, of course —an attempt to stifle Chinese education. Slightly over-mphatic denials were issued by the Government. The school noved out of its house into a temporary building in the garden vhich the pupils built with their own hands. They worked all lay and until late into the evening and stood guard like sentries t the gate with earnest expressions and a conspiratorial air. They were obviously thoroughly enjoying it all. But one could nly admire their determination and hard work and their bvious devotion to their school. I can hardly imagine myself loing a hand's turn to build up my school if it had been in langer of collapse and closure. I would have let the beastly, tinking, rotten old place fall down and danced with joy on he ruins. Meanwhile the school appealed to the public for unds and hung posters on its garden fence, drawn by the upils themselves, I presume, showing earnest boys and girls narching forward against a background of crops and factories, ammers and sickles and the New Dawn. In a few days IK $60,000 (between £3,500 and £4,000) had been con-ributed, and the school in due course moved back into its house.

On October 1st, which is the anniversary of the Communist evolution, the huge building of the National Bank of China, vhich towers even higher than the building of the Hongkong nd Shanghai Bank next door to it, is decorated with thou-ands of electric lights and with crimson Chinese lanterns, vith doves of peace and outsize figures of the inevitable earnest oys and girls. Similar decorations and motifs adorn all the nany other buildings, schools, shops and hotels affiliated to he People's Government. There are several of these, including large luxury hotel in Kowloon much patronized by American ourists, who would be horrified if they guessed for a moment. Communist flags, plain red with a circle of gold stars in the op left-hand corner, flutter from many tenements and from umble dwellings throughout the countryside on Red Revo-ation Day.

But ten days later, on October 10th, which is the day of

Nationalist China, known as the Double Tenth, there is an even bigger and gayer display of lights and flags. This time the flags are red with a blue sun and white rays in the upper left-hand corner. This is the flag of Chiang Kai-shek's exiled Nationalist Government in Formosa. Chinese feasts are held on that day and speeches are made.

Yet to whichever of these two flags the Chinese in Hong Kong profess allegiance they are all at heart thankful for the presence of that third one, much less often seen than the others, which hangs listlessly from its staff outside the police station.

On each of these two days in early October, when the summer heat is over and the weather in Hong Kong is at its best, the police patrol the streets in groups, heavily armed, and are ready for instant action with riot squads on the alert just around the corner out of sight. On October 10th, 1956, furious riots were touched off in the refugee tenement quarter of Kowloon when the police ordered the removal of some Nationalist wall posters. Several people were killed and many injured. Some Europeans, hearing that disturbances were going on, drove to the spot in their cars to see the fun. Some had their cars overturned and burnt and some were hurt. This was not considered to be playing the game, especially as the insurance companies refused to pay.

On the whole, however, Hong Kong is peaceful and law abiding. The Chinese are not much interested in politics, and everyone is too busy with the pressing business of making money or earning enough to live on. The correspondence columns of the local papers are mostly concerned with parking and traffic problems, the location of bus-stops and the efficiency or otherwise of the ferry service. This makes Hong Kong rather a dull place to live in. There is little cultural activity and society, what there is of it, is a business and commercial one—commercial travellers and their wives dining and playing golf or bridge with other commercial travellers and their wives. Life tends to tick on with the monotonous regularity of a clock. The changing seasons mark the passage of time. The summer is suffocatingly hot and damp, and in May or June torrential rains are liable to wash away the squatters' huts and cause landslides that block roads. In August and

eptember typhoons come sweeping up the South China
ea and may pass over Hong Kong, and warning symbols
re raised on a mast at the Observatory. From my windows
 cannot see these symbols, but I know when a typhoon is
pproaching because I can see hundreds of small junks and
ampans streaming across the harbour from the south side of
ie island to the typhoon shelter in Kowloon. They look like
 flock of frightened birds. When the typhoon has passed or
ie warning is over they all stream back again. In the middle
f September the temperature drops mercifully and quite
uddenly. Three months of lovely, cool, bright sunshine
ring the tourists, and up go the prices in the shops I never
requent. January and February are gloomy and chilly, and
ld friends like my old grey flannel trousers and my sports
acket with the patched elbows come out of their hot cupboards
or a brief spell. In March is the lovely short spring when the
ink Bauhinnia trees below my flat fill the air with the scent
f limes, the city's too few gardens are ablaze with azaleas
nd we go through the whole summer procession from jon-
uils through roses to chrysanthemums in the space of a few
veeks. In April we begin swimming to the music of juke-
oxes from Repulse Bay beach and all the little Suzie Wongs
rom the bars and clubs of Wanchai come there on Sundays
o pick up American sailors and lure them back to their lairs.
n May it is getting hot again and I melt and shrink into my
ir-conditioned bedroom.

12

On the Shelf

There are several fishing centres dotted round the indented coastline of the peninsula and on the islands. The largest is named Aberdeen, not after the Granite City but after the Marquess of Aberdeen who was Foreign Secretary in the middle of the nineteenth century. It lies in a cove flanked by steep green mountains on the south side of Hong Kong Island. The town itself is a fragment of the tenement slum of Victoria transported, as it were, bodily over the mountain side. It is only interesting by reason of its seething humanity and the spectacle of irrepressible vitality which it presents. Anchored in the harbour are three large houseboats, flamboyantly decorated in the Chinese style and brilliantly lit at night. These are the famous floating sea-food restaurants where you choose your own fish from a pen of depressed looking denizens in the murky harbour water alongside. They haul your fish out of the water and cook it for you. Each houseboat has its own landing-stage, from which Chinese ladies of robust charm scull you out to your dinner in a covered sampan while you admire their beautiful smiling white teeth and sturdy arms.

The fisherfolk of Aberdeen, like fisherfolk all over the world, are a race apart, a waterborne people. Their numbers have also been greatly increased in recent years by refugees from China. Their junks, one-, two- or three-masted and mostly yawl-rigged, are in most cases also their homes. They make a thick forest of masts in Aberdeen harbour and dot the far island-studded seas with wings of beauty, symbols of an ancient and indomitable people. Some of the larger ones are trawlers which always work in pairs, a single trawl hauled between two boats, and may go as far away as Hainan, three or four hundred miles to the south-west. Others are long-liners and carry two, four or more flat-bottomed sampans which are put over the side to act as 'dories' for paying out and taking

in their miles of line. These may go sixty or a hundred miles
from Hong Kong working on the mud shelf. But the greater
number of smaller junks work close inshore long-lining,
purse-seining, drift-netting, prawn-trawling or fishing with
lights and lift-nets. You can easily tell the drifters from the
others by their beautiful white nylon nets hanging from their
masts to dry. Prawners tow their nets, several on each side,
from booms projecting at right-angles from the ship's side.
Bright-light fishermen fish from small boats with kerosene
lamps hung a foot or two above the water to attract small
fishes, which they scoop up with a lift-net. Their lamps are
lit after dark all round the coast and fill the coves and inlets
with constellations of fixed stars, gleaming all night upon the
water.

Each small junk is a complete home for the family which
operates it, and fishing is a family co-operative business. All
the women and children go to sea and help with the work as
they can. The whole family lives and works in the boat, old
men and boys, women and young girls and tiny children. It
is their world and contains all their worldly possessions. Every
member is conceived, born, grows up, makes love, gives birth,
works and at last dies upon the water. Often they die by the
sea by which they lived, for casualties among the fisherfolk
of Hong Kong are many. The large junks may house several
families, and if there is more than a certain number of children
one of the crew has to be qualified to give them lessons. No
one asks what good the lessons do them so long as they are
getting a dollop or two of education of some sort.

The junks are not built for comfort. I went aboard a big
trawler junk in Aberdeen and was astonished at the sleeping
accommodation, which was a sort of shelf under the high
poop. Here the crew slept on mats side by side with the deck-
head within a few inches of their noses. There was no other
crew accommodation of any kind and they ate, as the Chinese
always do, where they worked, with their rice-bowls on the
deck. All the rest of the ship, except the engine space, was
a fish-hold filled with ice.

So far as fishing is concerned it is indeed true that the small
peninsula of Hong Kong and its few scattered islands are a
mere speck on the huge extent of the coast of China. The in-

shore waters of the peninsula have been fished for many years by hundreds of junks using every conceivable means of catching fish, including mass-poisoning and explosives, both nowadays strictly forbidden by law. The inshore waters of this small peninsula and its islands are now, therefore, exhausted. The majority of the inshore fishermen who land their catches in Hong Kong have for years been fishing along the interminable mountainous coast of China itself, with its countless bays and inlets, and in the estuary of the great Pearl River. But nowadays the Chinese People's Republic requires that all fishing-boats working in its territorial waters must hold a licence issued by its Government. For years Hong Kong fishermen have held both a Chinese and a Hong Kong licence, but landed their catch in Hong Kong, where they get a better price. Now, however, the People's Government says that all fishing-boats which hold a Chinese licence must call at Chinese ports, must join Chinese co-operative societies and hand over a large proportion of their catch. Many Hong Kong fishermen, of course, have fled from China and do not hold a Chinese licence at all. They cannot fish at all in Chinese waters. Meanwhile the Chinese Government has arbitrarily moved its territorial limits from the internationally agreed three miles to twelve miles from any Chinese land or island. Many of the islands that cluster round Hong Kong are Chinese territory and within a twelve-mile circle of them lie waters that are also the territorial waters of Hong Kong. The British Colonial Government, of course, does not recognize this extension, which, if it did, would in fact prevent ships from entering Hong Kong at all. But while the Chinese Government is prepared to enforce its ruling upon fishermen, and does so, the British policy is 'No incidents, please'. An incident would be really too embarrassing. There are quite enough gun-boats prowling around as it is. So the Hong Kong inshore fishing-boats crowd into the exhausted waters around the peninsula and islands. The forest of masts thickens in Aberdeen harbour, the little junks lie idle for weeks and the inshore fishermen are facing ruin. But they have faced that before, off and on, down the centuries. One lives. One exists. If one has a junk there are other ways of making a living besides fishing in these days.

The offshore fishermen who own and man the trawling junks and the big long-liners that go a hundred miles or so out to sea and to the distant grounds off Hainan are not affected by these chilly political and economic winds. The deep seas where they work are international and the fish population there barely tapped. But the number of these offshore fishermen is comparatively small. They are only a handful of the great fishing population of Hong Kong. Obviously their number must be increased and the number of inshore fishermen, who depend for their living on exhausted inshore grounds, must be decreased. But you cannot, by waving a wand, transform into deep-water, ocean-going fishermen thousands of inshore fisherfolk with all their wives and families, their homes and whole way of life centred in little boats, fishing with ancient primitive gear in shallow water within a few hours' steaming of some landlocked haven. It takes years and years of tradition, training and upbringing to make a trawlerman or a long-liner whether British on the Iceland grounds or Chinese on the equally forbidding South China Sea. Nevertheless, the fishing industry of Hong Kong has got to move out to sea into the deep waters beyond territorial limits where no restrictions can worry it any more. All this had a familiar ring when I first heard about it and reminded me again that life moves in circles. One constantly arrives back where one started.

A muddy shelf, very similar to that between Malaya and Borneo, extends outwards to about eighty miles from the coast of China and slopes gently to the hundred-fathom line. It is the silt washed down for countless ages by the great rivers of China, especially the great Pearl River and the Yang-tse. It forms a very rich fishing-ground, which becomes richer south-westward towards the island of Hainan. Since 1953 the research unit of the University of Hong Kong, of which I became Director at the end of 1957, has been trying to explore this mud-shelf with a small Hong Kong-built trawler drifter of 51 tons. She is named the *Alister Hardy* after Sir Alister Hardy, one of the most distinguished fisheries biologists living, an ex-colleague of mine in the *Discovery* and now Professor of Zoology at Oxford. But on the whole we have not found that her distinguished name has helped her much on the heavy, mud bottoms of the South China Sea during the black north-east monsoon.

When I plan a trip to sea in the *Alister Hardy* I make a special visit to the High Life provision store, where I buy my groceries. This is necessary because the crew of the *Alister Hardy* all eat Chinese food squatting on the tiny poop with their bowls and chopsticks, so that the Skipper and I, the only Europeans on board, have to bring our own provisions with us. We stock up with tins and the cook wrenches them open when we feel like eating, warming up the contents into a more or less savoury mess. I usually take to sea far more than I consume and buy tins which boast of being able to produce dishes far more elaborate than I feel I can face when, twelve hours out, I am spinning and bobbing giddily on the monsoon sea. For the *Alister Hardy* is a trial even to my inside, which I rather flattered myself, until I met this little ship, was lined with cast iron.

'Ah, good afternoon, Doctor,' says the little assistant in the High Life store, beaming through his glasses. 'It is I who have the pleasure to take your order every morning.' A Doctor (*Bok-si*) of the University has considerable prestige with the Chinese with their craze for education and their reverence for the knowledge which is power, but not with the European community, which is almost entirely commercial.

'Good!' I reply. 'And now you may have the pleasure of taking another order for me.'

'You are going away?'

'To sea—perhaps I shall never come back.' I always rather felt that way at the start of a voyage in the *Alister Hardy*. 'Give me a tin of that.' I choose a tin of 'delicious meat balls in savoury sauce. Just turn it out, and in an instant there is an appetizing meal!' I wonder if it will seem so appetizing eighty miles out to sea. I would like to take that horrible self-satisfied family on the paper wrapper (Pa, Ma and two kids) out to sea and ask them how they like their meat balls now.

'And two of that.' Pork and baked beans, sausages, corned beef, luncheon sausage, six eggs, one pound of oranges. I nearly always find I have forgotten something. On one trip I forgot to bring any bread. On another I brought no knife or fork and had to borrow the Skipper's, the only ones in the ship.

The ship lies at a buoy at Aberdeen looking tiny and somehow hunchbacked because of her tall upperworks, very squat funnel and short, blunt bows. Her trawl-nets, slung up to the fore-mast to dry, accentuate her top-heavy appearance. Her hull is painted a sickly green, the University colour. I pick my way gingerly down the foreshore opposite the buoy where the ship lies, because the stones are very slippery and I am wearing rubber soles. The land is being reclaimed from the sea here for building, but the building will not begin for years and there is meanwhile a wide, dusty level plain where a lot of young Chinese are playing football. They rush about in the sunshine for hours on end and only gleam slightly, even in the hottest weather. Some fishermen and women, dressed alike in black cotton suits and wide, circular straw hats like inverted bowls, are making sails from bamboo strips which they are weaving into a mat. Others are laying out small fishes in the sun to dry. They glance up from their work with only the curiosity that any European's appearance causes. Where I am going, what I am doing or where and what the ship and her crew are doing interests them not at all. It cannot possibly concern them. What do Europeans do anyway?

Presently the ship's flat-bottomed sampan arrives to pick me up, sculled by Old Cook.

Old Cook is neither old nor a cook. He is a thin, wiry young Chinese who joined the crew some months ago as cook but proved to be such a competent sailor and fisherman that he gave up cooking and now works on the deck. It then became necessary to get another cook, a new cook to replace the old cook. So the name 'Old Cook' has stuck to him, since it is easier to remember than his Chinese name. Chinese names, always in three syllables of three or four letters, are always very difficult for Europeans to remember at first, but become easier with practice. Old Cook is immensely resourceful and knowledgeable. 'Ask Old Cook' has become a sort of watch-word, a preliminary to any undertaking involving fishing or navigating around these islands and bays. He is a tireless worker, smiles all the time with very large teeth and wears a jade bangle above the elbow on his stringy left arm.

By the time I made my first trip to sea in the *Alister Hardy* the inevitable preliminary sifting and sorting process, which takes place at first in the crew of any vessel, was finished. We had as fine and well-trained and hard-working a ship's company as it would be possible to find. The Skipper, a burly Yorkshireman from Hull, was the opposite of Dave in almost every way, but not in the sagacity and resource which is common to all fishermen. Whereas Dave had been small and slight with fiery blue eyes, Tom was a big, robust man, slow of speech and seldom roused. He was devoted to his crew, whom he had chosen and trained himself, and he was wedded to his tiny ship in a way which no one unacquainted with the sea and with ships could properly understand. The *Alister Hardy* frequently broke down, for her engine was not powerful enough for the job we were trying to do with the ship. This meant many agitated conferences with Government and University officials, who had to find the money for the repairs. During one such conference an official of the Treasury suggested that the best plan would be for the Government to take over maintenance of the ship.

'And when anything goes wrong, don't you know, the Skipper just takes the ship to the Government slipway and leaves her there. After all, when I want my car serviced I just take it to the garage and leave it. I can't really see the difference between a car and a ship.'

'No,' I said. 'I don't suppose you can.'

Tom was a natural solitary, of whom there are many, especially among men getting on towards middle age or past it. He wanted nothing better than to be out in the South China Sea in his tiny ship with his tried and trusty crew of Chinese whom he knew and loved, though he could not speak a word to them except through the Bosun, who spoke English. Black north-east monsoon or flying-fish south-west made no odds. There was only one cabin in the ship, the small single-berth skipper's cabin abaft the wheelhouse. If any of the scientific staff ventured to sea, which, not surprisingly perhaps, was seldom, Tom gave up his cabin and slept, if at all, curled up into a ball on the deck of the tiny wheelhouse. Like all professional fishermen he seemed to have a capacity for going without sleep for days and nights together.

The Bosun, Mr. Chan, was a small, spry, active little man

who had been in the Chinese Nationalist Navy. He hopped about the deck shouting in a piercing tenor voice which occasionally gave way under the strain so that only a croak emerged, or no sound at all. He was always, perhaps justifiably, a little apprehensive when we went hazardously close to any Communist island, and once, when something lying close under one such island suddenly started to flash signals at us, he pulled in the trawl and set course back to British territorial waters with enthusiasm. He was always known as Mr. Chan, the 'Mr.' being important, and, as in all ships, as Bosun he occupied a key position between the English-speaking Skipper and his Chinese crew.

Old Cook guided the sampan between the many junks, some with their white nylon drift-nets hanging up to dry. The women on board them were cooking the evening meal, and from the stern of nearly every junk a thin spiral of blue smoke went up while the family squatted around under the hoop-shaped awning. On the square stern of every boat plants in pots gave a homely touch, and on many a mongrel chow-dog looked ready to defend his home to the death. The children waved and the tiny ones were held up by their mothers and made to wave too. They repeated 'Hallo! Bye-bye!' over and over again while their parents and family grinned approval at these first signs of budding genius. This is a kind of passport to friendliness between Chinese and Europeans in Hong Kong. Wherever you go these lunatic words greet you as a kind of salutation. I am always in any case a great joke to Chinese children, who always rush out and greet me with choruses of 'Hallo! Bye-bye.'

I climbed over the rail of the *Alister Hardy* and handed my parcel of provisions to Mr. Wong, the radio operator, to put in the cold room. Mr. Wong's duties as radio operator were fairly light, but, being an alert and intelligent young man, he also acted as scientific assistant and carried out many of the routine scientific observations on board, such as taking water samples, temperatures and collecting plankton. He was the only English-speaking member of the crew besides the Bosun. The Chief Engineer spoke a little, but only with hesitation and deliberation.

Directly I arrived on board the cook gave me a glass of

hot tea with no milk, sugar or lemon. This is a Cantonese custom. One was fed with glasses of this beverage throughout the day, and throughout the night too if one were up and about the deck. The little man who was the real cook, as distinct from Old Cook, who was not a cook, seemed somehow to be quite extraordinarily traditionally Chinese in appearance, one of those people, of whom one really sees dozens every day, who make one wish that gorgeous oriental clothes were not now extinct. Or what one has been led to believe were gorgeous clothes. These people, one feels, would look so much better in them. As things, alas, were the cook wore a white singlet and black calico trousers folding over in front. He always walked down the deck towards me smiling and holding my glass of tea in front of him at chest level with both hands. He held the glass out to me with both hands, inclining his head between his arms in a slight bow, in a gesture which seemed to be very old and quite perfect in its dignity and courtesy. This grave and courtly manner of offering this glass of tea always put me in something of a spot because, try as I would, I simply could not take the stuff and always had to wait until the little man's back was turned, and no one was looking, to empty it surreptitiously into the scuppers or over the side.

Mr. Chan gave several of his high-pitched shouts and we slipped from our buoy and glided between the junks where the children were still waving. Soon we were chugging round the low headland of the island of Ap-li-chau (Duck's Tongue Island), which guards Aberdeen.

On the first trip which I made in the *Alister Hardy* it was blowing a fresh breeze as we rounded the point. 'Cat's-paws' darted across the water, but there seemed to be little swell. It was a fine but cloudy evening with large lakes of blue among the clouds sailing over the high mountains of Hong Kong Island with their cubical blocks of flats perched in improbable positions.

'There's a strong wind warning up,' said the Skipper. 'I didn't know if you realized that.'

'Well, we can't bother about that,' I said with reckless abandon. The Skipper looked at me in a strange and meaningful manner for a moment, and then said:

'Right! Steer south-south-east!'

The entrance to Hong Kong harbour is guarded by constellations of green mountainous islands, many of which are
Communist territory. The Lemma and Ladrone Islands, for
instance, form a long chain about ten miles to the southward,
standing right across the entrance. Ships cannot pass through
them and mostly have to enter Hong Kong from the east-
ward round the easterly end of the chain of the Lemma Islands.
These islands are said to be armed with guns capable of blowing
Hong Kong sky-high. But most people of my age have spent
nearly all their lives within range of guns or bombs somewhere
which were said to be capable of blowing them sky-high, so we
do not worry very much.

It is not until you get outside these islands that you really
meet the monsoon. When the long eastward-pointing snout
of the easternmost of the Lemmas is on the starboard hand
you find, during the months of the north-east monsoon—that
is, from November to March—that a change has come over
the face of the sea and the sky. There may have been blue
sky and gently drifting fleecy clouds over Aberdeen, but now
the sky is covered with a low, uniform grey pall. The sheltered
channels among the islands may have been blue and gently
rippled, but as the tiny ship chugs on you notice with unease
a steadily increasing swell. When the Lemmas are well abeam
the sea has turned black and is streaked with evil flecks of white.
The ship now spins and whirls up and down, and that dreadful sinking nausea is beginning to creep over you, fight it
back how you will. When Mr. Chan or Mr. Wong asks
what I would like for my supper I find I am far from interested in
'delicious meat balls in savoury sauce. Watch the kiddies' faces!'
Nor in 'asparagus tips, ready for instant appetizing service'.

The *Alister Hardy* was exceedingly un-sea-kindly. She was
low down and short in the bows. Instead of dipping in the
troughs and riding triumphantly over each crest, she sliced
and butted her way through each oncoming wave, taking
large quantities of each one over her bows. Her decks from
bows to midships were continually awash, and cascades of
spray pelted at the wheelhouse. She not only rocked from side
to side like a metronome beating out three-four time but spun
also with a giddy circular motion.

Thus we staggered on into the night, reeling and lurching. I lay dismally in the tiny cabin, fully clothed, on the Skipper's very short bunk and kept my mind off meat balls. The ship pounded and vibrated with the frenetic heart-beat of her engine. Things took on a life of their own. Books, clothes, old newspapers, pencils, compasses, tumblers, catapulted down off shelves on to the deck. At first I heaved myself erect and put them back where they belonged, but they soon came clattering down again, so I let them lie. Between the door and the wardrobe a coat swung out, fell back, swung to touch the door, swung to touch the wardrobe, swung out, fell back.

I felt terrible and longed to die, but was not actually sick. From time to time my mouth filled with acrid bile and I had to get up and void this out of the door. The door opened on the starboard side and so was on the lee, but even so the deck of the cabin was covered with a film of dirty water that slopped to and fro. Without pleasure I thought that the door of the cabin would be on the weather side on the homeward journey. After each heave, belch and spit on the deck something seemed to clear in my inside and I felt a bit better, until the next crisis arose. About two o'clock I ventured to grope my way forward along the deck a few paces to the wheelhouse. The dark night seemed all whirling drops of water. Inside the wheelhouse I could see the Skipper, a huge, silent shadow leaning in a corner and gazing through the bespattered window forward into the dark night, out of which the white lines raced towards us and broke. Behind him the man at the wheel was another bulky shadow. Neither spoke to the other, nor could do so, but the bond between them was strong and complete. It was the bond that links two men of different races on the bridge of a very small ship in a rough sea on a dark night.

About four o'clock one of the Japanese scientists gave me a jab in the back with one of his innumerable propelling-pencils, and I jumped down from the hayloft on to a great bag of soft stuff like cotton-wool and lay there delightfully at rest. 'I always thought one was supposed to die if one actually landed,' I thought and felt under my shirt to see if my heart had stopped. It hadn't, but the ship had. The deck cluster light was on, and I heard Mr. Chan's shrill voice yelling commands. Glistening black figures in oilskins, sou'westers and sea-boots clumped to and fro along the deck. It was not raining, but the ship's rigging and housing gleamed and dripped from its recent dunking in spray. The sea licked hungrily around and hissed with white tongues, but no longer came leaping on board. The ship rocked and clinked, but no longer spun. But native crews, I have observed, always wear clothes appropriate to what the weather looks as though it might do, rather than to what it is doing. The weather looked wet and the air was damp, so the men dressed themselves accordingly.

The trawl went out for perhaps the sixtieth time in my life, but I should think the six-hundredth time in the Skipper's. Mr. Chan was always at the forward gallows and he yelled like a dervish as the door sank clattering away. Old Cook was at the after gallows but he only gave a short 'Hah!' as the door rattled into the water, because he was a silent man.

The Skipper rang 'ahead', and the little ship came round into the wind. The trawl sank into the darkness. Anchored by the heavy gear she made less of a frenzied dancing motion, but every now and then the South China Sea slapped her under the chops and an arc of spray flew over the foredeck. Her engine pounded away, labouring like an old man's heart.

In the dark void, with only the fleeting white lines on the sea to mark our progress, it was hard to tell whether the ship was going ahead or merely thrashing the water. To hear her you would think she was going hell-for-leather. The Skipper gazed at the water over the side and walked aft. He felt the steel warp with his hand. He came back and shook his head.

'She's anchored,' he said. 'We're making no way at all.' The engine thrashed on and presently he said:

'This is no good. She's not going ahead at all. What's to do? Shall we pull up?'

'Might just as well. We shan't catch any breakfast this way.'

The trawling winch was operated by a belt from the main shaft of the engine. But the belt shaft of the winch and the main shaft of the engine were, through some miscalculation of design or construction, inclined to one another at a very slight angle, only a matter of a very small fraction of a degree out of true, but it made all the difference. They should, of

course, have been dead true and parallel. It meant that perio-
dically, after uttering heartrending screeches, the belt would
slip off its pulley on the main shaft. It also prevented the
winch from developing enough power, so that its shaft revolved
within the belt without gripping. It was this that caused
the noise as of souls in torment atoning for their sins.

When the Skipper gave the word to heave in, these agonizing
shrieks began down below. The trawling warps came in slowly
and very reluctantly, and we all stood round the winch watching
it anxiously as though it were an animal about to spring,
steadying ourselves on the rocking deck by grasping the rigging, the housing or any other support. And presently the
warps, instead of inching inwards little by little, began to
hesitate, to pause, trembling, and then to slide backwards
again towards the sea. We said 'Ah!', because this was what
we had been waiting for. With a total absence of any expression, which the Chinese assume under adverse circumstances,
the tall young stoker pulled on the brake. The belt had slipped
off the shaft. We were sure this would happen. For the stoker
and his Chief Engineer this would mean at least an hour's
work in the rocking bowels of the ship in order to fix the belt
on again. Meanwhile any fishes we might have caught in the
trawl, now hanging idle in the water, escaped back into their
homely darkness laughing, if fish do such a thing.

The cook brought, and handed to me as though it were a
sacrament, another glass of hot tea.

'She hasn't the power, you see,' said the Skipper, as though
excusing his ship. 'And with a sea like this she's making so
much motion the winch doesn't get a chance to get a good pull.'

'This is worse than average weather, I suppose, is it?
I mean, it isn't always like this, is it?'

It was my first trip in the little ship, and I must say she
seemed very lost and half drowned in the black immensity of
the South China Sea. I felt I had never been so near to the heart
of the ocean before without actually being in it. The Skipper
considered.

'Perhaps you might say,' he said at length, 'that it's just
a little bit worse than the average.'

Now that the cook had gone back to his galley, I added to
the immensity by emptying my glass of hot tea into it.

Our Chief Engineer was a lanky young man with whom there seemed to dwell a settled melancholy. It is strange how certain callings place a certain stamp on people irrespective of their race, creed or colour. Those who are called to be engineers in small ships frequently wear this air of silent sadness. I had often seen it before, but usually thought it was more connected with being Celtic, a Celtic twilight in the engine-room, than with being an engineer. But recognizing the same characteristic in this young Chinese I came to the conclusion that it must be the engines or the little ships themselves that leave this curious imprint. Nevertheless our Chief was entirely master of his charge and knew all its tricks, and they were many. He disembowelled it once at sea while the ship drifted helplessly and the crew listened with anxiety to the sounds of clinking metal down below. But in the end, after about twenty-four hours down there in the oily gloom, he came up on deck wiping the oil off his forearms, like a surgeon washing down after an operation.

'O.K., Captain,' was all he said. 'I fix.' And she got back to port.

So now, silently and without registering any emotion, he went below with the young stoker, and they fixed and got the belt on again. When, after an hour, he came up on deck, all he did was to give a nod to the wheelhouse and walk aft. With eldritch shrieks, wallowing in the growing light of a grey dawn, we recovered the trawl. There was almost nothing in it and a large hole had been torn in the underpart, called the 'belly'. For in many parts of the mud-shelf there are rocks which cut through the meshes of the net, and we had struck one of these places.

Waste of a night? A lot of seasickness and discomfort and uninspiring toil for nothing? Not quite.

I made the trip to see for myself, and I had seen. Before I could really say that I thought the *Alister Hardy* was too small and underpowered, I had to see her at work on the trawling-grounds in the worst weather. I saw her again on many other occasions, though never again under quite such grim conditions. I learnt to respect those warnings at the Observatory. We went as far away as Hainan Island, two hundred and fifty miles to the south-west, on several occasions.

Here we took the Wave Sea Bream, which has a pink swelling on its nose as though it has had a drop too much, and the Lizard fish, which has a reptilian look about it and hundreds of needle-like teeth. The Golden Thread are here too, the staple fish of Hong Kong, pink and gold and silver with a golden filament on the tail. We caught the big Philippine crawfish and other small crawfish of a kind I had never seen before, translucent pearly-pink with red margins to the tail plates, and under the tail clusters of eggs of a miraculous sapphire blue. These are in my room as I write in jars of alcohol, but they are pale ghostly white now with all their colour gone.

Yet everywhere we went it was evident that the little ship was really too small for the job. She just had not enough power for trawling on the heavy, sticky mud bottom, and if the trawl got stuck the winch was often unable to pull it up again. Moreover she was really quite extraordinarily un-comfortable and un-sea-kindly. She was the only ship I have ever been in which could offer absolutely nowhere to sit down at all. You could half lie and half sit in the Skipper's bunk, but the bunk had immovable raised edges which cut you under your thighs. You could sit on the narrow brass-bound coaming of the cabin doorway. But not for long, because the coaming soon began to cut a groove in your buttocks. In fine weather you could sit on the deck, but this was very seldom and the deck was nearly always awash.

I showed her to a famous fisheries biologist who was visiting us from the Fisheries Laboratory at Lowestoft. He made a grimace.

'All right for pottering about the harbour, but for the open ocean—well!'

But it is in the open ocean far away to the south-west that the future lies. There lives the food for the two and a half millions of this teeming, pushful colony—soon to be three millions, four or five, where will it ever end? We must have a ship which can get to these far-off fishing-grounds and explore them, and in which scientists can live, sleep, work and eat—if they feel like it.

It happens that there are two research trawlers specially built for this very job. One is the ship which I still cannot help regarding as my own, the *Manihine*, though I shall never see her again and she is lost to me. At one time it looked as though I might get her back for work around Hong Kong, but the opportunity passed. The other is the trawler *Cape St. Mary*. She was specially built in 1949 for this kind of job off the west coast of Africa, and for years she was based on Freetown, Sierra Leone, and worked the continental shelf off Ghana and Sierra Leone. For the last two years she has been in British Guiana. Now she has been given to Hong Kong for the same job and is on her way here, a gift from the United Kingdom. At this very moment of writing she is running her easting down across the Atlantic on her way here and will call at Cape Town in a day or two. I wish I were on board her, for I should love to see that lovely mountain once again.

And this, gentle reader, I think, is where we came in.

13

Return to Singapore

It is seven years since I first landed in Singapore, and time moves swiftly in the East. We are witnessing what was spoken of with apprehension in the days when I was very young, before the First World War, as 'the awakening of Asia'. Perhaps it is a tribute to all concerned, and particularly to the British, that I am able to sit peacefully in Hong Kong writing this on a lovely day in September 1959, after all that we have gone through.

When I first landed in Singapore it was still a British Crown Colony. It seemed difficult to believe that anything could ever disturb the click of ball on bat on the Padang behind the cricket club, and the Tanglin Club was strictly for Europeans only. Orchard Road was bounded in those days, already hallowed with the nostalgia which belongs to the distant past, by market-gardens where orchids grew (*Cattleya*, *Arachnis* and *Vanda Miss Joachim*), and you were soon out of the town and into a countryside of ferny uplands, old rubber estates with vertiginous avenues, low-lying swamps with fish-ponds, coconut-palms and orchards of lichees. This pleasant untidy landscape was threaded by straggling, somehow light-hearted and uninhibited attap villages where children, hens, ducks and pigs joined with the inhabitants in a *mélange* of colour, laughter, noise and smells. But there were rumblings of approaching storms even in those days. The Bertha Hertog riots were fresh in the memory. They had been mainly religious in character, but Europeans had been killed, cars overturned and burnt and stones thrown through hotel windows. It is in this clamorous junction where East meets West, where the climate is hot and ill-tempered, that things boil up and time seems to move even faster and more jerkily than elsewhere in the East.

In 1954 a new constitution, drawn up by a special commission, gave the colony partial internal self-government with a mainly elected Legislative Assembly and limited powers. Singapore's first general election was held to decide the complexion of the new Government. Political parties began to sprout like mushrooms. Most of the electorate was illiterate and could neither read nor write, so that each of the parties had a symbol which was intended roughly to indicate what the party stood for. Each candidate also had his own symbol by which his supporters could identify him. The electors, who could not read the candidate's name nor that of his party, voted for his symbol instead. Political issues affecting the life of every one in the island city boiled down to symbols and slogans. I, who had never been eligible to vote in an election in my own country, was summoned to vote in Singapore. I went along to the polling booth and made a cross against a name which meant nothing to me at all. There was no one at the polling booth except the smiling Chinese officials who ushered me in as though I were the vicar arriving at a jumble sale. I came away enjoying private contemptuous thoughts about the futility of democratic institutions when transferred to the undemocratic East. 'No one even bothers to turn up,' I thought as I drove off. But someone must have turned up later, because my candidate was roundly defeated and an opposition candidate got in.

The Labour Front party, which won the election, was a party of the Left, anti-colonial and socialist, and the most formidable of the many which mushroomed into existence before the election. Its symbol was a spade with a pick-axe and its leader was Mr. David Marshall, whose real name was Martal and whose antecedents were largely Persian. He was a very clever lawyer and a persuasive speaker who professed a loathing for the colonial system under which he had made his reputation as a lawyer. In cases involving Asian individuals versus Europeans, or versus Authority, or versus Big Business, he accepted briefs for the Asians and often won with dramatic displays of oratory. This gift of oratory stood him in good stead during the election, when he addressed lunch-time meetings under a big peepul tree in Empress Place and thundered against colonialism, working himself into all the symptoms of towering rage. It was an easy horse to flog. To me colonialism, of which I am not in the least ashamed, means government by trained civil servants under a Governor and a Legislative Assembly, which is mainly nominated and not elected by voters who can neither read nor write and certainly do not understand what they are being called upon to vote for. Asia and Africa are dotted with great commercial cities which grew up and flourished under this system. As a system it involved no more exploitation than did any other system. Before the war, when there was no United Nations Organization and no cornucopia of American money, the full responsibility for the development of the Colonies fell upon these *élite* administrations and their devoted provincial and district officers, at whom it is nowadays fashionable to jeer. In Malaya, when independence came, there was trouble in some districts when the Malay peasants learnt that they were to lose their British officers. It has yet to be shown that the successors of these administrations can do better than they did or have raised the living standards of their people, for all the fine talk and the lavish outpourings of American money.

Mr. Marshall, however, did not see colonialism that way. He saw it as government by foreign bosses for foreign bosses, and saw it all the more clearly for being a foreigner himself. To this effect he thundered daily under the peepul tree, which the Press called 'the old apple tree'. The Labour Front party got in and Mr. Marshall became Chief Minister. Each of the former Government departments now had a Minister to answer for it in the Legislative Assembly. My Fisheries Research Station, after a good deal of argument as to who exactly should look after the wretched thing, finally came under the Minister of Commerce and Industry, a wealthy Indian textile merchant. All fisheries matters came under his wing, and whenever he made any pronouncement about them one thought how much better it would have been if he had stuck to textiles. Mr. Marshall as Chief Minister believed in the 'personal touch' and in bringing the Government to the People. To this end he held court once a week under the peepul tree, and the masses brought their individual problems and grievances to him. This was all right in theory, and many rulers have tried it before. But not for long. To the unfortunate civil servants who ran the Government departments it became an appalling nuisance, because individuals' requests, bearing the Chief

Minister's signature in green ink, kept getting out of line in the queue and clogging up the wheels of the machine. And inevitably the people whom the Chief Minister met under the peepul tree were usually the wrong ones.

The aims of the Labour Front were complete independence and full internal self-government for Singapore. A commission was set up to decide which expatriate civil servants could be dispensed with and how soon. Some of its meetings were held in public—which was a mistake—and its proceedings were marked by a good deal of backbiting and spite. Luckily for me I did not have to appear before it, because I was only partially employed by the Singapore Government, which paid for a small part of my organization. Many people who did appear before it, however, had an unpleasant time, for some members of the Commission thought it expedient to give displays of rudeness and ill-manners in public sessions while remaining polite enough at the private ones. Meanwhile the Communists were busy in the Chinese schools. There were schoolboy riots, led by schoolboys of well over twenty-one years of age, and inspired strikes which made people wonder where Singapore was going under its first elected Government. In 1956 Mr. Marshall flew to London to negotiate a new constitution for Singapore which was to give the city full internal self-government, but the Colonial Office was alarmed at the signs of instability in the colony and not convinced of Mr. Marshall's ability to keep the Communists in check. He came home with an empty portfolio with no independence in it. He had said that if he did not bring home the bacon from the London conference he would resign, but he did not immediately do so. With his curious capacity for working himself up into a towering rage it required several such rages, one on the steps of the Colonial Office in London, to blow themselves out like tropical storms before Mr. Marshall finally stepped down.

He was succeeded by Mr. Lim Yew Hock at the head of a coalition of parties called the People's Alliance. He was old sobersides compared with Mr. Marshall. He had been a solicitor's clerk and he puffed the pipe of reassurance, like Stanley Baldwin. At the end of 1956, about the time of the Suez crisis, there were more riots brought about by Chinese schoolboys. The actual rioting was done by about three thousand hired trouble-makers, who mostly ran around smashing traffic-lights. The vast majority of Singapore's million and a half people only wanted to be left alone to live their lives in peace, as all people do everywhere. Lim Yew Hock dealt firmly with the riots, and the fact that he was able to do so and remain in office was probably a sign of the general distaste for riots as a form of amusement which was developing in the colony. Many of the instigators went inside, where they remained for nearly three years. 'We had a most enjoyable riot,' said a young police officer. 'We really went to town.' He did not elaborate, but there have been no more riots since. Meanwhile the Colonial Office evidently became convinced that Lim Yew Hock really could keep order in Singapore, so that when he in his turn went to London in 1957 he returned triumphantly with a new constitution in the bag. Perhaps the pipe had something to do with it. Singapore was to get complete independence and full internal self-government in two years' time. Britain was to remain responsible for defence and foreign affairs and to keep her great naval base in the Johore Strait, her Army installations and R.A.F. aerodromes. A triumphal procession from the airport was arranged for the return of Lim Yew Hock, who stood up in an open car and acknowledged thin cheers from a rather sparse and silent crowd.

Meanwhile a new star had arisen on Singapore's horizon and glowed redder and brighter as the dawn of the new day approached. This was the People's Action Party, violently Left, anti-colonial and anti-European, under yet another lawyer. The step from the law to politics in the East seems to be an easy and inevitable one, Mr. Lee Kuan-yew, in the middle thirties, had a successful legal practice in Singapore, where he represented some of the big trades unions. He took a double first at Cambridge and it has been said that his bitterness against Europeans was due to the miserable time he endured at that University. He wears London clothes, calls you 'old boy' in conversation, plays golf with a high handicap, is knowledgeable about the London theatre and has a son at Cambridge, presumably now undergoing the same ghastly ordeal that his father went through. Lee Kuan-yew is usually depicted by the Press with his fist raised and mouth wide open uttering balloons of vituperation. 'We'll drive the white man into the sea' is one such balloon. 'The European may come here as a guest, but not as a swaggering ruler' is another.

A general election was to be held in April 1959, two years after Lim Yew Hock's bargaining with the Colonial Office, to decide what sort of government should rule the new city state in the first years of independence under its new flag and native-born Governor, the *Yang Dipertuan Negara*, or 'he who is made Lord of the State'. It soon became evident that the People's Action Party, whose symbol is a lightning flash, was the best organized of them all and was rapidly gaining ground. It stood for a policy largely based on repudiation of everything in the city's colonial past. Its programme was socialist and progressive, whatever that word may mean, and aimed at eventual union with Malaya. This last item is at present not regarded with enthusiasm by the newly independent Federation of Malaya whose population has about fifty per cent Malays. They do not want the turbulent Chinese of Singapore to come in and tilt the balance.

It became obvious long before the election that the fierce People's Action Party was romping home. The masses flocked to it in places like Tiong Bahru and Alexandra where the mercury-lit subtopias stretch out their arid perspectives and people live in what look like enormous incubators. Apprehensive European firms and not a few Chinese began to withdraw to the Federation of Malaya, and Kuala Lumpur waxed at Singapore's expense.

The people flocked to the P.A.P. because it shouted from every hustings that it would do away with the inequalities in living standards which a few minutes' walk through the streets of Singapore make obvious to anyone. It is very doubtful whether it will do so in fact, for the problems of Singapore arise mainly from over-population and under-production. Driving away trade from a city whose life-blood is commerce will certainly not achieve the end in view. But nevertheless there was to be more work and more money, more and better medical services, more and better free education, and more and more and more.

At the general election the party was far better organized than its opponents, drove electors to the polls in large fleets of motor-cars and told them to vote—or else. . . . People in

Singapore are easily intimidated, and no one really believes in the secrecy of the ballot. Intimidation often consists merely in making rude faces through the window at a man's wife when her husband is at work. The P.A.P. made ruder and grimmer faces through more windows at more wives than any other party. As a result the election was a landslide for Lee Kuan-yew and his men, including the near-Communist Mayor of the city, whose activities, beginning with the removal of the City Council's mace as a symbol of colonialism, had led to the Government taking over the public services. The P.A.P. won forty-three out of the fifty seats in the house, although it polled only about fifty per cent of the votes cast. So now a great question-mark hangs over the city-state, and everyone is wondering whether the Government will turn out to be as wild when in power as it sounded during the election campaign.

What happens to Europeans will depend on how they play their cards. A new day has come for better or for worse. In the rosy dawn it looks brighter for many than the day that went before it, but whether it will be as bright at high noon none can tell. But if the European community tries to cling to the régime and way of life which belong to yesterday it will be gradually squeezed out. I do not feel very optimistic. There seems to be almost no limit to the stupid prejudices perpetuated by elderly men who are blind to what is happening around them, and have thought for so many years about nothing but money and golf that they have grown a shell around themselves.

Not very long before the election at which Lee Kuan-yew swept the poll, I was sitting in the lounge of the Raffles Hotel with the head of a British engineering firm. A young man whom I knew slightly walked by and nodded as he passed.

'Do you know that young man?' asked my companion.

'Slightly, yes.'

'He seems to be very intelligent. Has a good degree, I believe. He applied to me for a job some time ago. I'd have liked to have taken him on, but I'm afraid it was quite out of the question.'

'Really? Why?'

'My dear fellow! He has a Chinese wife.'

'What on earth has that to do with it?'

'Oh, for God's sake, have some sense! My firm has to do with other European firms. What do you suppose they would think if I took on a European with a Chinese wife?'

'I suppose I must be very stupid or very ignorant or something, but for the life of me I can't see what the race, colour or creed of a man's wife has to do with his fitness to take a job with an engineering firm in this year of grace.'

'Well, if you're as ignorant as that there's not much point in discussing the matter.'

And there we left it, because I am, and shall remain until I die, as ignorant as that.

In an aeroplane flying from Singapore to Bangkok I sat next to a European. We talked. I do not usually make conversation in planes or trains, but this fellow-traveller was amusing and friendly, so I lowered my novel and listened. He was a newspaper-man and told me that he had been editor of one of the English-language papers in Singapore which has since been banned by the new Government, as part of its morality drive, as an undesirable publication. The paper was not indecent in fact, but it was so in intention and so grossly vulgar as to be objectionable for that reason alone. It catered for a moronic public and dealt with strip-tease, the less edifying activities of film actors and actresses and thinly disguised sex.

'Oh, that filthy rag!' I said, laughing.

'Sure, it's filthy! But it pays, boy! It pays. Of course from time to time the P.A.P. get a bit stroppy, so we close down a bit on the dirt. And down go the receipts. Then we slowly bring the dirt back and the receipts start to rise again!'

I must confess my heart was heavy when I heard these words. I thought that if this is what the West offers to the East it is indeed time we left.

Luckily I don't think it is. In the East today there is an enormous hunger for western education, knowledge and culture. The rush to learn English is embarrassing to education authorities, who are hard pressed to cope with it. In the Victoria Hall, Singapore, concerts by famous artists are packed with intently listening young Chinese, and libraries and reading-rooms all over the East are crowded. A Chinese once came to my house in Singapore and gazed around at my inexpensive attempts at decoration which went with my bamboo furniture and my pot plants.

'So European,' he said. 'So intimate and homely. We Chinese cannot achieve an effect like this.'

A great deal of the vituperation and abuse which preceded independence in Singapore resulted, I think, from a kind of love-hate, a sense of something elusive, intangible and unattainable. It cannot be achieved or grasped, so it must be reviled and belittled. It cannot be quite understood, so it must be cast out.

In March 1959, a few weeks before the election, when the torrent of vituperation was beginning, I returned to Singapore for a few weeks' holiday. I was touched by the welcome I received everywhere from people who, since I had been absent for nearly two years, might have been excused if they had forgotten my existence altogether. In Bugis Street, which was as beautiful and *louche* as ever, characters arose out of my less reputable past and shook me by the hand and sat at my table. I took the jolting red bus, called 'the Changi Express', out to the sand-spit to see how my temple of science was getting on. There it stood, forlorn and deserted and now sadly lacking paint, but the oleanders I had planted were doing well. Then I walked along the foreshore to look at the house that used to be mine. My casuarina trees had grown so high that the house was almost invisible behind them, and my red Bougainvillaea had obviously not missed me. Jakob was there, leaning on his fence and puffing his pipe. He gripped my hand and said, 'Very long time no see. When you come back to Singapore?'

As I walked towards the ugly but endearing village, which is a mile and a half away, the sky over Johore became ink-black, while jagged streaks of lightning forked down to the skyline. When I had gone an appropriate distance away from any shelter huge drops of rain, like small coins, began to fall, and a grey curtain of water advanced towards me over the mangrove swamp. There was no point in turning back now, so I might as well go on, and soon I was drenched in warm, soft water and looked as though I had been swimming in my shirt and shorts.

It was certainly not as a swaggering ruler that I squelched and dripped into Changi village on that teeming, gurgling, hissing afternoon, but I soon felt like a guest, and an honoured one at that. People ran out of their shops and dragged me in. 'Oh, Doctor, very long time no see. When you come back to Singapore? Very much lain? You no car? You stay get dry.' I made a damp, squidgy, triumphal progress under the spouting corrugated-iron verandas, from the bicycle-shop to the record-shop ('You remember—I sell your friend Chinese opela!'—it was still a joke), to the dignified lady still presiding behind the contraceptives. I had orangeade upon orangeade. Then to the Good-Luck Café, where the juke-box was blaring as though it had never stopped. They say it blares Beethoven and Brahms now, though it seems improbable and incongruous. But I wondered, when I read the election speeches later, who it could possibly be that was doing all the hating. When, in a few years' time, I straighten myself from the sweet peas, which all too soon now I shall be growing in an inexpensive part of the English countryside, the stars that I shall see before my eyes will not be, as the doctor will certainly tell me, due to my overworked liver. They will be the glittering, gold-toothed smiles of my dear but ugly village which I shall not forget.